FREE-RANGE RELIGION

WHERE RELIGION LIVES

Kristy Nabhan-Warren, editor

Where Religion Lives publishes ethnographies of religious life. The series features the methods of religious studies along with anthropological approaches to lived religion. The religious studies perspective encompasses attention to historical contingency, theory, religious doctrine and texts, and religious practitioners' intimate, personal narratives. The series also highlights the critical realities of migration and transnationalism.

A complete list of books published in Where Religion Lives is available at https://uncpress.org/series/where-religion-lives.

FREE-RANGE RELIGION

Alternative Food Movements and Religious Life in the United States

ADRIENNE KRONE

THE UNIVERSITY OF NORTH CAROLINA PRESS
Chapel Hill

© 2025 Adrienne Krone

All rights reserved

Designed by Jamison Cockerham
Set in Scala and Scala Sans
by codeMantra

Manufactured in the United States of America

Cover art: *Top*: A field of produce at the Adamah Farm Fellowship, July 2015. Photo by author. *Middle*: Swiss chard © Jonathan Kemper / Unsplash. *Bottom*: Cows grazing at Baldwin Family Farms, June 2015. Photo by author.

LIBRARY OF CONGRESS CATALOGING-IN-PUBLICATION DATA
Names: Krone, Adrienne, author.
Title: Free-range religion : alternative food movements and religious life in the United States / Adrienne Krone.
Other titles: Where religion lives.
Description: Chapel Hill : The University of North Carolina Press, 2025. | Series: Where religion lives | Includes bibliographical references and index.
Identifiers: LCCN 2025022066 | ISBN 9781469690315 (cloth ; alk. paper) | ISBN 9781469690322 (paperback ; alk. paper) | ISBN 9781469684215 (epub) | ISBN 9781469690339 (pdf)
Subjects: LCSH: Food industry and trade—United States—Religious aspects. | Food—United States—Religious aspects. | Food—Moral and ethical aspects—United States. | Food habits—United States. | BISAC: RELIGION / General | COOKING / Regional & Ethnic / American / General Classification:
LCC BL65.F65 K76 2025 | DDC 205/.68—dc23/eng/20250518
LC record available at https://lccn.loc.gov/2025022066.

For product safety concerns under the European Union's General Product Safety Regulation (EU GPSR), please contact gpsr@mare-nostrum.co.uk or write to the University of North Carolina Press and Mare Nostrum Group B.V., Mauritskade 21D, 1091 GC Amsterdam, The Netherlands.

To my parents,

BILL *and* MARTIE KRONE,

who raised me to pursue knowledge

and eat my vegetables.

CONTENTS

List of Illustrations ix

Acknowledgments xi

INTRODUCTION 1

1. Sustainable Agriculture at the Adamah Farm Fellowship 27

2. Live Foods for Living Bodies at the Hallelujah Diet Health Retreat 61

3. Cows, Chickens, and Certifications at Baldwin Family Farms 93

4. A Year of Rest and Restoration at Pearlstone Center 119

CONCLUSION 147

Notes 159

Bibliography 179

Index 187

ILLUSTRATIONS

- 11   Cows at Baldwin Family Farms, June 2015
- 28   View from an overlook, July 2015
- 44   Adamah Farm Fellowship food system poster, June 2015
- 52   Rainbow chard in the washbasin, July 2015
- 107   Baldwin Grass-Fed Beef display at Whole Foods, January 2016
- 120   Pearlstone Center farm, June 2013
- 121   Pearlstone Center farm, June 2015
- 149   "Feed me!" compost pile, July 2015
- 149   "Are we there yet?" compost pile, July 2015
- 149   "Still cookin'" compost pile, July 2015
- 149   "The good stuff" compost pile, July 2015
- 150   "The good stuff" compost pile, December 2015
- 155   Sign on the Adamah Farm compost yard gate, July 2015

ACKNOWLEDGMENTS

This book has my name on the cover, and all mistakes and misinterpretations are mine alone, but this was a collaborative project. It would not have been possible without all of my interlocutors at the Adamah Farm Fellowship, Baldwin Family Farms, the Hallelujah Diet Health Retreat, and the Pearlstone Retreat Center. I am grateful that I was able to spend time working, learning, and eating at each of these places. Many of the people who made those visits possible, fruitful, and enjoyable are anonymized here, but I hope they see themselves in their words and in my reflections of them in the pages that follow. Each and every person I met through this journey taught me, inspired me, and changed me.

As I began work on this book, Kate Bowler, Juliane Hammer, Laura Lieber, Eric Meyers, Grant Wacker, and especially David Morgan were there every step of the way with smart critiques and sage advice. In addition to the countless hours each of these busy scholars spent reading my drafts and offering feedback, they also provided the support and letters of recommendation that allowed me to find an academic job and keep this project alive. The Duke Center for Jewish Studies financed much of my early research including the fieldwork for this project, through the Nathan J. Perilman Fellowship and the Perilman Summer Stipend. I am grateful not only for the financial support but also for the intellectual community that the Duke Center for Jewish Studies provided throughout my time at Duke, with special thanks to Serena Bazemore and my boss and friend at Duke University Libraries, Rachel Ariel. In addition to championing all of my research endeavors over the last decade, Aaron Gross also arranged for a grant from Farm Forward and the Leichtag Foundation that enabled me to continue this research after I left Duke, and I am very thankful for his support. Michelle Crouch transcribed the interviews way back in 2015, and I appreciate her ability to bring the words of my interlocutors to life in a usable format. I additionally had a large community of friends at Duke and beyond who supported me throughout the early years of this project, and I am especially thankful for Lekha Shupeck, Jennifer Kryszak, Eric Chalfant, Ali Na, Erin Galgay Walsh, Yael Lazar, Brennan Keegan, Yasmine Singh, Andrew Coates, Jamie Brummitt, and Juanita Sikorski. The Americanists at both Duke and the University of North Carolina were gracious colleagues and excellent conversation partners in classes and in the Triangle Religion in the Americas Colloquium, and the Duke-UNC Religion and Theory Group community challenged my thinking and made my work better.

Academic jobs are hard to get and sometimes even harder to keep, so I particularly appreciate my friends, colleagues, and students at Allegheny College. Thanks go to my many colleagues over the years in the Department of Philosophy and Religious Studies, especially my friends and partners in the defense of religious studies, Dara Delgado and Matt Mitchell. My colleagues in the Department of Environmental Science and Sustainability took me in and treated me like one of their own, and I am proud and grateful to be in their department. I served on Faculty Council and a Shared Governance Task Force through a particularly tumultuous time at Allegheny, and my comrades in those spaces supported me with their wisdom, strength, and humor; I would not have made it through without them. I couldn't have asked for a better crew of people to write with on Saturdays than Allegheny's Writing Accountability Group and over the years UFOs, Thirsty Thursdays, Trivia Nights, Wines 'n Spines, and many less formal social gatherings provided much needed incentive and breaks from work. I served as Allegheny's director of Jewish life and Hillel advisor for six years, and I enjoyed getting to know all of the Jewish students, faculty members, and community members who made up our small and spirited community. The last stages of this project were completed during a sabbatical year, and I am very grateful to Allegheny College for granting me that time to focus on research. I also appreciate the support of Fulbright Canada and the Hadassah-Brandeis Institute during that year. I have been lucky to have Alyssa Ribeiro, Jennifer Franz, Lisa Whitenack, Brittany Davis, Uma Sureka, Mariana Silva, and Elisabeth Smith as my closest confidantes in and beyond Meadville, and it has been a joy to teach, write, eat, drink, adult, and laugh alongside them. Trips to the beach with Lekha Shupeck, Jessica Turner, Theresa Jorgensen, and a rotating crew of amazing people provided respite and joy in good times and bad. Finally, in a year when my position at Allegheny was particularly precarious, I had the opportunity to interview at an amazing institution. I didn't get the job, but the interview was the motivation I needed to finish and submit an earlier version of this manuscript, and I am thankful for all the generative advice those colleagues offered throughout my visit.

My interdisciplinary work has enabled my participation in numerous academic communities, and each of these communities has broadened my perspective and sharpened my thinking, particularly those in North American religions, Jewish studies, animals and religion, religion and food, and religion and ecology. I have become increasingly involved with the Society of Jewish Ethics in recent years, and I appreciate everything about our community and the enlightening conversations we have been able to have. I was fortunate enough to be a part of the 2022–24 Young Scholars in American Religion Cohort with Zaid Adhami, Lloyd Barba, Pete Cajka, Mike Graziano, Sonia Hazard, Helen Jin Kim, Laura McTighe, Kristy Slominski, and Barbara Sostaita and our dream team of mentors, Jennifer Graber and Omar McRoberts. I couldn't have asked for a better crew to learn, eat, and bowl with in Indianapolis, and our Zoom writing sessions kept me motivated during busy semesters and lazy summers. This remarkable group of scholars also provided valuable feedback and encouragement during a critical point in this project, and the book is better as a result. I can't wait to see all these wonderful people bang their cowbells and change the world.

My amazing friend and colleague Samira Mehta started a feminist reading group during the pandemic, and I have loved talking books and life with Sarah Dees, Kate Dugan, Sarah Imhoff, and Samira every month over the past few years. Our reading list kept me up-to-date in the field of American religion, and it has been an honor to be in regular conversation with the brightest in the business. I am particularly indebted to Samira and Sarah Imhoff, who read parts of this manuscript and offered their characteristic generous and generative feedback. It took some time for me to find the right publisher for this book, and I am very happy to have landed with the amazing and supportive team at the University of North Carolina Press. I especially thank Julie Bush for her expert copyediting. I am particularly grateful to the Where Religion Lives series editor, Kristy Nabhan-Warren, whose advice and enthusiasm for this book motivated me to start and finish the revision process. And thanks go to my editor, Mark Simpson-Vos, who found reviewers for this book in the middle of the pandemic and provided support for both it and its author throughout a multiyear process. I also want to thank Sandra Korn, who championed this project long before it became a book.

I also have a long-standing support team of friends and family for whom years are measured in decades. Zoey Glick and Maria Ciocca Basil have been more like family than friends since we were five, and I met Amanda Burns,

Lauren Coles, Megan Sorrentino, and Kristen Williams in college. It's been an honor to be a part of all of their lives, even from farther away. My siblings, Gregory Krone, Matthew Krone, and Rachel Clark, have been part of my life since they all came into the world on the same day forty years ago, and I can't imagine life without them. Ashley Krone and Liz Krone joined our family through marriage to my brothers, and they brought with them good humor and exceptional kindness. My nieces and nephew, Lily and Evie Krone and Delaney and Dougie Clark, have added new joy and energy to our family, and I am proud to be their aunt. Modern technology allows me to keep up with this crew through our endlessly entertaining family group chat, Attack of the Krones. Finally, I would like to thank my parents, Martie and Bill Krone. My mother has been feeding me tofu, sprouts, and wheat germ since I could chew, so it is no wonder that my research interests turned toward alternative food systems, and my father taught me that success is the result of hard work. Both of my parents were educators with strong inclinations toward the outdoors, and my best childhood memories involve reading books together, eating fresh tomatoes from our garden, and going on hikes that were much longer than we expected them to be. This project is just one of many things in my life that would not have been possible without their support.

FREE-RANGE RELIGION

Introduction

In 1969, V. Mac Baldwin purchased two certified Charolais cows and started grazing them on his wife Peggy's family farm. Charolais cows are white, and V. Mac found that they do particularly well in the North Carolina summer heat. In 1981, the Baldwins moved to a 331-acre farm in Yanceyville, North Carolina. V. Mac's business is about selling beef, but he considered himself a grass farmer. In the spring he planted Red River and Quick-N-Big Crabgrass. In the fall he planted ryegrass and Marshall ryegrass and crimson clover. He also set up an on-site chicken breeding operation, which supplied organic plant food for the grass and income that supplemented the beef operation. By 2015, his farm stretched over 1,100 acres, and the grass he grew fed hundreds of Charolais cows each year.

On the surface, V. Mac's pasture-raised beef operation looked pretty standard for the industry. But as we toured his farm on the back of an ATV, he let me in on what he saw as his secret to success. He told me he had a partner in the work that made it all possible: Jesus Christ. He asked me to recite Matthew 11:28, and when I revealed I didn't know it, he responded, "Come to me, all who labor and are heavy laden, and I will give you rest."[1] At Baldwin Family Farms, religion was inextricable from the agricultural operations. V. Mac was a dedicated member of Gideons International, an organization that emphasizes the importance of scripture and became known for distributing copies of the Bible. In keeping with his identity as a Gideon, V. Mac learned about animal husbandry from the Bible, and he saw his beef business as a ministry. But it wasn't just Christianity that shaped the production and processing of Baldwin Beef. When the cows reached their full weight, V. Mac sent them to Chaudhry Halal Meats, where the cows were slaughtered and processed in accordance with Islamic laws. V. Mac chose Chaudhry because it was a smaller processing plant, and he wanted his cows to experience minimal stress in their final moments. The meat that Baldwin Beef produced was grass-fed, antibiotic-free, hormone-free, extra lean, USDA-inspected, and halal. The labels on the packaged meat distributed to Whole Foods stores throughout North Carolina, South Carolina, and Virginia reflected the interreligious and interspecies relationships that formed the foundation of this enterprise.

The labels also revealed an aspect of the contemporary food system that is often obscured. In the cultural and academic imaginary, the alternative food movement is mostly seen as a secular movement of like-minded people who care about animals, the environment, and the food that they eat. Scholars Alison Hope Alkon and Julian Agyeman refer to the alternative food movement as "something of a monoculture" and note in particular the movement's white and middle-class character, and while they critique the lack of attention to race, class, and gender in analyses of the alternative food movement, they do not address religion.[2] Their critique of the alternative food movement as a singular entity is warranted, but it obfuscates the varied movements operating in the alternative food space. I use the plural "movements" where appropriate to acknowledge the diverse array of alternative food movements throughout history and today. Though the identities and motivations of the Whole Foods customers who purchase Baldwin Beef likely align with those in the more narrow, monoculture version of the alternative food movement and are worthy of further analysis under that framework, consumers' perspectives are not the focus of this book. Instead, in this book I focus on people like the Baldwins who are participating in and shaping one of many alternative food movements through their complex, collaborative, and distinctly religious approach to producing food.[3]

After spending four years studying the history of religious alternative food movements in the United States, I conducted ethnographic fieldwork in 2015 in order to analyze Baldwin Beef and three other religious food movement groups. These groups shared similar concerns, rooted in their own religious values, about the contemporary American industrial food system, and though their solutions varied, they were all working to change that system through the implementation of their religious ideals. At the Adamah Farm Fellowship, located at the Isabella Freedman Jewish Retreat Center, young adult Jews learned about sustainable agriculture, Judaism, and social justice.[4] Participants in Hallelujah Diet Health Retreats in Lake Lure, North Carolina, studied the biblical and scientific basis for the Hallelujah Diet, a mostly raw and plant-based diet, as they developed skills in food selection and preparation.[5] At Pearlstone Center, a Jewish retreat center in Reisterstown, Maryland, the staff integrated Jewish principles like *shmita*—the biblical agricultural sabbatical year—into their agricultural and educational work. I spent time with each of these groups in order to understand the alternative food systems they were developing and the role of religion in their work. And though I often refer to these groups and people as "religious," their religious identities were heterogeneous and dynamic rather than uniform and dogmatic, and their religious lives provide a window into the complex religiosities that have developed in alternative food movement spaces.

These four organizations serve as representative, though not exhaustive, case studies of contemporary religious alternative food movements in the United States. My argument in each case and throughout the book has two parts. First, religious people aren't just changing what they eat; they are working to revolutionize the food system from the ground up. Second, as religious people develop their own interventions into the food system, they incorporate ideas and practices from their own religious traditions but also draw on ideas and practices from other traditions, resulting in alternative food systems that are based in complex religious, secular, and scientific amalgamations. This kind of religious engagement with alternative food is not new, so I also contextualize these sites within the history of religious alternative food movements in the United States.

Taken together, these contemporary groups and the broader historical context demonstrate that religious people were and are part of alternative food movements and that understanding those alternative food movements in all their complexity requires attention to religion. I pay particular attention to ritual, human-animal relationships, and the environment along the way, but the primary focus of this book is the food systems and complex religiosities of these groups that are intentionally interventionist. In each of the case studies described here, people were motivated by their religious values to seek alternatives to American industrial food and then utilized a blend of religious and nonreligious frameworks, ideas, and practices as they developed alternative food systems.

ALTERNATIVE FOOD MOVEMENTS AND RELIGION

In 1830, the Presbyterian minister Sylvester Graham began to articulate his case in sermons and public lectures against the consumption of animal products and bread made by commercial bakers. Graham's Christianity motivated his teachings and informed his concerns that ingesting these foods would inflame people's inner passions and lead them into sexual immorality, thereby endangering their mortal bodies and immortal souls. Graham established boardinghouses where visitors could learn how to live according to his diet plan. And though that diet was grounded in the consumption of whole grain bread made from the eponymous whole wheat Graham flour, today his name is more often associated with crackers that bear his name but are made with the refined flours and sugars that he abhorred. If we want to understand today's religious alternative food movements, it is important to consider the broader history of religiously motivated food reform in the United States.

Sylvester Graham was one of the first in a long line of Christian diet reformers. His teachings inspired Ellen White, who integrated them into the dietary practices of Seventh-day Adventism, which she cofounded in 1863. The Kellogg brothers, both Seventh-day Adventists, then invented cornflakes to provide their coreligionists a healthy breakfast alternative to the meat- and grease-heavy meals common in their day. Against the wishes of his brother, John Harvey Kellogg, W. K. Kellogg commercialized the product and started the Battle Creek Toasted Corn Flake Company in 1906.[6] As with Graham crackers, the sugary and highly processed breakfast cereals that line grocery store shelves today are out of step with their historical roots, which speaks to the momentum of processed food and its contemporary dominance in the food industry in the United States.

Christians were not alone in their efforts to establish alternative food systems in earlier eras. In the last two decades of the nineteenth century, Jewish immigrants from eastern Europe established utopian agricultural communities in an effort to create their own autonomous food systems throughout the United States; in Canada, Argentina, and Brazil; and in what was then Ottoman Palestine, where they were called kibbutzim (collective settlements) and moshavim (cooperative settlements). The leadership at both Adamah and Pearlstone have imbued their work with a similar visionary spirit and found inspiration in some of the same Jewish texts and traditions as their predecessors. In the twentieth century, as Judith Weisenfeld has demonstrated, Black Christians and Muslims pursued food justice and alternative diets as part of their formation of religio-racial identities in Father

Divine's Peace Mission Movement, Ethiopian Hebrew congregations, and the Nation of Islam. In each of these cases, the incorporation of alternative food practices helped members of the group forge new identities in their new communities and distanced them from perceived harms in the mainstream food system.[7]

The contemporary groups I describe in this book shared many grievances and goals with those who preceded them. In some cases, the concerns were related to the potential harms that animal products or processed food might have on the health of those in their community. In other cases, marginalized communities sought to establish an autonomous food system based in their own values. For many of the historic and contemporary groups, these concerns and desires overlapped. The critiques of these religious alternative food leaders and groups were often grounded in the idea that God created the world and all its plants and animals, so human intervention and innovation was unnecessary at best and dangerous at worst. Graham warned his followers against buying bakery bread because it was made with processed wheat and additives. Today, there are alternative food movements dedicated to concerns about genetically modified organisms (or GMOs) and carcinogenic additives. The meat industry has raised concerns about the animal and human lives it impacts since the centralization of meat processing that occurred in Chicago (beef) and Cincinnati (pork) in the nineteenth century, and the contemporary vertically integrated systems continue to trouble religious people who hold particular convictions about animal ethics and human health.[8]

The similarities abound, but there are also differences between the historical and contemporary religious food movements. In the nineteenth century, Graham and his successors were invested in demarcating the differences between humans and animals so that humans could embrace their full potential as those who were created in God's image. Graham taught that improper foods would bring out "animal" tendencies and endanger humans in this world and the next. Contemporary religious alternative food movements tend toward an ecological perspective instead. The climate crisis has shifted many of these groups away from anthropocentrism and toward a more holistic view of humans as part of a broader ecological system with an emphasis on interspecies concerns. Because of factors like the industrialization and globalization of food and the climate crisis, the contemporary religious food movements differ from their predecessors in their more universal approach.

The twenty-first-century food movements described in this book condemn environmental, health, and animal welfare failures in the United States food industry. Adamah, for instance, was established as a response to environmental, health, and moral concerns about industrial agriculture. The Jewish farmers at Adamah cultivate local and organic produce for retreat guests at the Isabella Freedman Jewish Retreat Center, members of their community-supported agriculture (CSA) program, and customers at farmers' markets in northwest Connecticut. The Hallelujah Diet was a reaction to the "Standard American Diet," which founder George Malkmus believed was causing illness and premature death. The Hallelujah Diet is a raw and vegan diet, based on Malkmus's interpretation of Genesis 1:29—"And God said, Behold, I have given you every herb bearing seed, which is upon the face of all the earth, and every tree, in the which is the fruit of a tree yielding seed; to you it shall be for meat" (King James Version). The Baldwin family decided to raise beef cattle on pasture because factory-farming methods didn't align with their Christian beliefs. The Baldwin Beef cattle are not treated with antibiotics or hormones, and the farm is an Animal Welfare Approved organization. The staff at Pearlstone Center implemented shmita during the Hebrew year 5775 (2014–15). They cover-cropped their fields and created new educational programming for the schools and Jewish groups that regularly visit the farm. They reinvented shmita because the idea of a Sabbath for the land resonated with their ecological mindset, and they spent time during the shmita year engaged in ecological restoration instead of agriculture. In each of these examples, food reformers identified issues in the industrial food system and were motivated by their religious beliefs and values to create an alternative.

I use the term "religious alternative food movements" throughout this book because while these groups are all invested in food system change, they are not necessarily all invested in the kind of broader systemic change that tends to characterize groups in the food justice movement. In their book *Food Justice*, Robert Gottlieb and Anupama Joshi consider critiques of the global industrialized food system to be the first step and a critical entry point for food justice advocacy. Gottlieb and Joshi explain that as communities of color and low-income communities became involved in food justice, activists began to align food justice with the environmental, racial, and social justice movements, and collaboration across those movements became an essential component to food justice activism.[9] As the food justice movement grew and scholarship on the movement developed, this understanding of food justice as a component of broader social justice movements solidified. Alkon and Agyeman expanded on some of the differences between the food movement and the food justice movement in their book *Cultivating Food Justice*, noting that the food movement appeals to an audience of like-minded, predominantly white and middle-class people, while the food justice movement appeals to a diverse array of marginalized communities. Alkon and Agyeman brought together authors who described food justice projects led by low-income communities and communities of color that integrated social and environmental justice activism into their work.[10] Five years later, when Garrett Broad published *More Than Just Food*, he demonstrated that this perspective had been solidified. He described food justice as a "counter-force" not only to the industrial food system in the United States but also to earlier food movement efforts that had not placed social justice at the center of their work.[11]

As this conversation has developed alongside my fieldwork, the positionality of the groups described here have changed. Based on current understandings across activist and academic communities, Baldwin Beef and the Hallelujah Diet are best understood as part of the food movement because they appeal to an audience of predominantly white and middle-class people and do not integrate other social justice issues into their work. The Adamah Farm Fellowship and programs at Pearlstone Center appeal to Jews, many of whom are also white and middle-class, but they also incorporate social, environmental, and racial justice into their programming and collaborate with organizations in their local area focused on those issues, so their work does align with the food justice movement. I use the language of "food movements" or "alternative food movements" here because that terminology includes the broadest coalition of people working to change the industrial food system and is an accurate descriptor of all the groups described here.

Alternative food movement literature has not been particularly attentive to religion. My hope is that the examples here expand some of the broad understandings of who is participating in food movements and some of the religious diversity that complicates the perception of like-mindedness among food reform proponents. Jonathan Schorsch pointed out the disproportionately high number of Jewish people involved in alternative food movements and argued convincingly that their Jewishness influenced their engagement as "Jewish foodies" in ways that they themselves might not even recognize.[12] As I will show here, though the groups described here were all motivated by Jewish, Christian, and other religious values and traditions to change the food system, they were otherwise quite unlike-minded. For example, the mission of Baldwin Beef is to provide better beef from pasture-raised cattle, whereas the mission of the Hallelujah Diet is to convince people that the diet God intended for humans didn't involve meat at all. And in the same year, a shmita year, Pearlstone cover-cropped its fields and canceled its fellowship program and CSA program, while Adamah decided to rotate its fields through periods of rest and continued its programs during the shmita year with the addition of a community garden and new educational programs focused on shmita. Attention to religious difference provides a more holistic picture of who is involved in alternative food movements, and increasing awareness of religious participation may help the movement expand its coalitions and open up new avenues for engagement.

This book also serves as a contribution to the growing body of scholarship on religion and food. This attention to food has fostered a vital area of study, given the centrality of food in the lives of religious people (and all people). However, this scholarship has a heavy bias toward the consumption of food and the theologies and identities that are wrapped up in the act of eating, likely due in large part to the emphasis on eating, rather than on food production, within the religious communities themselves. This focus on food in its final, edible stage elides the majority of the interactions that humans have with food as it moves through the food system. It has to be grown, harvested, processed, and prepared. In this book, I build on the work of other scholars who have focused on agriculture and religion in their work. In *Religious Agrarianism and the Return of Place*, Todd LeVasseur identifies an increased level of engagement in sustainable agriculture among religious communities in the United States, which he terms "religious agrarianism.[13] In *Food, Farming and Religion: Emerging Ethical Perspectives*, Gretel Van Wieren emphasizes the ethical dimensions of religious engagements with sustainable agriculture, which she describes as "restorative agriculture."[14] In this book, I focus on the complexity of the religiosities that shape religious alternative food movements, which includes but is not limited to engagements with sustainable agriculture. Though eating is a feature of every chapter and agriculture is central to three chapters, the overall focus in this book encompasses both food production and preparation. Religion is certainly enacted at meals and in rituals, but it also plays a key role in decisions that were made long before mealtime in each of the organizations described in this book.

Just as religious alternative food movements are seen as marginal within the broader alternative food and food justice movements, their central focus on food activism similarly moves these organizations into the ideological periphery of the broader religious movements and denominations they belong to. This is not to say that people don't oppose the food industry within existing religious institutions. There are certainly religious institutions that run informational sessions about eating healthy and exercising, and community gardens have sprouted up on the grounds of many religious institutions in the last ten to twenty years. But initiatives like classes and gardens are a small piece of the religious programming offered by churches, synagogues, and community centers, and these types of programs tend to focus on seeking better options within the current food system. The organizations that are the focus of this book embrace food activism as a core principle. They advocate for structural changes to the way food is usually produced in the United States. The participants in these groups have often rearranged their own lives in an effort to live out their food-based ideologies by offering alternatives. The Adamah staff and fellows live on-site at the Isabella Freedman Jewish Retreat Center. Their days are ordered by the needs of their land and animals. Their Judaisms are innovative and ecological. Many Jews learn that Sukkot was an ancient harvest festival while they eat outside in sukkahs at their homes and synagogues each fall. At Adamah, they celebrate the holiday with kosher slaughter demonstrations and educational programs about ancient Israelite religion. The meat from the demonstrations is served alongside the fall squashes harvested from their own fields in a community sukkah that faces a lake and a mountain dotted with trees showing their fall colors. Physical distance separates these organizations from other religious institutions, and their focus on food distances them ideologically, but it also enables them to revive ancient traditions and create new ones.

RELIGION IN ALTERNATIVE FOOD MOVEMENTS

Free-Range Religion is primarily about religious engagements in the alternative food movement, but a holistic understanding of these groups requires attention to what religion looks like in these alternative spaces. Christians and Muslims collaborate in the production of Baldwin Beef, which appeals to diverse consumers and says more about the company's dedication to selling higher-welfare beef than the particular Christian and Muslim identities of the individuals involved. The resulting meat isn't Christian, Muslim, or secular; it is all three, and many other things at the same time. Religion is similarly complex within the other groups. The Adamah Farm Fellowship program brings together young adult Jews from diverse Jewish backgrounds and provides education on contemporary environmental, racial, and social justice issues; sustainable agriculture; and Judaism. Fellows are also encouraged to engage in Jewish and non-Jewish spiritual and religious practices like prayer services, ritual kosher slaughter demonstrations, meditation, and yoga. During my time at Pearlstone, the farm was managed by a director who practiced meditation at a Shambhala Buddhist center and by a Christian volunteer, and they worked alongside Jewish staff to implement shmita on the farm. The owners of the Hallelujah Diet Health Retreat site in Lake Lure, who identified as Messianic Jews, taught Christian visitors from a variety of backgrounds how to follow the diet while that retreat center was operational. Going even deeper, many of the practices these religious people are creating and revitalizing differ from those more frequently practiced by their coreligionists. According to Jewish law, shmita should be implemented only in the land of Israel. For many Christians, focusing excessive energy on the earthly body is theologically inconsistent with the prescribed focus on the status of the soul. So, is the farm Jewish? Is the diet Christian? Clear-cut categories like Christianity and Judaism work well in some areas of religious studies, but they are less useful in the complex reality of contemporary religion.

In the United States, religions have become increasingly intertwined through centuries of conflict, cohabitation, and cooperation, but in academic settings, the study of American religion often remains focused on particular religious traditions (for example, American Christianity, American Judaism, American Islam) or themes (such as gender, race, ritual). These approaches have helped us understand a great deal about American religion, and this book is a thematic treatment of religious engagement in alternative food movements. But the religious categories remain an issue because there is often an expectation that we could analyze data thematically and then work to understand what exclusively Christian or Jewish engagements in the food movement look like. As Sarah Imhoff argues in *The Lives of Jessie Sampter*, people in the United States have a tendency to act "both as a source of religious ideas, rituals, and worldviews and as the receiver of religious ideas, rituals, and worldviews." Imhoff calls this "religious recombination" and notes that even as people receive, give, and even give up ideas, they also retain "a sense of intactness," so they don't convert to something new or feel incomplete, they simply amend their religiosity, consciously or unconsciously, and continue living their life.[15] This model of religious recombination was visible in every group described in this book, though I am also adding a particular spatial element to my analysis, because the religious recombination that occurred in the groups described here happened outside of traditional religious institutions. In the spaces outside of religious institutions and between religious traditions, people intersect, ideas mingle, and new rituals develop. Notably, these are the spaces where we spend most of our time. They are our workplaces, schools, community organizations, and coalitions striving to address a myriad of concerning contemporary issues. I focus here on the spaces where religious people are collaborating across a variety of religious

Cows grazing in the shade of a large tree at Baldwin Family Farms, June 2015.

and nonreligious differences to change the food system. I call this phenomenon of religious amalgamation in the food movement space (and this book about it) "free-range religion."

Free-range religion has three key elements: It is happening outside of traditional religious institutions, it incorporates elements sometimes identified as "spiritual," and it is a combination of various religious and secular ideas, trends, and practices. The framework of free-range religion is more capacious than common categories used in religious studies, like "religion," "spiritual but not religious," and even "atheist" and "agnostic," because they are too narrow and therefore fail to capture the complex religious identities that people are building among and between these categories. I will explain all of these aspects of free-range religion below and expand upon them throughout the book.

The free-range religion label is convenient because the examples here are all related to food, but it also serves as an accurate descriptor of the religious groups participating in the alternative food movement. In the proper food industry terminology, V. Mac Baldwin's cows are pasture-raised, which essentially means they are raised entirely outdoors. In contrast, free-range means that the animals have access to the outdoors but generally spend their time indoors.[16] Similarly, many of the people described here spent some of their time "outside" in alternative food movement spaces but continued to attend worship services and events at mainstream religious institutions. This is the first aspect of free-range religion. Free-range religion is not embedded in traditional religious institutions, and its manifestations do not necessarily align with recognized religious denominations or movements.

The religious food movements I studied were not churches or synagogues, nor were they associated with particular churches or synagogues. Individual participants in these groups may or may not have affiliated with traditional religious institutions, but the religion they practiced as they engaged in these religious food movements looked at least a little bit different from their usual practice. Participants who rarely engaged with institutional religion at all found themselves praying, singing, and participating in ritual in the religious alternative food movement spaces. Participants who regularly attended worship services found themselves praying outdoors, singing new songs, and experimenting with innovative rituals. For example, some Adamah fellows arrived with little to no experience with formal synagogue worship; others arrived as regular attendees of Shabbat services in a range of contemporary Jewish movements (that is, Orthodox, Reform, and so on). While at Adamah, the fellows collaborated to create Shabbat services that worked for everyone in their group. So, fellows who didn't usually go to Shabbat services at all were not just going but participating in and creating Shabbat services while at Adamah. And fellows who usually attended services at a synagogue led by seasoned laypeople or professional clergy were designing services that they led with the other fellows, holding those services in the fellows' shared living room or outdoors or in the retreat center's worship space. In the end, all the fellows practiced Judaism in a slightly different way than they might have otherwise because they were in a new space with a new community of people.

Second, free-range religion incorporates elements that have often been identified as "spiritual" by religious studies scholars. This is related to the first point but also requires some discussion of what "religion" means and how it is most often used. Rather than distinguish "spiritual" from "religion" or "religious," I'll be using "free-range religion" as a broad term that encompasses spiritual practices because that is what I saw in the religious alternative food movement spaces. The categories that have been developed in religious studies were not well-suited to the experiences and identities of my interlocutors. Though many of them did engage in practices that might be considered "spiritual" and some of them spoke about how they connected to those spiritual aspects of the group they participated in, these spiritual practices were all occurring within the broader framework of a particular religious perspective. At the Hallelujah Diet Health Retreat, participants meditated, practiced yoga, and engaged in other forms of practice that might be considered spiritual. However, in interviews, many of the participants were quite clear that they identified as Christians and not as "spiritual but not religious" or "New Age." The rigidity of contemporary categories leaves little space for the kinds of spirituality that were previously understood as part of religion. Scholar Linda Mercadante notes that historically, "spirituality" was linked to "piety" and referred to an individual's personal practice and faith but wasn't distinct from that person's religious identity.[17] In my analysis of the Hallelujah Diet Health Retreat, this model of understanding of religion and spirituality as overlapping phenomena is much more useful than contemporary models that distinguish between the two.

Scholars Robert C. Fuller and William B. Parsons distinguish between the two terms in their book *Being Spiritual but Not Religious* even as they note that the terms have often been used interchangeably. They explain that the term "religion" has often been used to describe "shared, public, or institutional expressions of belief in the existence of something beyond the physical world," while "spiritual" is often associated with "more personal or subjective efforts to find connection with these more-than-physical aspects of reality."[18] This categorization prioritizes the aspects of religious expression associated with Christianity, and Protestant Christianity in particular, as it uses "belief" as the point of demarcation between that which is religious and that which is spiritual. Religion is about more than belief and is sometimes not about belief at all for millions of people, so suggesting that all such religious expressions are spiritual instead of religious reinforces Protestant frameworks and imposes hierarchies that have caused a great deal of harm to non-Protestant religious communities.

Work has already been done to accommodate the fact that categories like "religion" and "spiritual but not religious" are particularly ill-suited for describing the religious identities of those outside Protestant Christianity. In the case of Judaism, in particular, there are many who identify as Jews but not as religious. The Pew Research Center's sociological studies of Jews in the United States have developed alternative categories that work better for describing Jews who do identify as Jews but not as religious Jews. Pew uses "Jews by religion" and "Jews of no religion," which allows it to capture the population of Jews who engage in practices that are seen as spiritual or cultural but also Jewish.[19] Belief in God is not the distinguishing factor between the categories, as 17 percent of the Jews who identified themselves as "Jews by religion" indicated that they did not believe in either the God of the Bible or a higher power/spiritual force.[20] The categories allowed Pew to capture the kinds of Jews I spoke with at Adamah and Pearlstone who engaged in Jewish practices and identified as Jewish but didn't consider themselves "religious," which in the context of Judaism is often colloquially associated with regular synagogue attendance and adherence to Jewish law. But many "Jews of no religion" hold Passover seders, fast on Yom Kippur, and engage in a variety of Jewish cultural practices, so they are doing things often considered religious even as they are distancing themselves from the ways that term has been used, which suggests that our current definitions and terms are insufficient. Many of my interlocutors at Adamah and Pearlstone identified themselves as "spiritual," "cultural," "atheist," or "agnostic" Jews, but as I mentioned above, they attended and led Shabbat services in addition to other religious rituals. For these Jews, it was less important that Shabbat was commanded by God and more important that Shabbat provided a weekly opportunity to gather Jews together for education and celebration. In other words, religion was happening, even if God and Jewish law were not explicitly invoked. In this way, my approach to religion is similar to the one taken by Rachel Gross in *Beyond the Synagogue*, in which she emphasizes the role of nostalgia in American Jewish communities and argues for more attention to the broadest understanding of religion, which is "to provide existential meaning, answering questions about life's purpose."[21] The free-range religion framework I use here is inclusive of these kinds of complex identities and is intended to broaden our understanding of religion in accordance with how religion is being practiced today. So, rather than upholding this binary and attempting to place my interlocutors into one box or the other, I am using free-range religion in an effort to broaden the category of religion to include people who may reject belief in a higher power and rigid adherence to laws and texts but find meaning and purpose in exploring religious and spiritual traditions in new ways.

There are particular lineages of spirituality that are relevant to these religious alternative food movements. Religious studies scholar Andrea Jain suggests that spirituality, and particular forms of spirituality, like interest in health foods, is often an effort by people to control their lives and perhaps seek transformation, personal growth, or liberation. She notes that contemporary forms of what she calls "neoliberal spirituality" are a critical component of "global neoliberal capitalism" because they "relate spiritual practices to ethical values through marketing and purchasing activities."[22] During my fieldwork, the groups here were all involved, on some level, in marketing and purchasing activities, so they were inextricable from global neoliberal capitalism. Scholars Kathryn Lofton, Colleen McDannell, and Leigh Eric Schmidt have demonstrated that religious people engage in consumerism and capitalism as they impart and sell their religious ideals, wares, and holidays in the global marketplace, and the groups described here were no different, even as they were intentional about the products they produced and the consumers they reached.[23] All of the groups discussed here sold something, and whether it was Adamah pickles, Hallelujah Diet brand supplements, Baldwin Beef, or educational experiences at Pearlstone, these products all reflect the reality that these groups existed in a capitalist society, where they had to balance their budgets or make a profit to survive. This aligns with the argument put forward by Lucia Hulsether throughout her book *Capitalist Humanitarianism*—that nothing is outside of global neoliberal capitalism, and all attempts to do better remain tethered to the power dynamics of the underlying capitalism structures.[24] For example, Adamah is a nonprofit organization, but it still relies on philanthropic funds, grants, CSA customers, and the sale of goods at local farmers' markets to balance its budget, so its budget is as tied to the whims of the US economy as any other. Therefore, working within the broad structure of capitalism, the groups described here are setting up alternative food systems that are informed by neoliberal spirituality, but they are simultaneously motivated by long-standing religious texts, rituals, and traditions. For this reason, I find it useful to use the term "free-range religion" as a category that encompasses the spiritual, the religious, and many other things, too.

Free-range religion also includes forms of religion that are less easily identifiable with a singular religious tradition and therefore require attention to multiple traditions simultaneously. In *Between Heaven and Earth*, Robert Orsi suggests that departments of religious studies are "departments of the study of desirable religions."[25] In the broader field of religious studies, we tend to divide ourselves into subfields drawn from a short list of religious traditions. Scholars study Buddhism, Christianity, Hinduism, Indigenous traditions, Islam, Judaism, or new religious movements, among others. So, as I use free-range religion to open up our understanding of religion, it will help to begin with a more expansive definition of religion. Orsi's definition of religion as a network of relationships between heaven and earth works well for this book—with some caveats.[26] First, I'd amend "heaven" to include non-Christian conceptions of the spiritual world. In this book, people have religious experiences in fields, on walks, with animals, and while preparing meals. As they opened themselves up to these kinds of experiences, they were often sacralizing spaces and activities they may not have understood to be religious prior to their engagement in an alternative food movement group, and they were not narrow in their understanding of where spirituality might be found in those spaces. Rather than restrict themselves to religious institutions, or even to meals and food-based rituals, the religious alternative food movement participants described in this book often engaged all of creation as they sought to realign their diets, bodies, and worlds.

The third and final aspect of free-range religion is that it is an amalgamation of religious and secular ideas, trends, and practices. Though religious sources and traditions often carry the most weight, these religious food movements are in conversation with the other religious and nonreligious experts in their space. At the Hallelujah Diet Health Retreat I attended, the Bible provided the foundation for my and the other participants' raw vegan diet, but a cadre of scientists, doctors, religious and secular leaders, and cultural figures served as experts for the validity and effectiveness of the diet. We were told we were meant to eat a raw vegan diet because that was what humans ate in the Garden of Eden, but we were also told that a raw vegan diet was proved to be the healthiest diet by experts in the field. So, were we eating a raw vegan diet because that was what God created humans to eat, and we were religious people who believed that what the book of Genesis said was true? Or were we eating a raw vegan diet because scientists found that a raw vegan diet was a healthy diet, and we believed that what scientists said was true? I found that at the Hallelujah Diet Health Retreat, participants often believed both of these things and didn't dwell too much in the places where those beliefs might conflict. At times throughout this book, it may seem like these groups did not have a clear, logical, and coherent belief system because, like many other religious and nonreligious groups, they didn't. They drew from multiple sources, believed contradictory things, and sometimes acted in ways that didn't align with their stated beliefs. Like all of us, they were mere mortals trying to make sense of a complicated world and were using the sources available to them to try to make the best decisions possible within the scope of their worldviews.

It should be noted that in many cases, free-range religion involves the incorporation of ideas and practices from Buddhism, Hinduism, and Native American traditions and others, and in some cases, my interlocutors identified the complicated power dynamics involved. In other cases, they did not acknowledge those dynamics. And except for a few individuals, even those who were aware of the relevant power dynamics did not have relationships with members of the religious communities who originated those ideas and practices. Relatedly, these organizations were all located on land that was incorporated into what is now the United States through the violence of colonialism, and while some acknowledged that history, others didn't, and none of them had explicit intentions to return the land to Native Americans. Andrea Jain points to the common failure of people who engage in this kind of cultural adaptation or appropriation to engage with actual Buddhists, Hindus, or Native Americans, preferring instead to adopt "easily accessible wares and brand-name forms of self-actualization or enlightenment-ethics offered by entrepreneurs or corporations and available on television, through cheap paperbacks, or at their local grocery store, shopping mall, or gym."[27] Put another way, in her book *White Utopias*, Amanda Lucia argues that "long before the New Age dawned, Americans turned to religious others when dissatisfied with the dominant culture." Lucia connects this kind of "religious exoticism" with the "overwhelming whiteness of alternative spiritual communities" and notes the parallels to colonization in the ways that white people feel entitled to the religious texts, practices, and traditions of others, particularly those who are not white.[28] The people making up the groups described in *Free-Range Religion* were, indeed, predominantly white, so when they borrowed from the traditions of others, they did so from a position of power. Awareness of this power dynamic is essential to understanding religious alternative food movements as complicated and imperfect groups, even if their adherents see things otherwise.

In summary, *Free-Range Religion* offers a window into what religion looks like in the twenty-first century. It is less attached to traditional institutions, it incorporates spiritual elements, and it is a complex blend of religious and secular ideas and practices. I am not particularly interested in whether the religious expressions discussed here are "authentic" or "authorized." My work starts with the assumption that if people say they are part of a religious group, then they are, and if they see their practices as religious, then they are. The fact that religious people do not fit neatly in our prescribed categories is not a reason to ignore or discount their religious practices. Instead, it is an invitation to research religion without preconceived notions of what counts as "religion," "Judaism" or "Christianity." In *Free-Range Religion*, I'll provide a window into groups that want our food system to be better and to align with their religious values and ethics, and they are working to make it happen.

METHODOLOGY

I registered for the Teva Seminar on Jewish Environmental Education on a whim, so when I arrived on June 12, 2012, I was apprehensive. My research had moved toward religious food practices, but I was seeking ethnographic field sites and was uncertain of their existence. As part of the Teva Seminar program, I visited the farm at Eden Village Camp, where we harvested wheat, planted a tree, and visited with baby goats. I took a class on Jewish agricultural texts with Jakir Manela, who was the director of Kayam Farm at Pearlstone Center at that time. My discussion group leader for the seminar was Risa Alyson Cooper, who ran Shoresh, a Jewish environmental organization in Toronto, through 2021. I ate many of my meals with a friendly camp counselor from New York, whom I encountered again in 2015 when she was a farm fellow at Adamah. Arthur Waskow, a rabbi and leader in the Jewish Renewal Movement and the founder and former director of the Shalom Center, led a session about the importance of environmentalism for Jews. I made kimchi, took a course on permaculture gardening, and toured a double-stacked bus that runs on vegetable oil. I went to the Teva Seminar looking for a field site and found an entire world of people who were passionate about food, the environment, and Judaism.

Food offers a beneficial locus for the study of how religious and political ideologies are enacted in daily life. Anthropologists have been studying food and foodways—the collective set of cultural, social, and economic food practices—since the mid-twentieth century. Mary Douglas showed that food was used to develop and reify boundaries between religious communities in earlier periods, and her work suggested that the kind of interreligious cooperation around food that the groups in this book demonstrate was distinct.[29] Some of the differences I saw were the result of my methods, which emphasized religion as it was happening in day-to-day life rather than the kind of religion prescribed in sacred texts and debated by theologians. I utilized the lived-religion approach developed and popularized by David Hall and Robert Orsi, which is to say I studied religion as it was lived in people's everyday lives.[30] R. Marie Griffith, Courtney Bender, and Samira Mehta provided keen examples of how this approach can benefit the study of religion and food, in particular, as they analyzed Christian diet culture, the AIDS patient meal delivery nonprofit organization God's Love We Deliver, and interfaith foodways, respectively.[31] In this book, that means the religion(s) recorded was often the kind of religion that motivated people to weed beds, peel carrots, share a shade tree with cows, and prune invasive thistles and express gratitude for those activities even if they were sore, hungry, tired, or frustrated.

In keeping with the inclinations of my interlocutors, formal religious prescriptions and rituals associated with food do not receive much attention here. Instead, I describe the practices that reflected a community's intentional engagement with its concerns around industrial food, even, and perhaps especially, when those concerns raised questions about traditional religious foodways. Roasted chicken on Shabbat is such an ingrained tradition that some Jews consider meat on Shabbat a required part of the meal. Meat is kosher as long as the animal is clean and the slaughter is done properly. But is the meat kosher if the chicken spent its life in a crowded field house where its beak was clipped so it wouldn't peck at other birds, where it was pumped with antibiotics to stave off inevitable infections, and where it had no access to the outdoors? The laws of kashrut are dynamic, and Jews have adapted them in every context they have lived in. Adherence to kashrut has also varied widely, particularly in the contemporary United States, and many Jews have reconsidered their consumption of meat in recent years. In this book, I am interested in these moments, when religious traditions are reconsidered alongside evidence from environmental, animal, and food scientists, and in the practices that emerge from such investigations and collaborations.

After four days at the Teva Seminar, I had a vision for this project: There was a subset of religious people who were unhappy with the American food system and wanted to change it. In order to cover the different aspects of this multifaceted movement, I followed the food from farm to table to discover other potential places to visit. I lived in North Carolina at the time and prioritized sites close to home due to budgetary and time constraints. I also chose groups that were associated with either Judaism or Christianity—not because they are the only ones engaged in religious food movement work but because those were my areas of expertise. This focused approach also provided a sense of continuity between the sites as the alternative food systems that each site developed were based in the Tanakh/Bible even as the resulting food systems varied widely. This farm-to-table framework persisted and provided a useful organizational system for the chapters that follow. The first chapter is based on a Jewish produce farm. The second deals with a diet retreat focused on eating fruits, vegetables, and nuts in their raw form. The third moves us higher up the food chain, to cattle being raised for meat. The fourth chapter brings us to another Jewish farm where the land lay fallow after years of production. So, as the reader moves through the book, food will be grown and harvested, consumed raw, and fed to animals who are then themselves consumed, and then the land will rest.

After some preliminary fieldwork in the summers of 2013 and 2014, I packed my car and headed into the field in June 2015. I spent a week at Pearlstone, a week at a Hallelujah Diet Health Retreat, and two weeks at Adamah. Baldwin Beef was only an hour from my apartment at the time, so my visits there were shorter in length and more spread out through the summer and fall of 2015. I used my time in the field to fully immerse myself in each place and to conduct interviews. I wrote detailed notes in every class, meeting, and session I attended and spent many evenings recording field notes well into the earliest hours of morning. I ended up with over thirty individual interviews with staff, volunteers, participants, and leadership at the sites. I asked questions about their dietary practices, their relationship to land and animals, their motivation to work/learn at the site, and their religious beliefs. In every interview, the answers to those questions took us in a direction I had not anticipated, but I always learned a great deal. I conducted follow-up interviews with some of my interlocutors in the late summer and fall of 2015. I also took hundreds of photos during the visits. The photos mainly assisted in jogging my memory as I sat down to write, but some appear here. This intensive on-site fieldwork provided a wealth of material for much of what follows.

This is an undeniably anthropocentric project. In it, I studied religion and the human beings who expressed religion through the food systems that they created. But food systems cannot be created by humans alone, and I attended to all of the living species and the land they lived on as integral actors in a complex multispecies project.[32] Food, no matter where it comes from, is the product of a vast assemblage of humans and nonhumans who connect at different points to accomplish one particular aspect of the process that turns raw materials into food and subsequently into the energy that helps bodies act in the world. I did not manage to fully decenter the human, but whenever possible I tried to shine some light on plants, animals, microorganisms, and land to complicate the kind of human domination of the natural world that has led to environmental degradation, mass extinction, and climate change.

As an example of this attention to the nonhuman, I offer a description of Adamah's pickles. During my time at Adamah, the organization sold pickles as a value-added product to help support its nonprofit farm. Like all food, the pickle is ephemeral and dynamic. It moves through many different forms both before it becomes food and after its time as food ends. I was interested in the points at which agency shifted and changed on the trajectory of seed to plant to cucumber to pickle-in-process to pickle to lunch to vitamins and nutrients absorbed by the body to digested matter to waste to compost to fertilizer and back again to planted seeds. I was curious about how the human-plant interactions changed along with the cucumbers and about the moments when religion got entangled in this system. For example, once a cucumber was washed and brought into the kitchen at Adamah, it was subject to the laws of kashrut, and adherence to those laws would determine the cucumber's fate. If someone dropped a ham into the pickling barrel, the cucumber inside would never become a pickle or go through a human body. It would end its life on the compost pile, fodder for hungry chickens and future plants.

Cucumbers work well to illustrate what Ian Hodder has called the "flow of materials." He proposed that we engage things like cucumbers differently as they transform.[33] It is easy to ignore a cucumber when it is growing on the vine. Humans may weed around the vine to make sure it is not obstructed, water the vine, and ensure that it is receiving sunlight, but the cucumbers themselves can be ignored—until the day when they can't be ignored. There is a brief window of time when cucumbers can be harvested so that they are the right size for pickle jars. One afternoon at Adamah, we were harvesting cucumbers and encountered a number of them that had been missed a few days prior. They were now too large for pickling and would instead be sent to the kitchen to use in salads. The cucumbers changed human plans that day. They grew too much while we were ignoring their material presence, and Adamah lost money as a result, because pickles are worth more than cucumbers. Examples like this from all my field sites speak to the nature of the human-nonhuman relationships that foodways require. To deal with the changing states of people, plants, and animals, each account of food or food-in-process is offered with context, and the described condition of the food or food-in-process should be understood as temporary. Religion is similarly contextually dependent.

The religious character of the sites I visited varied, and my status as an insider or outsider differed at each site. I am white and come from a middle-class background. These characteristics were shared by almost everyone I encountered doing my fieldwork. The food described in each chapter was relatively expensive, so the choices made by my interlocutors to produce or consume fresh, local, organic, plant-based, and pasture-raised foods were choices that were not available to many Americans. At each organization I visited, there were people who lived and worked on-site. In addition, there were also temporary laborers, visitors, and participants at each site. These groups of people were not necessarily less invested in the goals of the group, but they were active in the group for a limited period of time. The farm fellows at Adamah worked on the farm for three months; participants at the Hallelujah Diet Health Retreats stayed for one to two weeks. Then they left and enacted their new alternative food system in their homes and at their local farmers' markets, grocery stores, and restaurants. My own experience as a temporary resident in these spaces paralleled theirs.

My religious identity as an agnostic Reform Jew remained consistent throughout my fieldwork, as it has for the last two decades or so. I argue throughout this book that the religious labels often applied to organizations and movements are not as simple as they appear. However, for the purposes of positioning myself in relation to these sites, I will attempt to offer a basic description of the religiosity of each site. Adamah and Pearlstone were both pluralistic Jewish spaces. This allowed me to function as an insider at both sites. I understand the language(s) of American Jews, I share their communal set of experiences, and I have robust training in Jewish texts and traditions. However, I also spent most of my time at Pearlstone with non-Jewish staffers, and some staff members at both retreat centers were more observant than I was and wouldn't consider me Jewish at all, so my insider status at both sites was relative.[34]

Baldwin Family Farms was managed by faithful Christians, and a devout Baptist wrote *The Hallelujah Diet*. A family of Messianic Jews organized and ran the Hallelujah Diet Health Retreats at the Lake Lure location. My interlocutors at Baldwin Family Farms and the Hallelujah Diet Health Retreat were simultaneously interested in my project and concerned about the state of my non-Christian or non-Messianic Jewish soul. Conversations with people at both of these sites often took on a missionary tone. I have spent a great deal of time in Christian and Messianic Jewish settings, for academic and nonacademic reasons, so I was more comfortable in these situations than others might have been. But I was certainly not an insider at either site. Beyond religion, this often had more to do with the social conservatism of the participants and staff members. My ability to set aside differences in these areas stemmed from the fact that our ideologies converged at other points that were central to this project.[35]

Religion is not the only aspect of one's identity, and frequently throughout my fieldwork, it was not the main point of connection between my interlocutors and me. My fieldwork was about food, and that was how I created and maintained relationships at each site. I told everyone about my project and answered interested individuals' extensive questions about my research. And whether I was helping to grow it, pick it, process it, or prepare it, my participant observation was all about the food. Interestingly, in the realm of food, my beliefs and practices proved susceptible to the influence of my ethnographic and written sources. In the summer of 2014, when I was researching shmita, I embarked upon a canning and pickling project that occupied my days and my kitchen for about a month. I was about seven flavors and fifty jars of jam into that experiment before I connected it to the focus on food preservation in the shmita literature I was reading. While drafting an early version of chapter 2 of this book, I looked down and noticed that the cold-processed (raw) vegetable juice I was drinking was similar to the one I drank numerous times at the Hallelujah Diet Health Retreat and grew to enjoy.

Beyond jam, pickles, and juice, I also found myself adapting my own diet based on the research I did and the experiences I had. In 2011, I became a vegetarian while reading about the food industry in the United States. I became a vegan on June 21, 2015, my first day at the Hallelujah Diet Health Retreat. During the retreat, all participants follow the Hallelujah Diet, which involved veganism and abstention from caffeine and alcohol. It took me four weeks prior to the retreat to wean down my coffee intake so I could participate fully. While at the retreat, I noticed that I felt energized and my digestive system was running smoothly, so I decided to keep up the vegan diet at my next field site, Adamah. It wasn't hard because the Isabella Freedman Jewish Retreat Center kitchen staff offered a vegan option at every meal. By the time I left Adamah, caffeine and alcohol were back in my diet, but the dairy and eggs I had stopped eating no longer appealed to me. As I write this, I am still a vegan who spends many of my summer evenings canning jam and pickles. I note these dietary changes with the caveat that this is my past and current situation. I don't dare imagine what I will or won't be eating in the future. I don't believe that my evolving food practices are unique, and the fact that dietary practices are not stable is a basic assumption of this book.

My own engagement with food is dynamic and subject to external influence, and the same applies to my interlocutors in the field. I attend to the historical lineages and cultural contexts that enable and inspire the religious food movements described here. I investigate the aspects of industrial food that motivated them to action and the familiar character of their responses. In order to properly contextualize these groups and consider their historical predecessors, my ethnography is supplemented by printed materials produced by these sites, sources that were mentioned in those printed materials and in classes and conversations, and the websites of each of these groups.

I have been on email and mailing lists for these sites since 2013, which provided an overabundance of prescriptive and promotional material. I examined the secondary sources written about these and similar sites and the primary and secondary literature that provides historical context for these groups.

ORGANIZATION

As I mentioned above, the chapters in this book are ordered to move us up the food chain and then back down again. We'll begin at Adamah, where fellows grew produce; head to a Hallelujah Diet Health Retreat, where participants consumed only raw vegan food; visit a cattle ranch, where beef was produced and sold; rest along with the land at Pearlstone, as we might after a hearty meal; and end in the compost pile, where ideas were recycled and renewed. In order to fully articulate my argument that religious people are creating alternative food systems and doing so through an amalgamation of religious ideas and practices, I dedicate separate sections to each aspect of this argument in each chapter. I also provide historical context for each contemporary expression of religious food activism before describing the alternative food system the group was working to enact and exploring the religiosity of the group.

Chapter 1 focuses on the Adamah Farm Fellowship at the Isabella Freedman Jewish Retreat Center in Falls Village, Connecticut. This fellowship program, still running, is geared toward young Jews in their twenties and thirties from the full spectrum of Jewish backgrounds. The fellowship runs three times per year in the spring, summer, and fall seasons for three months each session and provides participants with an immersive and educational experience in farming, Judaism, community building, and social justice. In this chapter, I set Adamah within the context of Jewish environmentalism and describe the sustainable agriculture system that the organization implemented to help young American Jews reshape their relationship with their food while they simultaneously cultivated their own Jewish identities.

Chapter 2 considers how the book *The Hallelujah Diet* by George Malkmus was put into practice at the Hallelujah Diet Health Retreat in Lake Lure, North Carolina. The Hallelujah Diet fits within a well-documented tradition of Christian diet reform in the United States, and the chapter includes an overview of this history before exploring the Hallelujah Diet system and the religiosity of the Hallelujah Diet Health Retreat. My discussion of the religiosity of the Hallelujah Diet centers on the interplay between "New Age" ideologies, scientific knowledge, and biblical sources that together formed the authoritative foundation of the diet.

Chapter 3 follows the Baldwin Family Farms cows as they moved from grassy hills to the meat counters at such grocery stores as Whole Foods and Kroger. I provide some background on Christian perspectives on human-animal relationships before explaining the inner workings of this pasture-raised beef operation and the poultry breeding operation that made it financially sustainable. The religiosity of this site was particularly tied to a broader network of certification agencies and consumer demand, so I consider Christianity and Islam as they related to the processing of the USDA-certified halal beef alongside these factors in this chapter. This includes attention to the more innocuous marketing of this religious food movement product as the meat made its way to a less religious public.

Chapter 4 delves into the shmita year, an agricultural sabbatical practice that was reimagined and implemented at Pearlstone Center in Baltimore during 2014–15. I begin this chapter with an overview of shmita as it has been interpreted in Jewish tradition before recounting the agricultural and human-centered shmita practices that Pearlstone introduced. Pearlstone's location slightly outside the center of the Baltimore Jewish community gave it the freedom to be a space for innovative Judaism, and shmita exemplifies this. The observance of shmita continues to expand within Jewish environmentalist spaces, so this chapter ends with thoughts on the growth and future potential of shmita in the United States.

Compost is the heart of healthy soil and the foundation of a sustainable agriculture system. In compost, leftovers and food waste are repurposed and allow the cycle to begin again. The conclusion discusses the past, present, and future of religious alternative food movements through the lens of the compost process, wherein food breaks down slowly over time, aided by humans and chickens, until it becomes nutrient-rich compost, ready to be spread over the fields and help new things grow.

CONCLUSION

All four of the sites discussed here grounded their work in the Tanakh/Bible, so I'll end where they began. According to the book of Exodus, after the ancient Israelites were freed from enslavement in Egypt, they were wandering in the desert. They couldn't find food, so God provided them with manna from heaven. The manna would appear each morning, like dew on the grass, and Exodus says that it sustained the Israelites for forty years until they were allowed into Canaan, which was often referred to as the "land of milk and honey." The groups described in this book might be seen in parallel to the ancient Israelites. They were free, but they did some wandering and could not find food they wanted to eat. What they found was produce covered in pesticides, water filled with microplastics, and processed foods containing carcinogens outlawed in other countries. They saw land that was becoming barren due to monoculture farming and fertilizers, and they learned about the millions of animals that spend their short lives on factory farms. The people described here, faced with food they didn't want to eat, looked inward to their religious values and traditions and outward to scientists and activists to provide alternative food. Unlike manna, these alternatives were not provided directly by God, nor did they appear in the wilderness. Instead, they were developed by thoughtful people who built on previous traditions as they established new practices. In this book, I seek to record their presence, their collaborations, and their innovations as they pursue a better food system here in the United States with the hopes that it, too, can become a land of milk and honey.

CHAPTER ONE

Sustainable Agriculture at the Adamah Farm Fellowship

And God saw that this was good.

GENESIS 1:12 (JEWISH PUBLICATION SOCIETY)

July 4, 2015, fell on a Saturday. At the Adamah Farm Fellowship at the Isabella Freedman Jewish Retreat Center in Falls Village, Connecticut, the fellows have Saturdays off for Shabbat.[1] Instead of spending the day working on the farm and attending classes, the fellows, young Jews in their twenties and thirties, tended to spend Saturdays taking leisurely walks and trips into town. As the sun started to set, I joined two of the fellows, Shana and Debby, on a hike up to Lookout Point, an overlook that sits on the Appalachian Trail adjacent to the retreat center.[2] Shana and Debby were very patient with me (and my recently reconstructed knee) as we trudged up the steep trail. I arrived at the top exhausted, but the view was well worth the climb.

We had just settled in when Ari, an Isabella Freedman employee, joined us. The sun was setting, so even though other folks hadn't made it up the mountain, we decided to start the Havdalah ceremony. This Saturday evening

View from an overlook on the Appalachian Trail at sunset, July 2015.

ceremony delineates the separation between Shabbat and the rest of the week. Four blessings are recited: one over wine, one over spices, one over the candle lighting, and a blessing when the candle is extinguished.³ We brought a braided Havdalah candle with us, but we had to get creative to come up with the other Havdalah supplies. Ari's scented oils took the place of a spice box, and we used water instead of wine. As the first July 4 fireworks started to dot the horizon below us, we sang the blessings together. After we finished, more fellows, staff, and visitors from Isabella Freedman joined us. A rabbi who was working at Isabella Freedman at the time reached the top and wanted to do Havdalah, so we took out the candle and the oils once more. A few of the other fellows who had joined us brought beer with them, so we used that in place of wine in our second ceremony. After we finished the blessings, we continued singing. Instead of the usual cacophony of fireworks, our ears were treated to a choir of about twenty voices singing in harmony as we watched the colorful displays below us. When the fireworks ended, we hiked down the mountain by the light of our headlamps and spent the rest of the evening enjoying kosher burgers around a campfire.[4] This July 4 celebration epitomizes Judaism as it was (and still is) practiced at Adamah. Our celebration was earth-based, innovative, and Jewish—we hiked up a mountain, performed an improvised version of the Havdalah ceremony (twice) with a creative collection of supplies, and enjoyed the standard American July 4 fireworks.

I argue in this chapter that the Adamah Farm and the Adamah Farm Fellowship program have developed and enacted an alternative food system based in both Judaism and sustainable agriculture. *Adamah* is the Hebrew word used for the earth in the Genesis creation narrative. The word *adamah* is related to the Hebrew word *adam*, which is often translated as "human," but the term "earthling" more accurately represents the relationship between the two words in Hebrew.[5] This evocative name, Adamah, speaks to the heart of this organization—the relationship between humans and the earth. Adamah seeks to bring young Jews into a relationship with the earth that reflects Adamah's interpretations of relevant biblical and rabbinic texts. The Adamah food system has also been shaped by the history of Jewish agriculture and environmentalism, and it has been animated by an eclectic, dynamic, and pluralistic form of Judaism that helps fellows shape their own Jewish identities. The current mission statement of the Adamah Farm Fellowship emphasizes that it is growing not just food but also people: "Adamah cultivates the soil and the soul to produce food, to build and transform identities, and to gather a community of people changing the world. We grow vegetables, fruit, herbs, goats, flowers, eggs, and we grow people through experiences with ecology, food production, social justice, spiritual practice, a vibrant evolving Judaism, and intentional community."[6] I'll open this chapter with an overview of the fellowship program, followed by sections dedicated to the historical context for Adamah, the alternative food system at Adamah, and free-range religion at Adamah.

THE ADAMAH FARM FELLOWSHIP

The Isabella Freedman Jewish Retreat Center leadership hired Shamu Sadeh to start a farm in 2003. Sadeh also established the fellowship program and has directed it since the beginning.[7] During my time there in June and July 2015, Janna Siller was the farm director and Rebecca Bloomfield was the associate director of Adamah. Then and now, the central component of Adamah is its three-month fellowship program, which runs three times per year in the spring, summer, and fall. During each of the three-month fellowship periods, the fellows live, cook, and eat together in community in the Beit Adamah (Adamah House), often shortened to "BA."[8] Through classes and practical experience, the fellows learn about growing food using sustainable techniques on the six-acre Adamah Farm.[9] The fellows seed, plant, weed, water, harvest, wash, and package produce throughout their three months in the program. The produce is split about equally between the Isabella Freedman Jewish Retreat Center's dining hall and the Adamah community-supported agriculture program, which provides paying participants with weekly or biweekly shares of Adamah's harvest. The fellows also learn to care for chickens and goats and help make value-added products like jam and pickles in Adamah's commercial kitchen, selling those products at local farmers' markets. I describe the food system at Adamah in more detail in the third section of this chapter.

In addition to their agricultural work, fellows also attend classes, prayer services, holiday events, and other activities intended to expand their knowledge about Judaism, social and environmental justice, and themselves. A typical day at Adamah begins with a morning prayer service, called Avodat Lev (Service of the Heart), followed by breakfast and morning chores, which during my time there included milking goats, letting the chickens out and collecting eggs, and transporting compost from the dining hall to the compost yard, among others. Morning chores are followed by a three- to four-hour work session on the farm, then lunch, and then another three- to four-hour work session on the farm followed by a class or experience, dinner, and another class or experience.[10] I'll describe many of these work sessions here in more detail, but because I was there in the summer, our work sessions were often dedicated to harvesting, weeding, washing produce, and making jam or pickles. In my time with the Adamah Farm fellows, I attended classes on anti-oppression, fundraising, active listening, and compost, among others. Some of the experiences included visiting a nearby farm and swimming in its quarry, leading farm tours and doing activities with retreat center visitors, and spending time with staff of the Jewish environmental education program Teva (Nature) and touring its Topsy Turvy Bus.[11]

The activities, prayer sessions, and classes at the farm encourage the fellows to consider the connections between Judaism and the environment, often opening their eyes to new aspects of their own Judaism, their diets, and their environmentalism. In terms of food and diet, the fellows are guided through community discussions about how to set up the kitchen in the Beit Adamah, and they spend time working in the kitchen at the retreat center on-site. They also take classes focused on the issues in the contemporary food system and on Jewish values and practices related to food, labor, and ecology. Just before I arrived, the fellows participated in a kosher slaughter demonstration, and many of the fellows were in the process of rethinking their consumption of meat during my visit.[12]

One of the fellows, Rayna, explained that she didn't seek out Adamah for its Jewish components. However, her experience at Adamah helped her understand Judaism differently: "I think at this point, there is something about Judaism that you can no longer deny. It's just the earth and the soil." She ended her thought, reflecting, "You get to sort of learn about your roots, literally."[13] Classes and experiences at Adamah utilize the Hebrew Bible and other Jewish texts to explore ancient Israel as an agricultural society. Adamah fellows are encouraged to imagine and embody an environmental form of Judaism inspired by its foundational texts. This environmental Judaism necessarily extends the interests of its adherents beyond the boundaries of the Jewish people and their lands. When I asked Sam, a fellow from London, what his plans were upon returning home, his answer illustrated this desire: "There's also a kind of Adamah-y thing starting up in London. But I'm not sure whether I want to help out with that or not, because I want to save all of humanity, not just the Jews."[14] Sam voiced an opinion that was shared by many of the fellows. They were at Adamah to learn more about food systems and how to produce food in a sustainable way and then bring that knowledge back into the Jewish and non-Jewish worlds they inhabited. Sam's comments also point to the wider network of Adamah alumni that connects young, environmentally minded Jews all over the world.[15] Many Adamah alumni are leaders in the growing Jewish environmental and food justice movement. Adamah alumni have started educational programs, food businesses, and farms all over the country.[16] In many cases, Adamah alumni have turned toward activism during and after their time as fellows. Alumni are currently working as activists on issues such as climate change, animal welfare, and food insecurity.

I spent the bulk of my time at Adamah with eight summer 2015 farm fellows (Amy, Andie, Debby, Elisa, Rayna, Rose, Sam, and Zack), two field apprentices (Maya and Miri), and three Isabella Freedman Jewish Retreat Center staff members (Ari, Max, and Shira).[17] The three Adamah leaders, Shamu, Janna, and Rebecca, taught our classes, guided our work sessions, and provided support for the fellows throughout the program. At times, we also attended classes and worked alongside other Isabella Freedman staff or visiting instructors. Both field apprentices and all three of the retreat center staff members were alumni of the fellowship program. The fellows, field apprentices, and staff members were all in their twenties and thirties. It is worth noting that there was a significant gender imbalance in this group with more women and nonbinary people at every level. This is common in Adamah Farm Fellowship cohorts, though Janna informed me that there were fewer people than usual who were "experimenting with their gender identity."[18] The gender dynamics at Adamah suggest that this community feels accessible to women and transgender and nonbinary Jews and enables them to experiment with gender identity but also with community building, leadership, and religious ritual and worship in fruitful ways that I will discuss further in the fourth section of this chapter.

Within this community, as demonstrated by the mountaintop Havdalah ceremonies, there is space for experimentation with Judaisms and a wide range of earth-based religious practices, so religion at Adamah is based on and embedded in Judaism, but it also incorporates ideas and practices from other religious traditions.[19] The Isabella Freedman and Adamah staff and the fellows represented a wide range of Jewish upbringings, from secular or culturally Jewish to Reform to Orthodox, though again Janna noted that this cohort represented a narrower range than she was used to, as some cohorts include Haredi (ultra-Orthodox) Jews as well.[20] As I discuss in the fourth section of this chapter, time in the Adamah Farm Fellowship had many of the fellows rethinking their Jewish identity, so their backgrounds had a lot of influence, but their very presence at Adamah suggests they were seeking something at least a little bit different from the Judaism that they knew. The Judaism at Adamah has its roots in the agrarian forms of Judaism, Jewish environmentalism, and the spirit of innovation that has long defined Judaism.

HISTORICAL CONTEXT FOR THE ADAMAH FARM FELLOWSHIP

The Tuesday after Independence Day, the fellows met on top of Beebe Hill for Avodat Lev, which takes place at six each weekday morning. That morning, Shamu asked us to participate in an "Interdependence Day" celebration. Standing between Adamah's Kaplan Family Farm, where we spent most of our work sessions, and Beebe Hill, which sits just beyond Isabella Freedman's property line, he asked us to look at the world around us and really pay attention to it. He wanted us to consider the plants, the animals, the sounds, and the sights that the fellows often miss as they bustle about their work around the farm. After Shamu finished giving us instructions, he led us on a mostly silent walk through the forest. We stopped a few times to admire trees, fungi, and the sound of the birds. After walking for about ten minutes, we reached a grass meadow overlooking the valley. Shamu started the first verse of "Ashrei,"[21] a question-and-answer song based on Psalm 84, which translates to "Happy are those who dwell in Your house; they forever praise You, *Selah!*"[22] We continued to walk through tall grass as different people spontaneously sang out the call portion of this call-and-response song. When we reached the other side of the hill, Shamu led us in the Shema, which is the prayer that Jews say to affirm the oneness of God and their relationship with God.[23] He gave us time to reflect silently on where we were and what we were seeing during the Amidah portion of the service, which is the central component of the morning shacharit prayers. I am not sure how long we sat in the dewy grass, but eventually Shamu brought us back together to sing one more song, "Oseh Shalom," a song about peace, before we headed back down. We stopped a few times on the way to admire some interesting mushrooms and then dispersed to do morning chores.[24]

Shamu's "Interdependence Day" celebration encouraged us to see ourselves as part of the local ecology. A few of the fellows remarked later that they hadn't fully realized until that morning that the retreat center sits in a valley. A walk through the forest with Shamu as our guide alerted us to the flora native to northwest Connecticut. He also helped us see that the species considered invasive on the farm were an integral piece of the local ecology beyond its borders. For example, when we were on the farm, grass is a weed, but on the hillside the tall grass helps prevent soil erosion and feeds numerous animals. When Shamu and I sat down the next day for an interview, he expanded on this idea of "interdependence." He told me that a holistic approach to spirituality, food, and farming can help reshape our understanding of ourselves, our tradition, our spiritual life, and our ecological life.[25] The verse that adorns the gates to the Kaplan Family Farm, where most of the vegetables and fruits are grown, reads, "And God saw that this was good." This phrase, repeated throughout the creation account in the first chapter of Genesis, shapes Shamu's ecological approach and emphasizes the Jewish lineage of that ecological approach. According to that account in Genesis, God created everything and then declared that this creation was good. Humans, Shamu insisted, should stop trying to master nature and instead learn to work with it. He brought this up during a compost class that week, encouraging us to compost at home without purchasing compost starter kits because everything humans need to grow food and process the waste is already there, and this is good.[26] The Avodat Lev walk combined the morning Jewish prayer ritual with a walk intended to raise our ecological awareness. This particular combination of Judaism and ecology has its roots in the lengthy history of Jewish agriculture and the relatively recent history of Jewish environmentalism, and the mobile and musical Avodat Lev service was characteristic of a particular kind of innovative Judaism that developed in the late twentieth and early twenty-first centuries. I will discuss each of these lineages in brief below to provide some context for Adamah's agricultural, environmental, and Jewish foundations.

Jewish Agriculture

Many of the classes I attended at Adamah stressed Judaism's agrarian roots. Jewish agricultural history was also frequently invoked on farm tours and food demonstrations led by the fellows or the Adamah staff. The staff at Adamah tended to invoke biblical principles when they were discussing Jewish approaches to agriculture, animal husbandry, and the ideal relationship between humans and creation. These aspects of Adamah will be discussed in the third section of this chapter in more detail, but the community-building aspects of Adamah resonate with particular trends in Jewish agricultural history. The kibbutzim (communal settlements) in the state of Israel were seen as a model for the communal living aspects of the Adamah Farm Fellowship. Like the residents of kibbutzim, fellows at Adamah live together and share the labors of growing and preparing their food. And though it is less well known, even among American Jews, the United States has its own history of Jewish agriculture.

In the late nineteenth century, as Jews were emigrating en masse from eastern Europe, organizations like Am Olam (Eternal People) worked to educate Jews in practical tasks and set up communities where groups of Jews could live off the land and be self-sufficient together. The communes they established in Ottoman and Mandatory Palestine were the earliest iterations of the kibbutz movement that continues today in the state of Israel. Jewish agricultural colonies were also established in the wilderness areas of Louisiana,

Oregon, Michigan, North and South Dakota, Colorado, and New Jersey. And though many of these colonies were abandoned within a few years, their efforts to establish their own autonomy through their relationship with the land were not dissimilar from the goals of Adamah and other contemporary Jewish agricultural enterprises. Uri Herscher, author of *Jewish Agricultural Utopias in America, 1880–1910,* identified numerous factors for the failure of this American Jewish agricultural enterprise, but he argued that the major problem was that the communitarianism of this effort ran counter to the spirit of American individualism.[27] He posited that if individual Jews had settled as farmers in the nineteenth century, they might have succeeded.[28] Instead, many of these early Jewish agriculturalists moved to urban and suburban areas, sought work in other industries, and eventually moved into the American middle class, as scholar Rachel Kranson demonstrated.[29] So it is interesting, then, that Adamah and other modern farms have organized themselves as community farms and their work often involves efforts to create temporary and permanent intentional communities. This suggests that contemporary Jewish farmers are reconsidering their relationship to American individualism and are pursuing collective projects once again.[30]

Todd LeVasseur noted a political connection between the nineteenth-century Jewish agricultural colonies and the contemporary movement in his book *Religious Agrarianism and the Return of Place.* He suggested that the socialism of the nineteenth-century Jewish farmers served as part of a foundation of political activism among American Jews that influenced the contemporary Jewish social justice movements, including the environmental and food justice movements. LeVasseur included Adamah and the Jewish environmental organization Hazon in his discussion of religious agrarianism, which he argued is a "developing set of practices that brings explicit religious environmentalist concerns, values, and ethics into the perennial problems of soil destruction."[31] This certainly aligns with the mission of Adamah and its particular expression of Jewish environmentalism, but LeVasseur missed a key component of the Jewish agrarian movements. These movements also sought to provide Jewish people with a connection to each other in tumultuous times. The farms created space for Jews to come together and build new lives on the land after a period of disconnection from agriculture helped them assert their autonomy through the development of their own alternative food systems. In the past and the present, farming certainly offered Jewish urban dwellers better food options, but more important than that, agriculture provided them with community support and practical skills that would allow them to sustain themselves. Whether the threat was Czarist

Russia or industrial food and climate change, Jews have responded by living and working together to create food systems that will enable them to be self-sufficient. And like their historical predecessors, the farmers at Adamah found agricultural wisdom in Jewish tradition.

Jewish Environmentalism

Adamah's community and social justice-oriented ethos is aligned with the Jewish agriculturalists of the late nineteenth century, but its agricultural work is inextricable from Jewish environmentalism as it developed in the late twentieth century in response to environmental crises as they were understood at that time.[32] The editor of *Judaism and Ecology*, Hava Tirosh-Samuelson, identified the early 1970s as the beginning of "the creative weaving of Judaism and ecology" and pointed to efforts like Jewish activist Mike Tabor's "Trees for Vietnam" program and his later "Diaspora Kibbutz" program designed to be the American version of the Israeli kibbutzim.[33] Zalman Schachter-Shalomi, a Renewal rabbi, also began using the term "eco-kashrut" to critique unsustainable kosher food in the 1970s, and his colleague Arthur Waskow called on Jews to engage the environmental aspects of Jewish holidays in the 1980s. Both Schachter-Shalomi and Waskow are cited frequently in Adamah programs and materials.[34] Ellen Bernstein established Shomrei Adamah (Keepers of the Earth), the first national Jewish organization that focused solely on the environment, in 1988, and her work, which primarily focused on reconnecting Jews to the ecological values in the Hebrew Bible, similarly influenced many of the educational programs and Jewish ritual programs at Adamah.[35] In the 1990s, the Teva Learning Center began providing experiential environmental education to young Jews at Surprise Lake camp in New York, and another national organization, the Coalition on the Environment and Jewish Life, was founded.[36] All of these organizations expanded Jewish environmental thinking, trained Jewish environmental leaders, and established environmentalism as a Jewish value. When Adamah was founded in 2003, it provided a space for environmentally minded Jews to enact their values through sustainable agriculture.

A number of Jewish environmental principles form the basis of Adamah's approach to the land, to agriculture, and to animal husbandry. Many Jewish environmental principles stem from an interpretation of Genesis, where humans are seen as stewards of creation rather than as having dominion over it.[37] In her book *The Splendor of Creation*, Ellen Bernstein suggests that humans' "job is to minister to all of creatures' needs" and notes that humans are not meant to "harm the creation or interfere with the Creator's design."38 Much of the work of Jewish environmentalists has followed Bernstein's thinking and sought to do the work of restoring a relationship between humans and creation that is not based on harm or interference. This approach undergirds many of Adamah's sustainable agriculture practices, which aim to grow food without harming the soil or interfering with nature via the use of nonorganic herbicides or pesticides. In an essay that Shamu Sadeh wrote before founding Adamah, he added an additional perspective to this interpretation of creation. He analyzed the biblical story of Job and argued that only through a visionary experience with the wilderness was Job able to see "that his life, that indeed the entire drama of human society was no longer center stage" and that he had a "shared origin with all of Creation," for "he, too, was of the dust."39 Sadeh saw the kind of experience that Job had as transformative and suggested that everyone needed "a pilgrimage into the natural world to regain our sense of balance" because humans could not understand "our famous 'dominion'" otherwise.40 Sadeh brought this emphasis on decentering humans from creation into his work at Adamah. In the Adamah binder that was provided to fellows in 2015, there were Jewish textual resources on *shmita*, which prioritizes the land's need to rest over humans' need to grow and harvest annual crops. Shmita is the focus of chapter 4 of this book, but Adamah's shmita practices are described in this chapter.41 The binder also included resources related to the principle of *tza'ar ba'alei chayim*, which translates as "suffering of living creatures" but is actually a requirement to prevent the unnecessary suffering of living creatures.42 Following a page of biblical and rabbinic texts about *tza'ar ba'alei chayim* were two additional resources about contemporary factory farming and the suffering that animals endure in that system. Adamah's husbandry practices will be discussed in the fourth section of this chapter.

The focus on Jewish texts, principles, and laws that pertain to the relationship between humans and creation demonstrate Adamah's particular focus on the aspects of Jewish environmentalism that inform its agriculture program, though other environmental issues like energy and water were frequent topics of conversation during my time there. Within the Adamah Farm Fellowship, environmental education takes the form of classes on topics such as climate change, soil degradation, and factory farming. Fellows are also encouraged to respond to these injustices in their choices during the program and in their work with plants and animals on the farm. The Jewish environmental values that shape their work will be discussed in the next section of this chapter. The fellows also engage in environmental activism during their time in the program. This often includes legislative advocacy on the Farm Bill and other related issues, antiracist activism, climate activism, and an array of other areas of social justice activism as issues arise for each fellowship cohort. I will focus on the Adamah Farm fellows here, but each year thousands of Isabella Freedman Jewish Retreat Center visitors are also offered opportunities to learn about and experience Jewish environmentalism.

Jewish Innovation

Adamah is a relatively new organization, and it epitomizes an innovative approach to Judaism that has arisen outside legacy Jewish institutions like synagogues, Jewish community centers, and camps. Like other innovative Jewish organizations, Adamah attracts a significant number of Jews who are otherwise unaffiliated with Jewish institutions, which is common among the Adamah Farm Fellowship audience of Jews in their twenties and thirties. In his book *The New American Judaism*, scholar Jack Wertheimer describes movements like Adamah as unexpected, unconventional, and marginal. But this characterization fails to account for a history of Jewish innovation on the margins that includes movements from Hasidism to Reform Judaism and diminishes the importance of these so-called religious start-ups in the twenty-first century.[43]

Alternatively, scholar Shaul Magid has identified these organizations within the framework of what he calls "postethnic" or "post-Judaism" in his book *American Post-Judaism*. Magid described this move toward a postethnic Judaism as having two distinct periods. He identified the first as romantic/nostalgic, beginning in the 1960s and ending in the late 1990s. He used the examples of the Havurah movement and Chabad to illustrate this period's focus on re-engaging tradition in the face of secularism. Magid then described the constructive/illustrative period, which began in the late 1990s and included an alignment with New Age spirituality and politically progressive principles. Magid clarified that these Judaisms use traditions from the past but do not "hold them to be anything more than creative resources with which to reconstruct a new Jewish spirituality." He suggested that this new Jewish spirituality "is open to the conscious use of religious syncretism and the sharing of texts and rituals with other religions." Magid offered Renewal Judaism as an example of this syncretism and described its development alongside the rise of other spiritualities in the 1960s.[44] I use the framework of free-range religion to describe this kind of syncretic religion because

Jews are not the only ones who do this, but my framework generally aligns with Magid's. The Judaisms at Adamah were heavily influenced by Renewal Judaism, and rabbis and scholars of that movement figure prominently in educational materials used in the fellowship program. However, the unique syncretic forms of Judaism at Adamah also blur the lines between Magid's two periods of Jewish innovation. At Adamah, nostalgia for a Jewish agrarian past animates syncretic Judaisms that draw ideas and practices from a wide variety of Jewish and non-Jewish spiritualities.

Jack Wertheimer contended that many of the forms of spirituality that are practiced by Jews in America have "no discernible relationship with Judaism." He cited communing with nature, deriving uplift from natural wonders, and engaging in meditation specifically to propose that while these are acts of spirituality, "there is no good reason to assume they necessarily are acts of Jewish religious activity." As a caveat, he suggested that this is because these practices may not be connected to "teaching and expectations of a religious system known as Judaism." Given this caveat and his overreliance on congregational rabbis as interlocutors, it is clear that Wertheimer missed the element of Jewish innovation that Magid saw in Renewal Judaism and that I saw at Adamah. At Adamah, fellows' engagement with nature and spirituality falls entirely within the "religious system known as Judaism." Classes, rituals, educational materials, and even signage at Adamah include quotes from the Hebrew Bible and rabbinic sources in order to reawaken, rather than invent, a Judaism that centers environmental and food justice. And though he perpetuated their marginalization by dismissing them as outside of Judaism, Wertheimer did note that these approaches to Judaism are flourishing and are "increasingly influencing the core."[45] In addition to the influence of organizations like Adamah on "the core," by which Wertheimer essentially means legacy Jewish institutions like synagogues and Jewish community centers, Jewish community farming continues to grow and attract otherwise unaffiliated Jews. Since Adamah's founding in 2003, over twenty-five Jewish community farming organizations have been established all over the United States and in Canada. These organizations collectively engage thousands of Jews annually and have become an established aspect of Jewish life in a number of major Jewish population centers like Baltimore, San Diego, and Toronto. Adamah was founded to reconnect Jewish people to the land and to food systems, and over twenty years later the organization is still fulfilling its mission to "grow people" and "transform identities" by engaging young Jews in a vibrant and constantly evolving form of Judaism that they can carry with them as they build Jewish lives in their own communities. At Adamah,

Judaism forms the basis for its sustainable agriculture system and provides structure and educational material for the farm fellowship program.

THE ADAMAH FARM FELLOWSHIP'S ALTERNATIVE FOOD SYSTEM

During my time at Adamah, each work session started with one of the staff members or apprentices providing an overview of the tasks that needed to be done. Then the fellows and I would self-select into those tasks. I tried to choose new tasks each time, so when a greenhouse option came up one day, I volunteered. I spent the session sitting underneath large tables in the greenhouse, weeding between the stones that covered the floor. Although I found the task surprisingly pleasant, I was not sure why the floor of the greenhouse needed weeding. When I posed the question to Miri, a field apprentice and our supervisor that afternoon, she explained that the newly planted seedlings in the greenhouse needed protection from pests and diseases. When weeds are in the same family as the crops planted, they may attract pests and diseases that would attack the vulnerable seedlings.[46] As one of the fellows, Elisa, and I crawled around on the floor pulling weeds, three other fellows, Rose, Zack, and Amy, planted seeds with Miri above us. This seemingly simple task, weeding, protected both the seedlings and the fall harvest. The daily lives of the Adamah fellows and the food system they work to support are shaped by Jewish values that prescribe their relationships with the plants and animals and form the foundation of their sustainable agriculture system. As described in the previous section, humans are seen as stewards of the earth and plants, so if seedlings need protection, a human must hand-weed between the stones in the greenhouse. In this section, I will describe the ways that human lives and labor are shaped by their stewardship of the Adamah Farm and provide an overview of the alternative food system that has been enacted by the Adamah Farm Fellowship and the Isabella Freedman Jewish Retreat Center.

At Adamah, all hours, days, and weeks are structured around the needs of the plants grown there. Fruits and vegetables need to be harvested when they are ripe. There is not much leeway in this system, because overripe cucumbers are too big to fit in pickling jars and raspberries left on the vines too long will rot. Rebecca told me that scheduling the work sessions for the fellows takes a surprisingly large amount of time, in part because of the aspects of the schedule that lie outside human control.[47] During the weeks I was at Adamah, the raspberries were ripe and needed to be picked every other day. I spent a number of the three-hour work sessions with a cardboard box hung around my neck picking ripe red raspberries alongside two to five fellows. Raspberry vines are prickly and the berries are often hidden among the brambles. To get all the berries, one often has to switch between standing up and crouching down. Max, who supervised the raspberry picking, has been working on the farm periodically since she completed the Adamah fellowship in 2012. Under Max's leadership, we became an expert berry-picking force. She made sure we picked only the reddest raspberries but also checked to see that we were getting all the raspberries as we moved along the rows. More than once during the raspberry harvest, we were unable to cover all the rows during a work session. Instead of leaving the berries, a few of us would be assigned to complete the harvest in the next session instead of moving on to a different task. We couldn't leave ripe raspberries for an extra day or two because they would rot before our return. An extra work session was added on Sunday mornings in early July to accommodate the increased need for harvesting sessions. Meanwhile, at the cultural center, which is what Adamah calls its commercial kitchen, the pickle apprentice, Tara, ordered her days so that she could turn the fresh berries into jam. Farmers adhere to the schedules that their crops require.

Harvesting also provides the fellows with an important lesson in the seasonality of produce. In the United States, we have grown accustomed to eating produce from all over the country and the world. Many Americans have lost track of when raspberries are in season and may not even know what they taste like freshly picked. The Adamah fellows leave the program with a solid sense of the produce seasons in northwest Connecticut. Many of the fellows talked to me about how their proximity to and participation on the farm changed their relationship with the land. Debby explained that she had spent time "contemplating the connectedness of all things" through songs and meditation, and it had affected her. "I think through even this short month, my relationship to the land has become more spiritual, where it's like I will stop and notice and allow myself to feel curious and struck by things and excited about things."[48] Debby's reflection exemplifies the ecological sensibility that operates at Adamah. The fellows spend large portions of their time outside working the land and the rest of their time in classes and prayer sessions dedicated to enhancing their relationship with the land.

The Isabella Freedman Jewish Retreat Center is nestled between three mountains and contains Lake Miriam, which lends a sense of enchantment to everyday experiences on-site. When I asked Elisa whether her relationship with the land had changed during her time at Adamah, she said, "Just being in a beautiful place like this, I feel like it's not hard to feel more connected to nature." She continued, "That has changed my experience completely, just being outdoors all the time. It really just gives you a greater appreciation for nature."[49] There was even something at Isabella Freedman for Zack, a fellow who came to Adamah as a seasoned farmer. He was used to spending time outside and lamented the fact that the sky was hard to see surrounded by the trees on-site. For him, it was early morning walks by the lake that provided a new experience. "I love seeing the mist on the lake every morning. That you just don't see very often, even though I lived by water for a while."[50] Adamah immerses the fellows not just in the agroecology of the farm but also within the wider Berkshires ecosystem—fellows spend time by the lake and take hikes on the Appalachian Trail, and it all adds to their experience.

Ari, who also went by the title "mayor of the woods" and stayed on as part of a work trade program after completing the fellowship in the fall of 2014, identified the opportunities to experience interconnectedness as a key element of Adamah. Ari talked about their involvement with the whole process, "putting my food waste into the compost, and then hauling the compost to the compost yard, and then putting the compost on the field, and having the chickens eat the compost, and then eating the chickens' eggs every day." Seeing this full cycle resonated with Ari: "Having all these things so intricately connected all the time just really laid a groundwork for me to find more connection and meaning in my life. That was really big. That was really important."[51] Adamah is set up so that fellows experience the interconnectedness of their world with the plants and animals that are entangled in the human food system. When those connections are explicit and combined with the curiosity and openness that Debby possessed and with the basic beauty of the location that Zack and Elisa mentioned, an authentic spiritual relationship with the land develops. As Ari's experience shows, through participation in Adamah, interdependence moves from being a concept that Shamu teaches in early morning prayer sessions to an integral component of a new relationship between the fellows and their environment.

The work at Adamah also altered the fellows' perspectives on their own bodies. Fellows at Adamah tend to spend multiple work sessions a week weeding, harvesting, and planting, but these are not activities that they typically performed daily prior to their arrival at Adamah. Sometimes, their transition into this work was uncomfortable or even painful. Sam described the adjustment process his body went through in his first couple of weeks at Adamah: "I don't crouch. I've never crouched for that long. Now I have to do it so much."[52] Techniques of the body, like crouching, are socially constructed, and the fellows learn the techniques of farmers in the program.[53] Fruits and vegetables are rarely harvested at heights that would allow humans to stand or sit comfortably. Human bodies have to adjust to spending time down near the ground, where root vegetables grow, or climb ladders into the trees, where stone fruits ripen. Weeding also keeps bodies busy in a way that allows minds to rest. Rose mentioned to me that she tended to philosophize farming and enjoyed the idea of it more than the actual act of farming. However, she found weeding quite enjoyable: "I do love being in the dirt. I find weeding very cathartic."[54] Many of the other fellows echoed this sentiment.

Since Karl Marx first lamented the alienation of labor, reformers of many kinds have sought to reconnect workers to the pleasure of physical labor.[55] At Adamah, many of the fellows were enthusiastic about farming, often because they were able to see the literal fruits of their labor. Shira was working as the associate registrar for Hazon after finishing the spring 2015 fellowship when I visited. Given her recent transition back to office work, she was able to see and feel the difference: "It feels really nice to work with your hands and to see—to really see the results of your effort." She explained it wasn't like working at a desk, where individuals might not be sure that anyone notices their work. In contrast, she noted, on the farm, "if you have to weed a row of plants, you spend whatever, an hour, weeding a row of plants, and at the end it looks totally different. It transforms right in front of your eyes."[56] My experience aligned with Shira's. Regardless of the particular task, after a work session at Adamah, we were usually able to see what we had accomplished, whether that was weedless stones in the greenhouse or berryless raspberry bushes.

Beyond the sense of connection to labor and accomplishment with completed tasks, some of the fellows found the physicality of the labor meaningful. Amy told me that she'd learned she really loves farming, and the act of working the land was part of what attracted her to farming. "I just connect with—it sounds weird, but . . . I connect with hard labor. I find that I'm most mentally at ease when I'm just completely physically busy."[57] Because she enjoyed hard labor, Amy was usually the first to volunteer to use the wheel hoe and other tools that required more strength and effort to operate. The fellows also got creative with adding social elements to their work. For example, sessions with Rose always involved answering her "question of the day," which helped the fellows get to know one another. The fellows also worked out their interpersonal issues, vented frustrations, exchanged gossip, and planned their futures while they weeded and harvested.

Once a week, some of the fellows are assigned to "homesteading" for an afternoon work session. My first week at Adamah, I joined Shana, Sam, Rayna,

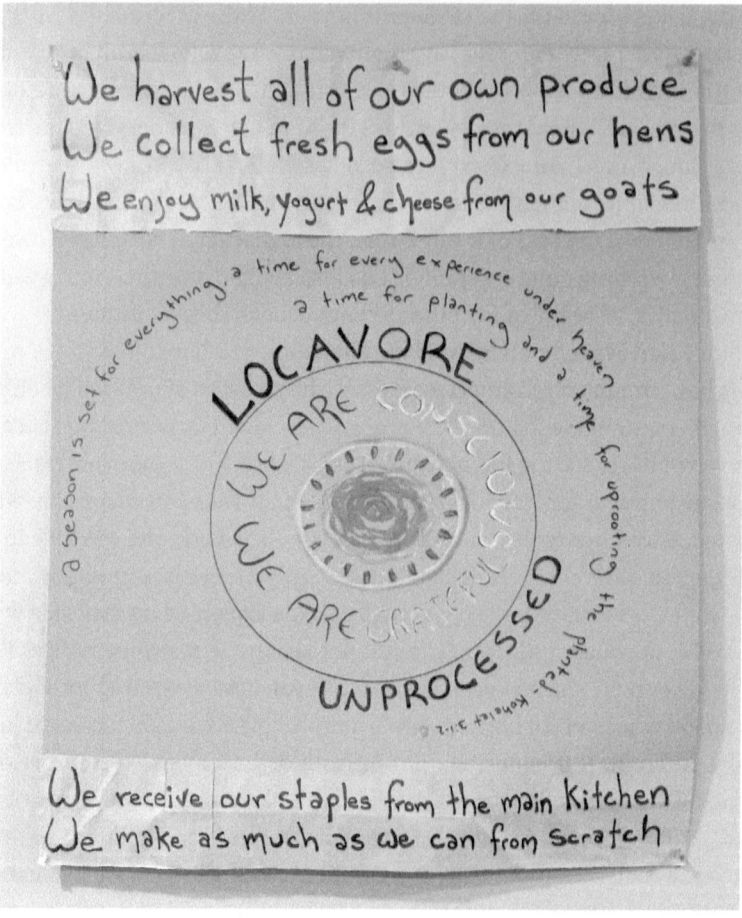

Adamah Farm Fellowship food system poster, June 2015.

and Zack for a homesteading session. Music from the Adamah soundtrack created by the fall 2014 cohort played on a laptop and kept our spirits up as we worked.[58] Shana made granola that all the fellows had requested from the homesteaders. Sam and I washed and chopped freshly harvested vegetables and stored them in mason jars in the refrigerator for use during the week. We also washed chard, kale, and beet greens, wrapped them in towels, and placed them in the refrigerator. Zack and Rayna made honey lavender cheese using milk from the goats. After finishing the cheese, they juiced carrots, apples, beets, greens, and lemons into a rich purple liquid that they poured into mason jars for storage. Sam, who was now providing a soundtrack of his own *kirtan* (yogic chanting) because the Adamah soundtrack had ended, paused his chanting to insist that the fruit and vegetable pulp be used instead of composted. I washed dishes while Sam and Zack cooked up "fakin' loaf" made from vegetable pulp, shawarma seasoning, tomato paste, and eggs. Sam rolled the remaining pulp into balls bound together with peanut butter. Homesteading tended to be a favorite work session for the fellows. It was also an important one, as the food the homesteaders prepared became the basis for their meals in the following days. Fellows ate breakfast at the Beit Adamah every morning. They also ate lunches and dinners at the house during certain retreats and on Shabbat.[59] In order to cook meals in a reasonable amount of time, produce preparation was required. The other products created that afternoon—the juice, granola, cheese, and pulp balls—supplemented meals throughout the week. Processed, prepackaged food was nowhere to be found in the BA kitchen.

A poster hung next to the refrigerator that describes the Adamah food system. The text at the top and bottom of the poster, printed on brown butcher paper and glued to red posterboard, read as follows:

We harvest all of our own produce
We collect fresh eggs from our hens
We enjoy milk, yogurt & cheese from our goats
We receive our staples from the main kitchen
We make as much as we can from scratch[60]

That afternoon, we followed the script of the poster quite closely. We washed and cut produce harvested from the farm. Eggs from the hens were added to the "fakin' loaf," milk from the goats was made into cheese, and oats, honey, and cinnamon provided by the kitchen became granola. The fellows and I made all of their food for the week from scratch. The rest of the text on the poster pointed to the motivation behind this focus on local and homemade foods. In the center of the poster, words encircled an abstract design. They read, "We are Conscious, We are Grateful." The fellows grow and harvest the food themselves. They know exactly where it came from and how much work goes into each meal they eat. Because Sam was both conscious and grateful, he couldn't fathom wasting the pulp from the vegetables they had grown, so he and Zack repurposed it to make additional food items for the week.

The words "Locavore" and "Unprocessed" are written along the circumference of a circle in the center of the red posterboard. Technically, the fellows and I did process food during our homesteading session—we cleaned, cut, juiced, and cooked the raw, unprocessed vegetables. But the fellows use

Sustainable Agriculture

"unprocessed" to distinguish their foods from industrial processed foods. "Locavore" is the term used to describe people who eat food produced close to where they live, and religious studies scholar Benjamin Zeller has suggested that locavorism can itself be considered a "quasi religion." He described the movement, popularized by writers Michael Pollan and Barbara Kingsolver, as one that identifies some foods and practices as good. These "good" practices include things like growing one's own food or buying food from farmers nearby. The "bad" foods in this system would be things like processed food, fast food, and some restaurant food.[61] This moralization of food based on distance applies at Adamah, though in this context fellows' locavorism is understood as part of their Judaism and not as a quasi religion unto itself. The Kaplan Family Farm, where most of the Adamah food is currently grown, is located about a thousand feet from the BA.[62] Locavores are often concerned about the fuel used to transport food long distances. At Adamah, fuel is rarely involved, and food is most often transported from the farm to the house by foot or by bicycle.

The poster also incorporates Jewish elements to distinguish Adamah's food system from other local food systems. Two abridged verses from Ecclesiastes complete the poster: "A season is set for everything, a time for every experience under heaven. A time for planting and a time for uprooting the planted."[63] These verses connect the food values of Adamah to Judaism through the use of this biblical text and call attention to the seasonality of its local food system. When all of its elements are taken together, the poster reminds the fellows at every meal that they plant their food, harvest their food, prepare it from scratch, and eat it in season, and they are inspired to do so by Jewish tradition.

The fellows, for the most part, had not eaten this way prior to their arrival. I asked Shira to describe her experience with food at Adamah as a recent alumna, and she explained, "I feel more comfortable and more empowered, knowing more about where my food comes from. I can just walk into the field and be like, I'm going to pick this cucumber and just eat it."[64] Shira felt this was very different from her previous experiences with grocery stores, where she takes the extra step to wash all the produce she purchases. I spent one evening harvesting vegetables with Shira, and then we made dinner together. Her confidence working in both the fields and the kitchen was evident. We snacked on snap peas while we weeded in the shmita garden at the entrance to Isabella Freedman, and she helped me identify the different kinds of kale we harvested to make a salad. Back at the home she shared in the staff housing section, nicknamed "the suburbs," I acted as her sous chef while she made *mujadarra*, a Middle Eastern dish comprising primarily lentils, rice, and onions. Max joined us as we sat down to eat. When I spoke with Max a few days later, she offered her thoughts on how her approach to food had changed since she came to Adamah three years prior, explaining that when she's in the city, she loves grocery stores and enjoys complementing her "entirely picked-right-before-I-ate-it meal of all local vegetables" with items from far away."[65] Adamah had not changed Max's affinity for grocery stores, but it had inspired her to eat more local produce. In talking with the fellows and Adamah alumni, it seemed that although the changes they made were often small, they understood them to be meaningful.

Many of the changes that fellows adopted were made possible simply by being at Isabella Freedman. The retreat center kitchen also used local produce and avoided foods that fellows identified as problematic when possible. For example, the kitchen did not serve almonds or almond products during my time there. Shira explained that this was because most almonds are grown in California, which was in the midst of a major drought.[66] During a compost class, Shamu told us that the kitchen also chooses meat based on the retreat center's dedication to ecological eating. The kitchen staff at Isabella Freedman do not use prime cuts of meat, which include cuts like tenderloin, strip steak, and porterhouse. They also do not use boneless meats. Shamu explained that there is more food value and flavor in bone-in meats and that the retreat center was trying to change the way staff and visitors thought about eating animals by reducing waste. The staff at Isabella Freedman work to ensure that their meals better incorporate the whole animal.[67] The kitchen also sourced meat from distributors who were certified kosher and raise their animals "in alignment with our ethical and ecological standards."[68]

These decisions made Debby and others confident in the ethical nature of the food they were served in the Isabella Freedman dining hall. However, Debby did wonder what would happen when she returned home and had to cook for herself again. She also expressed concerns for the majority of Americans who do not have access to local organic produce at every meal: "I think that's a major question in food systems work right now.... How can we make this kind of food the norm when financially it's totally inaccessible to a majority of people?"[69] This speaks to the mission of Adamah. The program isn't just about raising consciousness among the fellows who participate in the program. It also encourages them to bring what they see and what they learn into the world. Debby told me that she volunteers with many food justice organizations in and around her home city. She may not have had a solution to the problem yet, but she was driven to find one and chose to participate in the Adamah Farm Fellowship with these aims in mind.

FREE-RANGE RELIGION AT THE ADAMAH FARM FELLOWSHIP

I spent one entire day at Adamah in various stages of wetness. The day started when my five a.m. alarm was almost drowned out by the sound of thunderstorms. It was pouring as I left my room for Avodat Lev. I had to walk only a few hundred feet to the synagogue, but by the time I got there I was both soaked and late. I stepped into the synagogue, removed my rainboots, and joined the fellows who were sitting cross-legged in a circle on the floor singing "Mah Tovu" ("How Good").[70] Maya, a field apprentice, led Avodat Lev that morning. She talked about her childhood admiration for her rabbi, who wore a large tallit (prayer shawl). She invited us to walk around and try out the different tallitot she had laid out in the synagogue and then select one to wear if we felt comfortable doing so. After we had selected our tallitot, we returned to our seats. Some of the fellows wrapped their tallit around their damp bodies as a source of warmth. Others covered their heads and faces. We sang "Modeh Ani" ("I Give Thanks") and the Shema together. When we finished, Maya explained that she had also put out different prayerbooks. She wanted us to pick up a book that was not familiar to us so that we could experiment with different versions of the Amidah prayer. I picked up a Jewish Renewal prayerbook and read through the prayer while lying down on my stomach. Some of the fellows sat reading through the prayer, while others were lying down, enjoying a moment of quiet meditation. We came together for a few songs at the end and headed back out into the rain for morning chores.[71] That morning's service was pretty characteristic not just of Avodat Lev but of the way Judaism was practiced at Adamah. It was lay-led and informed by tradition, it incorporated singing and experiential elements, and participants were offered space to explore new things and make the service work for them. Judaism at Adamah is also defined by its complex engagements with halakah (Jewish law), pluralism, and innovation, and I'll discuss all three of these elements in this section.

Amy, who told me she's "not into Judaism" but "really likes the cultural kind of Judaism," was surprised to find that she really enjoyed Avodat Lev. She recalled experiences from her childhood at a Jewish day school where they had morning prayers every day. She told me they would pick up the siddur (prayerbook) and go through the prayers in order until they finished. She found that Avodat Lev at Adamah was noticeably different. She explained, "We meditate; we sing the beautiful songs. Even though they are prayers, they're just beautiful. They make it more of a spiritual experience than just saying it because you're supposed to be saying it."[72] Amy found that the songs, in particular, helped her feel more connected to the prayers and to the experience of prayer than the day school services had, and that was a common experience among the Adamah Farm fellows.

The musical aspects of Avodat Lev, and Adamah in general, came up repeatedly in my conversations and interviews with the fellows. Rayna described herself as a "very cultural Jew" who likes to celebrate Shabbat and say the basic prayers. She felt that the more classes she took about the Jewish laws, the less she connected to a rules-based Judaism, which is what she was distancing herself from as she identified herself as a cultural, and not religious, Jew. However, she was also really enjoying the prayer services at Adamah. "I love singing," Rayna emphasized, and she explained that if there were places with people, food, and singing, "I'm there." She had found that Adamah was like that "all the time, which is really cool."[73] Zack also brought up singing in his reflections on the program. He told me that his favorite Jewish part of the program was learning the songs. He had enjoyed singing as a child in Hebrew school, but he saw this as a different type of experience. He felt that learning the translations of the songs was helping him use them as "a way to bring in peace and tranquility and joy." He emphasized that the singing was his favorite part of being a fellow.[74] Zack and the other fellows saw Avodat Lev as distinct from their previous Jewish experiences. It was flexible, it was musical, and it was experiential. Amy reflected on this larger purpose of Avodat Lev: "It's more just a holistic idea that the morning prayers are meant to start you. It's more about you than it is about reading a text for the sake of reading the text."[75] Avodat Lev gave the fellows experience with one of the daily Jewish prayer services, whether they generally said morning prayers or not, and many of the fellows found that Avodat Lev helped them to connect to their Judaism and prepare for their day.

Halakhah at Adamah

After Avodat Lev, I walked down to the barnyard with Andie and Leah. There were four goats that needed milking—Feta, Bagel, Talia, and Zola. They came into the milking hut in pairs. When they were situated in their spots, Leah and Andie sprayed their udders with iodine and then pulled a stream of milk for Maya to check. Maya inspected the milk carefully to make sure it was the proper color and consistency, and once she gave her OK, Leah and Andie started milking the goats. I watched for a while, until Leah offered to show me how to do it. I found it fairly difficult, having no experience with milking prior to that morning. I returned my seat to Leah when it became clear that I was slowing down the process. When Andie and Leah thought they had gotten all the milk, Maya sat down and pulled every last bit of milk out of their udders. The goat milk was tested every week, and the week before the tests had shown a higher-than-normal number of somatic cells, which can indicate inflammation, so she wanted to be sure their udders were completely empty to avoid infection. When Maya finished, the milk was poured into a large stainless steel container and weighed. The goats were treated with udder massages and another iodine dip before they were sent back into the yard. Leah and Andie repeated the process with the other two goats and then headed off to the cultural center to wash the buckets.

I stayed in the barnyard to help Maya move the goats out to the pasture for the day. I mentioned that I had seen a special note about goat milking on Shabbat in the Adamah binder and asked Maya what they had decided about milking on Shabbat. According to Jewish law, milking is prohibited on Shabbat. However, Adamah considered this prohibition alongside one of its central Jewish values, *tza'ar ba'alei chayim*, which forbids humans from inflicting unnecessary pain on animals. So, with this principle in mind, the Adamah staff decided to milk the goats on Shabbat because leaving them without milking for twenty-four hours would cause pain. In other words, the Adamah staff decided that the health of their goats took precedence over the human Shabbat prohibitions.[76] However, while all the milk collected on other days is used in the BA, the fellows do not use the milk that is collected on Shabbat. Instead, they give it to a neighbor outside the retreat center. This is because the BA keeps a kosher kitchen, and milk collected on Shabbat is not kosher because of the prohibition against milking on Shabbat.[77] The milking example offers a glimpse into how Judaism is worked out in practical situations on the farm.

Most of the halakhic (Jewish legal) issues that have to be worked out at Adamah are related to Shabbat. The Adamah fellows rotate through assignments associated with Shabbat. Each week, someone is put in charge of cooking dinner and someone else leads the Shabbat worship at the Beit Adamah. The fellows can choose to open their home to the Isabella Freedman community for Shabbat, they can invite their own friends or family to visit, or they can hold a fellows-only Shabbat. Shabbat is meant to be inclusive, and the goal is to create a meaningful experience for all of the fellows. This is a difficult task. The first week I was at Adamah, Rose was in charge of cooking dinner and leading the Friday evening Kabbalat Shabbat service. She worked hard to ensure that everyone had something to eat. There were two vegan challahs made by Elisa and Zack. They took different approaches to baking the two loaves, so one was long and flat and the other was short, puffy, and undercooked in the middle. Both were delicious. After a dinner of zucchini lasagna, pasta, black-eyed pea soup, and salad, we moved into the living room for the service. Rose led us through a series of prayers and directed readings. We ended with a community song session that went on for quite a while. We sang Hebrew songs, African American spirituals, a Rumi poem set to music, and a song that Sam wrote about the farm.[78] In between songs, people posed questions to the group (such as, "What were you like as a kid?") and told stories from their pre-Adamah lives. A few days later, Elisa reflected on the Shabbat experiences she had at Adamah. She said she wasn't sure the fellows had reached a point where they'd found a Shabbat that everyone could appreciate as beautiful. However, she was optimistic that once people got more comfortable with each other and with Judaism, they could get there.[79]

The next Friday, I spent the morning work session walking the perimeter of the Isabella Freedman campus with Elisa and the mashgiach (kashrut supervisor) from the kitchen, to check the eruv (boundary). This line of string connected by posts and trees encloses the Isabella Freedman site and allows staff and retreat guests to carry items outside of their rooms and push strollers on Shabbat. And even as Isabella Freedman is set up to ensure that observant Jews are able to visit, during Shabbat at Isabella Freedman many of the staff members, fellows, and visitors also turn on lights, make phone calls, and drive. Isabella Freedman and Adamah are pluralistic Jewish communities, so they strive to make people with more stringent levels of observance feel comfortable without forcing those who are less observant to adopt restrictions they wouldn't normally practice.

Pluralism at Adamah

After the goat milking session, I reported to the cultural center for the first of two work sessions I would spend at the wash station. The rain had stopped, but I was still damp from walking around in a downpour before Avodat Lev. As it happens, the wash station is a place where wetness is inevitable, no matter how dry you are when you arrive, so I fit right in. I worked with Shana and Max to wash produce and separate it into bins headed for the CSA customers and the retreat center kitchen. In the morning session, we washed greens.

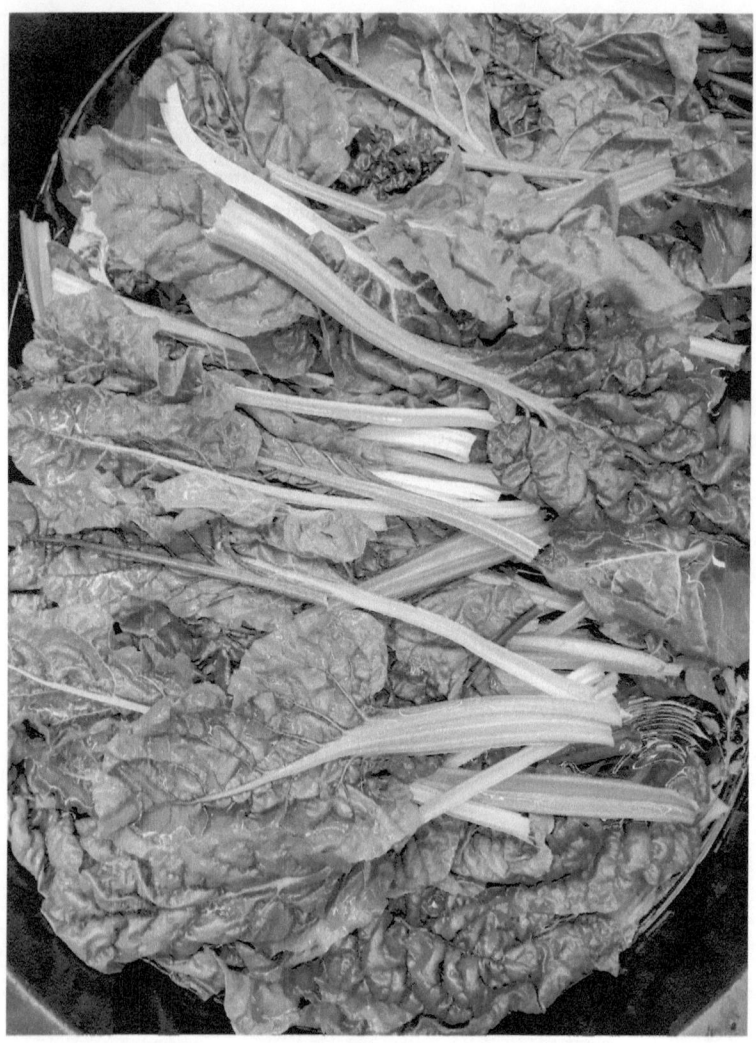

Rainbow chard in the washbasin at the Adamah Farm Fellowship, July 2015.

We dumped bunches of kale into a giant washbasin and moved them around gently to ensure that the water spread throughout the leaves. Romaine lettuce proved to be the most difficult to wash. Each head was covered in dirt, and the leaves were filled with straw. It took us a while to get fifty-six heads in good shape for the CSA bins. They didn't have to be perfect, because we imagined that people would wash their lettuce at home again, but they had to be presentable. The lettuce and greens headed to the kitchen would endure more intensive washes and the bug inspections required in kosher-certified kitchens. Washing the rainbow chard was the highlight of the work session for me. Bright yellow, orange, pink, and red stalks of chard interspersed with vibrant green leaves was aesthetically pleasing, but the colorful blend was also reminiscent of Adamah's pluralism. This is a community of people with similar interests, values, and goals but different levels of observance, and they have to work out some of those differences together.[80]

The Adamah Farm fellows come from all different backgrounds, and during their time at Adamah, they are exposed to different practices and offered opportunities to try new things. For example, in Orthodox Judaism, women usually do not wear a tallit. At Adamah, anyone who would like to wear a tallit may wear one. Janna told me that she thought the pluralism component of Adamah was one of the most interesting aspects of the program. She had worked on secular farms in Washington state and tended to find that while they shared an excitement for local organic produce, their political views were very different from her own. What she liked about Adamah was that it brings Jewish people together. She explained that something special happens "where people are encountering each other where they wouldn't otherwise" and added that she thought this was because food "speaks to people across this religious spectrum." Janna recalled cohorts with Haredi, cultural, and other Jews living, working, and praying together.[81] Though there were no Jews with a Haredi background in the fellowship program while I was there, there were Jews who had been raised in or had experience with Orthodoxy. Elisa explained, "I've led prayers since I've been here, and I hadn't done anything like that beforehand, because I grew up Orthodox and women weren't really allowed to do that. So that's been really cool." She thought that this experience helped her grow spiritually, and she ended her reflection by saying, "I love this type of Judaism."[82] Elisa wasn't sure how she would practice Judaism when she returned to finish her senior year of college in the fall. She hadn't been participating in Jewish life on campus and still wasn't sure that was for her. However, she thought that she might seek out a Renewal community in the city where her university was located.

Miri had a similar experience when she was at Adamah as a fellow. She remembered that when she arrived, she was still recovering from time she had spent at an ultra-Orthodox Jewish seminary school in Israel. She had a hard time there, especially with the gendered aspects of the program. She had dealt with some judgmental people and with many men who wouldn't even talk to women. Miri identifies as a queer woman, which added to her discomfort there. "It just felt dehumanizing when I was at this seminary, because I would be ignored because I was a woman. Just the idea of being also a young queer woman in an ultra-Orthodox place just felt really hard." When she arrived at Adamah, she began to understand that "it's OK to be who I am and also Jewish. All parts of me are OK and they don't conflict with each other, even though I was told that they do."[83] Miri had sought out Jewish experiences prior to her arrival at Adamah, but none of them had allowed her to fully embrace all of the parts of herself. At Adamah, Miri brought her graduate degree in soil science, her Judaism, and her identity as a queer woman and found a community where every aspect was celebrated.

This is not to say that Adamah's pluralistic community is perfect. One morning a few of the male Isabella Freedman staffers were assembling a minyan (quorum). They moved through the campus, seeking ten Jewish adult males, as is required in Orthodox Judaism.[84] When they approached Rose, Debby, and me, they did not invite us to join them and instead asked us where the male fellows were. We were at the BA a short while later, where they found the male fellows, Zack and Sam. However, they ignored Zack while they pressured Sam to join their minyan. In the wake of their departure with Sam, Rose explained to the room that the women and Zack, whose mother was not Jewish, were not counted as Jews according to these particular staffers' interpretation of the laws. Throughout the day, fellows expressed their frustration with the minyan situation that morning. The women saw this as the most recent in a series of situations where they weren't invited into Jewish practice because of their gender, and Zack fumed about his exclusion from the minyan despite a lifetime of Jewish education and participation. However, by the end of the day, all the fellows began talking about the minyan incident as a minor blip in the midst of a generally positive pluralistic experience. Complications and difficult moments inevitably arise when Jews from across the spectrum meet. At Adamah, a shared sense of purpose related to food helped the community move through the rough patches to find common ground.

Adamah's dedication to pluralism extends beyond Judaism. As evidenced by Avodat Lev, practices that originate with other religious groups, like meditation, have made their way into Jewish experiences at Adamah. Adamah has also established a formal relationship with Wake Forest University School of Divinity. This program started after Fred Bahnson spent time at Adamah while writing his book *Soil and Sacrament: A Spiritual Memoir of Food and Faith*.[85] Shamu recalled that Bahnson connected to the place and "really thought that we had something to offer the larger faith-based food and farming movement."[86] As the director of the Food, Faith, and Religious Leadership Initiative at Wake Forest's divinity school, Bahnson worked with Shamu to create opportunities for Christian divinity students to visit Adamah and receive course credit.

In the spring before I arrived, a group of divinity students had visited the farm for a week. Rebecca told me that ten students, whose ages ranged from mid-twenties to mid-fifties, joined the regular Adamah schedule. She said it was "a beautiful opportunity for everybody" and that when the group left, the Adamah staff and fellows were really sad.[87] Shira, who was a spring fellow, liked having the students there because they brought a different perspective to the issues that inspire the fellows. She remembered that the divinity students were also interested in using faith as a lens to look at food, and she believed they were able to relate because they were also passionate about connecting faith and healthy food. Shira also talked about how they came to Avodat Lev and got really into the Jewish prayer experience alongside the fellows.[88] Shamu remained in awe of the excitement that each new group of people—the fellows and the Wake Forest students—bring to the program and told me that it's renewing his "own sense of wonder."[89] When he sees new people learn about how nature works and what prayer can look like, it inspires him.

Religious Innovation at Adamah

After a day spent in the rain and at the wash station, I had grown accustomed to being damp. I had almost dried off by the time we attended our evening class, but I was still looking forward to a warm shower afterward. However, after the class ended, Sam and Debby started talking about that evening's blue moon, the second full moon that month, and they wanted to mark the occasion. I sat with them for a while in the library while they discussed their plan. Sam and I perused the books on ritual and Renewal Judaism to see whether we could find any resources for a full moon celebration.[90] We were unsuccessful. Sam, Debby, and Elisa decided the best way to celebrate would be to go down to the lake and skinny-dip by the light of the blue moon. I was hesitant about joining them, but Elisa pointed out that this was a Jewish ceremony, my exact area of interest, so I shouldn't miss it. I found myself susceptible to this particular form of researcher pressure, so I went back to my room to grab my towel and headed down to the dock.

Debby, Elisa, Sam, Rayna, Shira, and a visiting Adamah alum, Blake, were already there. We put our bags down and sat in a tight circle at the corner of the dock. It was about sixty-five degrees and quite dark, and the sky was cloudy. The moon was not visible. Rayna started off the very informal ceremony by comparing the Jewish people to the moon. She talked about how the Jewish people have waxed and waned throughout history: Sometimes they are powerful and sometimes they are weak, but they are always there. We sang four Hebrew songs about the moon, love, God, and peace. During the fourth song, a faint light began to appear behind a lone tall tree at the top of Barrack Mountain. We started another song to encourage the moon. During the sixth song, the moon cleared the mountain and became completely visible. Our little group erupted into cheers and howls. Someone somewhere else on the retreat center campus howled back. We stood up and began to undress. We all jumped into the lake together. People swam for a few minutes, and then we quickly redressed and headed our separate ways.[91] As seen in this event, fellows are enthusiastic about experimenting with Jewish practice at Adamah. Sam told me that he'd spent a lot of time since his arrival reading books about Hasidism and Kabbalah from the Isabella Freedman library. He was excited by this opportunity, remarking, "I've been given the space to read a lot and explore that and understand really what Judaism actually stands for on a much deeper level, but also on a practical level." He said that his reading had helped his sense of and desire for spirituality to grow.[92]

The openness to experimentation also helps the fellows when they are facing difficult moments. Debby found out that her great-aunt passed away while she was at Adamah. She was upset after her mom called to tell her, so she decided to skip the morning work session and hike up to the overlook. While on the mountain, Debby spent some time thinking about her great-aunt, who was the last person in her family from that generation. As she did, she reflected on the things that her aunt and others in that generation of Debby's family had dealt with. Debby then had an experience where a thought came to her: "I am Jewish and I'm proud and I'm not going to be afraid and I'm not going to be ashamed." Debby said she didn't think it was a "message" but did feel it was important, and she and I both had tears in our eyes as she told this story. She explained that she has been working to navigate her Jewish identity. Her father was an immigrant from Hungary, and she felt she had "internalized fear and shame of being Jewish." This experience and others at Adamah allowed her to let go of that.[93]

The atmosphere at Adamah enables fellows to experiment and determine what Jewish prayers, rituals, and experiences will work for them. And the practices don't necessarily have to have their origins in Judaism. Zack told me that he felt like he was learning a lot of Buddhist tenets at Adamah. I asked what he meant, and he clarified, "Just about being in the moment and let things not affect you. Just sort of have a middle ground and be balanced."[94] There's a long history of Jews engaging with Buddhism in the United States, and Buddhist ideas about things like being present and balance, which Zack mentioned, are often invoked at Adamah.[95] Jewish texts and traditions are amended as non-Jewish elements are incorporated in ways that make experiences meaningful for the fellows. This flexibility allows people to feel comfortable in a Jewish community, often for the first time.[96]

Maya remembered feeling too embarrassed to go to Jewish events before she came to Adamah. She didn't feel like she was as Jewish as the other people in those spaces, but at Adamah she found that people could experience their Judaism differently, together. She now felt more comfortable in Jewish spaces and told me that she had learned to love being around Jews. Maya attributed her love for the Jews at Adamah to the connection between Judaism and the agricultural work that she does. The interdependence that Shamu makes explicit encourages the fellows to reflect on their work in the field during prayer services and consider their Judaism during their work. Maya explained, "The Judaism and the gratefulness and the awe and the celebration isn't separate from what we do. It's like, whoa, this is amazing, what we're doing." She continued, "This is a miracle. Science is a miracle and plants are a miracle. Just like the joy—it feels like a place where you're really allowed to be joyful."[97] The joy Maya identified ran through all of the work sessions, classes, prayer services, and meals that I participated in while at Adamah. The program encourages the fellows to connect to the land, the animals, and their Judaism, and each point of connection is meant to bring a sense of awe and joy.

CONCLUSION

On Friday afternoons, all the fellows and apprentices were assigned to work in the *sadeh* (field). This field, which is located down the road from Isabella Freedman, contains four acres of land. About a quarter acre was planted that summer. The field is susceptible to flooding during big storms, and the staff decided to stop using the *sadeh* as their main field after two catastrophic losses. Adamah had suffered a recent and devastating complete loss of everything in the field when it flooded after Hurricane Irene swept through the area in 2011. Janna referred to the small amount of planting they did at the *sadeh* as their "Hail Mary." She remarked on her use of this particularly

Christian metaphor before explaining that they planted a small piece of it and tended to the field once a week. If anything came from it, it would add to their fall harvest.[98] But if something were to happen, they wouldn't lose everything.[99] We moved through our tasks at the *sadeh* quickly. This wasn't the careful weeding we did in the fields at the Kaplan Family Farm. We alternated between hands and hoes to figure out which worked best to pull weeds efficiently.[100]

My last day at Adamah, I worked in rows of squash at the *sadeh* that were so overrun with weeds that the outlines of the squash plants were difficult to discern. I chatted with Miri, Debby, Rayna, and Sam as we worked. They were all tired from a long week and were excited for the rest that Shabbat would bring. After three hours, Janna gathered everyone for a closing conversation. We stood overlooking the field and reflected on the week. People shared high points and things that they had learned. We sang. Then we split into two groups—male-identified and female-identified—and headed off to separate sections of the Housatonic River, which borders the *sadeh* and serves as the mikvah (ritual bath) for Adamah. Janna, Miri, Maya, Rayna, and I stood naked at the edge of the river and shared an intention for the week to come before saying the blessing and immersing ourselves in the cold river.[101] Immersing oneself in water is a method of purification that fellows and staff use at Adamah to mark the end of their workweek and the beginning of Shabbat. The mikvah is also used to mark conversions to Judaism. Just like the mikvah, the Adamah Farm Fellowship transforms Jews: The fellows immerse themselves in this intense program, and three months later they re-enter the world with a new sense of who they are and who they want to be.

Many of the fellows had heard that Adamah was life-changing before they arrived. Rayna recalled that everyone told her it was "a really transformative place," but she was skeptical. And yet, when we sat down to talk, Rayna acknowledged a shift: "Something that's happened since I've been here is my plans for the future have drastically changed." She was originally intending to move to a large city after her time at Adamah, but after just a few weeks in the program she now had a loose plan to move to a more rural area and work on cultivating the soil and being as self-sufficient as possible instead.[102] I asked Rebecca why she thought Adamah was able to inspire people to change their lives. She said, "There's just something about the program . . . that's just really transformative for a lot of people in a way that I haven't heard of other programs being. It's just, like, I feel really connected to anyone who's done Adamah because we've shared this—it's an intense experience. It's a really hard schedule. It challenges people physically, emotionally, spiritually, and so there's something about that that really brings people together."[103] The intensity of the program seems to be a key aspect of its success. The fellows live and work together separated from their friends, family, and "regular" daily lives for three months. They are encouraged to be flexible and open. They are surrounded by natural beauty and learn new things about their food, their environment, and Judaism every day. These ingredients seem to enable and encourage personal transformation.

There are Adamah alumni all over the world whose lives changed course after their experience. They have started businesses and nonprofit organizations to spread their knowledge and move Jews, Americans, and humans in general toward food justice. I asked Shamu whether this is what he had imagined for the program when he started it in 2003. He laughed and told me that when the program started, "Farming wasn't that popular. Food wasn't a thing. There was no Jewish food movement."[104] There is a Jewish food movement now, and Adamah has had a lot to do with that. In the two decades since Adamah was founded, around twenty-five Jewish educational farms have spread throughout the country, and Adamah alumni work in their fields and offices. Adamah alumni started the Shmita Project, which encouraged American Jews to imagine a yearlong sabbatical for agricultural land and will be discussed further in chapter 4. There are now two companies selling higher-welfare kosher meat, and one of them, Grow and Behold, is owned and operated by a husband-and-wife team who met at Adamah. For many years beginning in 2006, hundreds of people gathered annually for the Hazon Food Conference at Isabella Freedman, which kept Adamah at the center of the Jewish food movement.[105]

There is a song that we sang frequently throughout my time at Adamah. A Hebrew verse is sung first[106] and then its English translation: "Love the earth, love the sky, heat of fire, drop of water, I can feel it in my body, in my spirit and in my soul."[107] This song began to feel like the Adamah anthem, in part because the first Hebrew word sung is "Adamah" (Earth), but also because the verses indicate the key components of Adamah. The fellows are taught to love the earth, sky, fire, and water that form the basis of the farm and its alternative food system. They learn to feel that love in their bodies through hard work and the consumption of the plants, eggs, and milk they help bring to their table. Prayer services and classes make the connections between the environment, food, and Judaism explicit and accessible through innovative spiritual practices. The Adamah experience transforms spirits and souls by awakening participants to the injustices in the food system and their appropriate place within their environment, their food system, and the Jewish community. And, through the continued efforts of a strong network of alumni, Adamah is assisting with the transformation of Jewish food in the United States and beyond.

CHAPTER TWO

Live Foods for Living Bodies at the Hallelujah Diet Health Retreat

And be not conformed to this world: but be ye transformed by the renewing of your mind, that ye may prove what is that good, and acceptable, and perfect, will of God.

ROMANS 12:2 (KJV)

It takes about a pound of carrots to make eight ounces of carrot juice. During my time at the Hallelujah Diet Health Retreat in Lake Lure, North Carolina, I went from knowing nothing about juicing to knowing the process, start to finish. We had to juice about 100 pounds of carrots over the course of our six-day retreat to make enough carrot juice for nine people to enjoy twice a day. Juicing the carrots was a three-part process. During one juicing session, Chef Robert supervised as Danni, Cathy, and I peeled the carrots, put them into the juicer, and finally strained the juice to remove any remaining pulp.[1] On the other side of the kitchen, Kendall juiced red chard, celery, cucumber, and green apple to make green juice. We needed both of these components for our "sun and juice breaks." These breaks were carefully orchestrated.

We started with a Hallelujah Diet brand Barley Max supplement drink, and then we grabbed a two-toned cup of juice—half carrot and half green—and moved outside. We spent a good portion of these breaks chatting in our matching red Adirondack chairs and chasing the shade as the temperatures climbed into the mid-nineties. These sun and juice breaks exemplify the alternate food system of the Hallelujah Diet. The Hallelujah Diet's alternative food system of mostly raw and plant-based food with prescribed elements like juicing and time outdoors mirrors similar secular diets, but the religious basis for the Hallelujah Diet subsumes the common secular goals around health and weight loss into its broader effort to return human bodies to an Edenic state of perfection.

In this chapter, I argue that the Hallelujah Diet is a distinctly religious diet but is best understood as something more complex than a "Christian diet."[2] The Hallelujah Diet is based on both biblical and scientific evidence, and during my time at the Hallelujah Diet Health Retreat, other religious ideas and practices were incorporated into this alternative food system as the diet was implemented. In my experience with Hallelujah Dieters, I found that while the diet may have developed in a Christian context, it was also amended over time as participants engaged the diet at the retreat center and in their daily lives. I'll begin this chapter with overviews of the Hallelujah Diet and the Hallelujah Diet Health Retreat before moving into sections that detail the historical context for the diet, the alternative food system of the diet, and the complex religiosity of the diet.

THE HALLELUJAH DIET

In 1976, according to his narrative, the Reverend George Malkmus was the pastor of a Baptist church in New York state when doctors found a tumor the size of baseball under his lower left rib.[3] Malkmus's mother had recently gone through chemotherapy and radiation treatments for colon cancer but had died. When he was diagnosed with the same type of cancer, he couldn't bring himself to take the same medical route that he believed had killed his mother. Malkmus explained this decision in his book *The Hallelujah Diet*: "In so many cases, even prayer didn't seem to make a difference. I had watched some of the most dedicated Christians, who used personal prayer as well as collective prayer, get sicker and often die after going the medical route." Malkmus decided to contact an evangelist friend, Lester Roloff, whom he knew to be a "health nut."[4] After switching out cooked food for raw fruits, vegetables, and carrot juice, by 1977 his tumor was gone.[5] Malkmus noticed other benefits of the diet beyond his disappeared tumor, including improved vision. Impressed by the results of his diet experiment and inspired by Genesis 1:29, Malkmus began spreading the word. He even gave it a name: "Filled with gratitude, I nicknamed this new (or actually ancient) way of eating, *The Hallelujah Diet*."[6] He published his first book, *Why Christians Get Sick*, in 1989. Malkmus's answer to the question posed by the title is simple: Christians get sick because they eat the same food as non-Christians. According to the Hallelujah Diet website, more than 1 million copies of *The Hallelujah Diet* are currently in print. Malkmus also met his wife, Rhonda, through his diet ministry and reported that one year after Rhonda started the eating plan, she had lost eighty pounds and saw her severe arthritis vanish. George and Rhonda were married in 1992, and then they worked together to found Hallelujah Acres the same year.[7] Malkmus described Hallelujah Acres, the organization that promotes the Hallelujah Diet, as "a Christian ministry that teaches health from a biblical perspective," but in my experience, throughout the diet's publications, seminars, and retreats, that biblical perspective is almost always supplemented with additional sources.[8]

The Hallelujah Diet is promoted as "biblically based, scientifically validated and personally evidenced," and this tagline encapsulates the three primary aspects of the alternative Hallelujah Diet food system.[9] The Hallelujah Diet is based on one biblical verse, Genesis 1:29: "And God said, Behold, I have given you every herb bearing seed, which is upon the face of all the earth, and every tree, in the which is the fruit of a tree yielding seed; to you it shall be for meat" (KJV). This verse is quoted throughout Hallelujah Diet materials in the King James Version translation. Hallelujah Dieters interpret this verse as an indication that the diet that humans were meant to consume is one comprising raw and plant-based foods, such as those that might have been found in the Garden of Eden. Like Malkmus, they also believe that many modern diseases and conditions are the result of humanity's divergence from the original diet prescribed by God. George Malkmus was concerned that humans were relying on what he termed SAD, the "Standard American Diet." The leaders at the Hallelujah Diet Health Retreat I attended taught another version—"Satan's Alternative Diet." Both versions of SAD describe the diet that most Americans eat, which includes animal products and processed convenience foods. In his books and seminars, Malkmus taught that SAD's so-called dead foods were the root of common ailments like cancer, heart disease, diabetes, and a number of other degenerative illnesses that plague Americans. Malkmus's plan is based on the idea that living bodies need food that is alive. In his words: "L-i-v-i-n-g f-o-o-d. It spells out the basic foundation of *The Hallelujah Diet*. It is primarily a raw-food diet in which people eat as many foods as possible in their natural, uncooked condition." Malkmus intended the diet for a Christian audience, but as the Hallelujah Diet world expanded, so did its audience. Inspired by biblical images of Adam and Eve eating their meals straight from the trees, Malkmus determined that theirs was the diet that would allow all humans to enjoy long and healthy lives. Malkmus used scientific language and evidence throughout the book to support aspects of the diet, and retreat leaders did as well. The "scientific validation" of the diet comes mainly from scientists and doctors who also promote plant-based diets. In the case of juicing, Malkmus proposed that juicing enables the core nutrients in fruits and vegetables to feed bodies without using energy to separate the juice from solids.[10] The Hallelujah Diet also incorporates an array of contemporary practices like the use of essential oils and naturopathic remedies.

The Hallelujah Diet Health Retreat

The Hallelujah Acres ministry has grown significantly, and Paul Malkmus, George and Rhonda's son, now runs it.[11] The organization's initiatives have included a store in Gastonia, North Carolina; corporate offices in the United States, Canada, and Nigeria; training seminars in churches all over the United States; and weekly emails, informational books, recipe books, videos, a product line, and three health retreat centers.[12] I attended a weeklong health retreat with eight other participants at the Hallelujah Diet Health Retreat in Lake Lure in late June 2015. Seven of the participants, including myself, were women (Cathy, Danni, Erica, Faith, Kendall, Lori, and me), and two were men (Mike and Calvin), both of whom were attending the retreat with their wives. Most of the participants were middle-aged or older. Our hosts were a married couple (Andrea and Tom) and their adult son (Chef Robert). All of the participants, except me, were practicing Protestant Christians. Andrea and Tom identified as Messianic Jews and brought their religious perspective into many of our classes and informal conversations throughout the week. Our days at the retreat included classes on the diet and on food preparation, "sun and juice breaks," meals, walks, and film viewings in the evening. We all lived together in Andrea and Tom's home for the week. Many of us shared rooms, and while we had some time to ourselves, most of our time was spent with a least a few other retreat participants. We rarely left the retreat center grounds except for our walks and a boat ride on Lake Lure in the middle of the week.

The Hallelujah Diet is a rather expensive endeavor. The retreat cost $1,295 in 2015, and many of the participants whom I spoke with during the week mentioned that they had saved up for the program and were sure the diet would stick because they had already invested so much.[13] To fully follow the diet at home, we would also have to add on the cost of all the necessary kitchen appliances, the required Hallelujah Diet brand supplements, and weekly fresh produce purchases, so this diet is really accessible only to those with the means to afford such things. The Hallelujah Diet has become a commercial enterprise, and the company sells the equipment and supplements through its website. Malkmus also addressed the financial requirements of the diet throughout the literature as he reminded his readers that medical care costs more than fresh vegetables.

Throughout this diet empire, one common theme pervades: The Hallelujah Diet is all about the food. In 2015, the tagline on the Hallelujah Diet website read, "Fall in love with food again."[14] The retreat similarly focused on food. All our food was included, and we learned by doing as we helped prepare all our meals and snacks. We practiced new techniques and recipes, tried new foods and supplements, and prepared for our transitions home through group and one-on-one discussions focused on helping us follow the diet in our own lives. Throughout our time at the Hallelujah Diet Health Retreat, religious and secular sources were blended together in classes, film presentations, and informal discussions, and we were encouraged to explore using the resources that appealed most to us. In order to understand the Hallelujah Diet, it is helpful to understand its predecessors and the ways that previous efforts to establish Christian diets in the United States were similarly focused on food and were also developed through the blending of religious and secular sources.

HISTORICAL CONTEXT FOR THE HALLELUJAH DIET

In the summer of 2013, I managed to convince a friend to travel with me to Charlotte, North Carolina, for a day of raw vegan food with the promise of a stop at IKEA on the way home. We started our day with the Hallelujah Acres "God's Way to Ultimate Health" seminar at the Sheraton Charlotte Airport Hotel led by George Malkmus himself. During the seminar, Malkmus described his discovery and early experience with the Hallelujah Diet. He went over some of the scientific studies that suggest eating raw and vegan food is better for human health and shared anecdotes of people he had met who found success with the diet. He called on people from the audience to share testimonials. He talked about the diet in detail and offered specific advice in response to questions from the audience. Late in the seminar, Malkmus responded to a question about how healthy the diet was by showing off his muscles. Malkmus was in his eighties at the time, and his muscled arms and legs were meant to serve as compelling testimony all on their own.

After the seminar, we visited the Hallelujah Acres store in Gastonia. The store was small but well stocked. A row of juice machines featuring all the Barley Max flavors greeted customers as they arrived. Barley Max is a nutritional supplement that serves as an essential component of the Hallelujah Diet, so I tried them all. The original Barley Max flavor, which tastes a lot like eating grass, ended up being my favorite. The beet, berry, mint, and carrot flavors all tasted a bit like juice that had been sitting out for too long. Those odd flavors lingered in my memory two years later, and I selected the original flavor for the sun and juice breaks throughout the entire retreat. The store in Gastonia stocked all the Hallelujah Diet brand products, plus numerous additional health food products, beauty products, and supplements. You could also purchase juicers, blenders, and other kitchen appliances at the store. The refrigerators were filled with fifty-pound bags of carrots and an assortment of other produce. After browsing the store for about an hour, my friend and I moved on to a late lunch at a raw foods restaurant in Charlotte that was not affiliated with the diet. However, as we were eating, we overheard the table next to us talking about the Hallelujah Diet. This suggested that there was some overlap in the secular and religious raw and vegan worlds in and around Charlotte.

After our IKEA stop, we drove home to Durham, North Carolina, with fresh juices in our cupholders, and my friend asked about the difference between the Hallelujah Diet and the restaurant where we enjoyed a completely raw lunch. She was interested in what made the Hallelujah Diet successful enough to warrant a store, two lifestyle centers, and thousands of followers. She wanted to know more about how the diet was related to other religious diets and to the broader raw food movement. The answers to her questions can be found in the development of the diet and the broader Hallelujah Diet ministry. Secular raw vegan dieters and Hallelujah Dieters are likely to believe that eating a raw vegan diet is the best way to stay healthy and achieve or maintain their ideal body weight and to support their beliefs with scientific sources. But the Hallelujah Diet is also bolstered by its religious foundations in the Bible. Hallelujah Dieters believe the diet is healthy, in part because scientists say it is, but mostly because George Malkmus reminded them that it was the diet that God intended for humankind. For many Christians, the religious foundations of the diet authenticate it and make the diet more accessible to them. This appeal to central religious ideas is not unique to the Hallelujah Diet. In the United States, there is a well-documented history of religious people promoting vegan and vegetarian diets for religious reasons.

On the first day of the Hallelujah Diet Health Retreat, we were given water bottles with our names on them and were encouraged to drink water throughout the day. All our water came from a water distillation system set up downstairs. In *The Hallelujah Diet*, Malkmus explained that tap water often contains chemicals like chlorine and fluoride and well water is often tainted by pollution, concluding that the most reliable source of clean water is distilled water.[15] At the retreat center, a Hallelujah Diet product called Hydroboost was added to the distilled water to incorporate some minerals back in. The final product had an odd taste and a bewildering inability to quench my thirst. And the water rules didn't stop there. We were not permitted to bring our water bottles to meals with us. We were also told that we should stop drinking water about thirty minutes before meals and should not resume drinking until about thirty minutes after meals. Meals were to be ingested without the assistance of liquids so the liquids would not impede our digestive process. We were permitted to put ice in our water only one time during the retreat, for our boat ride on Lake Lure, and the few precious ice cubes we got to put in our water bottles for that outing melted long before we reached the lake. Hot drinks were similarly discouraged, but the last few evenings a few of us enjoyed cups of hot herbal tea to help battle issues with congestion and insomnia. All of these recommendations are based on ideas that have been around since the nineteenth century. The basic premise of water rules like the ones we followed is that food and liquids change the composition of a body's interior systems, and extreme temperatures or the consumption of liquid and solid foods together can have dire effects on those systems. In the nineteenth century, these warnings were paired with the idea that hot foods, as well as stimulants and spices, would heat blood and excite passions, awakening the animal nature contained within human beings. These temperature warnings are one of many characteristics that the Hallelujah Diet shares with its historical predecessors.

In 1817, William Metcalfe left England with a small group of Christians who practiced vegetarianism. His arrival marked the beginning of religious vegetarianism in the United States as he preached about the practice at his church in Philadelphia. He often cited a familiar biblical verse as the basis for his vegetarian views: "At the very commencement of the book of Genesis we find this plain and important commandment prominently set forth, as one of the laws of direction, essential to the health and happiness of new-created."[16] Metcalfe then quoted Genesis 1:29. Given its usage by Metcalfe and other early Christian advocates of vegetarianism, it is no surprise that Genesis 1:29 became central to the Hallelujah Diet. In the decades following Metcalfe's arrival, a wave of vegetarianism swept through the Northeastern United States. Coinciding with the first moments of the Second Great Awakening, this alternative food movement was explicitly religious in nature. Preachers taught that changing one's diet was a moral imperative and failing to do so would have consequences in this life and the next. This discourse was based on a collective understanding that "animal" refers to living creatures who were created by God but lack the self-control, morals, and souls that distinguish humans from them. Nineteenth-century religious diet reformers were concerned that consuming animals would bring out the animal nature of human beings. Relying on a Cartesian mind-body dualism, these writers felt that the mind was constantly endangered by dalliances of the body. The control of sexual impulses and general physical health were of utmost importance to preachers. Early vegetarianism was seen as a way for Christians to control their bodies in order to cleanse their minds and souls.

Sylvester Graham, a Presbyterian minister, was so influenced by Metcalfe's vegetarian message that he also began lecturing about the dangers of animal foods in the 1830s. He invented the Graham diet, a plant-based diet of unprocessed foods and whole grains, and started a movement of "Grahamites." In 1850, he helped found the American Vegetarian Society, which was established to "induce the habits of abstinence from the flesh of Animals as food."[17] Ellen G. White, cofounder of the Seventh-day Adventist Church, also adopted and promoted a vegetarian diet based on Graham's.[18] These early religious vegetarian leaders focused their teachings and writings on the biblical support for this diet and on the subsequent beliefs that adhering to a vegetarian diet would heal human bodies, protect human souls, and end human suffering. These diet reformers were adamant that they had uncovered the true diet meant for humanity. Sylvester Graham taught that humans had turned away from their God-given diet and were suffering from diseases and dying as a result. Daniel Sack, historian and author of *Whitebread Protestants*, explained that Graham blamed his own poor health and that of his fellow Americans "on ignorance of God's design and the onslaughts of modern civilization."[19] Graham took particular issue with bread made in bakeries with bolted wheat, which he referred to as "the most miserable trash that can be imagined." He informed his readers that bakers used "poor flour," added chemicals, and adulterated their bread with beans, potatoes, and chalk to increase the weight of the bread. Graham was also deeply concerned with processed food of all types and urged his followers to eat foods in their natural, or raw, state. He wrote, "It is nearly certain that the primitive inhabitants of the earth, ate their food with very little, if any artificial preparation." Graham was most concerned about wheat, but his interest in "natural state" food aligns with the raw-food focus of the Hallelujah Diet. Food served at the wrong temperature was similarly problematic for Graham. He believed that hot food would agitate the blood and cold food would disrupt digestion, so food was best eaten raw to avoid these temperature-related issues. As Graham wrote, "If man were to subsist wholly on uncooked food, he would never suffer from the improper temperature of his aliment."[20] For Graham, food served uncooked and in as natural a state as possible was the ideal.

In addition to his concerns about bread and both hot and cold foods, Sylvester Graham was also convinced that a great deal of human suffering was a direct effect of the consumption of animals. He focused a good portion of his writing on the relationship between the consumption of animal foods and increased sexual appetite. He believed that eating animal foods altered the state of one's body and brought it closer to that of an animal. In 1839, Graham published *A Lecture to Young Men on Chastity* and explained his belief that nonhuman animals lack the necessary rational and moral powers to control their sexual appetite. He then argued that when humans consume animals and incorporate animal flesh into their own bodies, they risk becoming like nonhuman animals and losing control over their sexual appetites. Graham was also adamant that all of the physical pain people experienced could be avoided by abstaining from animal foods. His confidence in this solution was due to its source—God.[21] Graham's diet became fairly popular in the Northeastern states and gained traction in the new religious movements that were flourishing at that time. According to Stephen Nissenbaum, author of *Sex, Diet, and Debility in Jacksonian America*, Graham's teachings "were adopted, directly and virtually intact, by the Seventh-day Adventists; and on a more secular level, they ultimately led to the rise of the modern American breakfast cereal industry."[22] Ellen White also highlighted the connection between a diet of animal foods and sexual propensities in her 1865 book, *Health; or, How to Live*. In a piece about sexual excess, she wrote that "flesh meat is not the right food for God's people. It animalizes human beings," and she warned her readers that consumption of flesh meat results in "animalism."[23]

She clarified that this was a negative state because animals are inferior to man. Beyond the concern for the souls of individual Christians, White also suggested that the consumption of animal foods was the underlying reason that Christian civilization experienced a slow growth.[24]

These nineteenth-century diet reformers were striving to save souls, but they were also concerned about human health and suffering in this life. Graham was clear throughout his lectures that humans had the tools to live healthy and happy lives free of physical and mental suffering. God had gifted them with the knowledge of what food would nourish their bodies, and according to Graham, animal foods were not on that list. "God made you to be happy. He gave you all your powers and faculties for good; and if you suffer evil, depend upon it, it comes not from the legitimate and undisturbed economy of your original constitution."[25] Graham's ideas were incorporated into the dietary practices of Seventh-day Adventists and continued to be persuasive in many American religious communities. Seventh-day Adventists retained their vegetarian diet, which led to the recognition of their impressive overall health by Dan Buettner. He included the Seventh-day Adventist community in Loma Linda, California, on his list of "Blue Zones," which he defines as areas where people tend to live longer than average.[26] In the late twentieth century, teachings related to the dangers of processed, industrial foods gained traction with the broader public again. Stephen Nissenbaum wrote that "the figure of Sylvester Graham and the movement he helped define . . . achieved new and unanticipated salience in the 1970s." He explained that after the publication of Rachel Carson's *Silent Spring*, which brought public attention to the issue of pesticide use, there was growing concern about the modern food industry, including the use of pesticides and a propensity toward overconsumption. Nissenbaum suggested, "Sylvester Graham would surely have understood these fears."[27] Of course, there is no way to know what Sylvester Graham would be concerned with were he alive today, but Nissenbaum was right that Graham and his successors shared concerns about the effects of processed and animal foods on Christians.

Malkmus and Graham shared grievances and proposed similar solutions—a diet of unprocessed, plant-based foods—but their motivations differed. As Nissenbaum explained, the nineteenth-century diet reformers focused on anxieties and moral questions about sexuality and the body.[28] Graham was worried about processed food and animal products, but his concern was that the impurity of the food would lead people, and men in particular, toward sexual deviance. Malkmus identified those same impurities, but his concern lay in their relationship to health. Graham was concerned with morality and behavior; Malkmus was more worried about disease. Daniel Sack similarly highlighted the early religious food reformers' emphasis on morality, noting that "food carries a moral value in America. In this culture, a particular foodstuff is not only good or bad for your body but also can be good or bad for your soul."[29] Christian diets, especially those that emerged in the nineteenth century, tended to revolve around the morality of food decisions and the state of stomachs and souls. Malkmus diverged from this pattern and focused instead on whether food is good or bad for bodies. He was less concerned with the moral consequences of food than with the physical. He even included a lighthearted reference to the Christian emphasis on the afterlife in *The Hallelujah Diet*. "Although I know Heaven is a better place, I really do enjoy life! I enjoy physical life. I know where I'm going to go when I leave this world; but if it's just the same to you all, I'd rather put it off a while."[30] Rather than align his diet with earlier versions, Malkmus clarified the difference between the diet he promoted for health reasons and the early religious diets that were aimed at altering the morality of Christians.

Differences aside, Malkmus also utilized the model of those early diets. Graham established Grahamite boardinghouses so people could come learn about and follow his diet. John Harvey Kellogg, a Seventh-day Adventist inspired by Sylvester Graham and Ellen White, started the Battle Creek Sanitarium to teach people how to live healthy lives, and his brother, W. K. Kellogg, eventually began selling the "Corn Flakes" they developed at the sanitarium in order to provide all Americans with an accessible alternative to animal-based breakfasts.[31] Like his predecessors, Malkmus decided to provide trainings, products, and support for dieters because he understood that their journey was going to be difficult. He explained, "Friends, I promise you this is not a magic cure. The Hallelujah Diet is merely getting back to nourishing the body as God intended and then letting the body function naturally, the way God designed it. It's that simple."[32] The basis of the diet may be simple, but implementing the diet in the context of the Standard American Diet is not. The Hallelujah Diet requires an alternate system, and it has thrived by virtue of the system Malkmus created.

THE HALLELUJAH DIET'S ALTERNATIVE FOOD SYSTEM

When I arrived at the Hallelujah Diet Health Retreat, my main concerns were hunger and lack of caffeine. Prior to my arrival, I spent four weeks decreasing my coffee intake from four cups a day to none. We were asked to start eliminating animal foods from our diets prior to our arrival to lessen the impact of detox symptoms during our week at the center. I had already been a vegetarian for four years at that point, so I figured cutting out dairy and eggs for the week wouldn't be too difficult. That said, I was worried about the raw food. I wasn't really looking forward to what I imagined would be a week of salads. We all arrived on a Sunday in the late afternoon and introduced ourselves, settled into our rooms, and unpacked. Andrea led our first class to introduce us to the basics of the diet and to the retreat center. When we were told to move into the dining room for dinner, I was hungry and a bit nervous. What I found was a beautiful table set for twelve. Huge platters of bright green raw zucchini manicotti adorned with raw tomato sauce provided an impressive centerpiece. Large serving bowls of broccoli and pea salad and Italian salad were interspersed with the manicotti platters. After Tom led us in a quick prayer to thank God for the food, we served ourselves family-style and began to eat. Almost immediately, the table filled with audible gasps and excited reactions. The manicotti was remarkable. A raw cashew filling stood in for cheese and provided a creamy and salty counterpart to the bright, crispy zucchini and the bold-flavored tomato sauce. After dinner, we were served a sweet and hearty raw carrot cake for dessert. The food was filling and satisfying, and dessert was an unexpected treat. I settled in and started to look forward to meals. That first meal, like many others we enjoyed at the health retreat, was entirely raw. "Wholly alive" is a phrase that Andrea and Tom used to describe raw food and the Hallelujah Diet in general. Throughout the week, the wholly alive approach of the Hallelujah Diet was compared to the Standard American Diet. From the perspective of our hosts, Hallelujah Diet foods were living, raw, plant-based foods, and SAD foods were dead, processed, and filled with additives.

The focus on raw foods makes the diet particularly difficult and requires dieters to make drastic lifestyle changes. The materials for the Hallelujah Diet promote some practicality in this regard and propose an 85 percent raw and 15 percent cooked food split to enable dieters to follow the diet and live in the world. The other participants and I talked frequently about what we would be able to eat when we returned home, and most of our answers involved at least some of our 15 percent cooked food allotment because the addition of foods like beans, rice, and some whole grain products opened up a lot of possibilities. This Hallelujah Diet concession is not too dissimilar from those allowed in other alternate food systems in the United States. For example, many local food advocates purchase as much of their food as possible locally but continue to purchase items not found locally, like coffee, chocolate, and bananas, to supplement their diets. Hallelujah Dieters similarly carved out space for their alternative system within current food system structures. They learned to shop in different sections of the grocery store, prepare raw foods at home from scratch that taste like familiar favorites, attend social events built around SAD foods, and even order at restaurants. Dieters were able to find educational and commercial support through the Hallelujah Diet materials and communities as they developed their own individual alternative food system built on living food.

George Malkmus dedicated a large portion of *The Hallelujah Diet* to the importance of eating food that is alive. He began with Genesis, as he often did: "In the Garden of Eden, God revealed that all animals—including humans—were designed to take energy directly from plant life." He continued, explaining that plants were God's way of turning light into energy. He referred to this as the "life-force," which humans access by consuming plants. He concluded, "This is the simple yet brilliant way God designed to pass along the life-giving energy from one living thing to another in the form of *living foods*." Malkmus went on to remark that despite this system set up by God, humans set up advanced civilizations wherein they learned to kill and cook their food. Incredulous at the ignorance of mankind, Malkmus continued, "We share this planet with over 700,000 other species of animals, but we are the *only* ones who have tamed fire in order to cook our food." Malkmus also listed the damage inflicted upon food in the cooking process: "Enzymes are lost, proteins are denatured, heated oils and fats convert to trans-fatty acids, which are carcinogenic, sugars are caramelized, vitamins and minerals become less available, water is reduced, and fiber is refined to the point of losing much of its benefit."[33] For these reasons, Malkmus proposed a diet of raw, living foods.

The conceptual argument that Malkmus made is interesting for two reasons. First, it is curious to call plants and fruits that have been uprooted from the ground or picked off trees, plants, or bushes "alive." Aware of potential critiques, Malkmus suggested that his readers try an experiment to prove that these types of foods are alive, asking them to cut the tops off five carrots. They should leave one raw, boil one, steam one, bake one, and microwave one. Then all five should be placed in separate glasses of water. The raw carrot will sprout and the others will not. For Malkmus, this proved that the raw carrot is alive and the others are dead. Malkmus also noted that the enzyme content is the key: "Living foods still contain their life-force, which is indicated by the presence of active enzymes. Those enzymes supplied in all living foods are crucial to proper digestion and absorption of the nutrients found in that food." Here Malkmus equated the presence of a food's "life-force" with the presence of active enzymes. This is persuasive, but do active enzymes really distinguish between what is alive and what is dead? Malkmus would not permit dieters to eat yogurt, which has active enzymes but is an animal product, so there are still some blurry edges to his argument. Malkmus also pinpointed a specific temperature at which food moves from being alive to being dead—107 degrees Fahrenheit. He explained that at that temperature, the life-force starts to break down and die. He wrote that by 122 degrees Fahrenheit, enzyme activity is gone and food is dead. He also noted the degradation of proteins at 150 degrees Fahrenheit. Malkmus finished with the suggestion that dead food, or food heated to 122 degrees Fahrenheit or beyond, is no longer acceptable food for humans. He explained that this is because "a body is comprised of *living* cells, which were designed by God to be nourished with *living* food!"[34]

The second compelling aspect of Malkmus's conceptualization of live food is the cooked foods concession. In the book, Malkmus proposed an 85 percent raw, 15 percent cooked food ratio. At the retreat center we were taught 80 percent raw and 20 percent cooked foods. Either way, dead foods are being consumed. Malkmus explained his leniency: "I used to teach all raw, and people were cheating, feeling guilty about it, and then falling away altogether. So we started adding a little cooked food at the end of the evening meal. And we started getting the same, if not better results than the 100-percent raw diet we had previously been teaching." In the end, this means that the Hallelujah Diet materials, which include lengthy discussions to discourage people from eating dead food, actually allow people to consume 15–20 percent of their diet in dead foods. More fascinating is the fact that this concession occurred without the usual biblical and scientific evidence that Malkmus relied so heavily on throughout his book. Rather, we are offered a psychosocial explanation—people cheat less if they are permitted to eat some cooked food each day. Whatever the reason, Malkmus permitted 15 percent dead foods, and readers are left to assume that the raw foods they are eating are enough to nourish their living cells. Malkmus summarized this point, writing, "In a nutshell, we need to eat a diet rich in living foods in order to fuel the living cells that comprise the physical bodies God gave us: Living Food = Living Fuel → Living Cells = Healthy Body."[35] And it seems Malkmus determined that 85 percent is "rich" enough in living foods to fuel living bodies.

There are other interesting aspects of the diet that don't align with its biblical foundations. This is a diet that, as mentioned earlier, requires a lot of juice. Curious readers of *The Hallelujah Diet* may wonder how a diet based on the foods available to Adam in the Garden of Eden came to rely rather heavily on juicing, an activity that requires modern equipment. Malkmus informed his readers that our produce today simply does not live up to the standard of the food available to Adam: "Even those fruits and vegetables grown under superior organic growing conditions today are nowhere near as nutritious as the vegetables man grew in our ancient soils." As mentioned above, Malkmus believed that living cells need living nutrition, and a lot of it. So, Malkmus let his readers know that they should plan for this inevitable situation by consuming more food. This was an easy enough solution, except that eating fruits and vegetables continuously throughout the day wasn't really an option for most people. Malkmus had a solution to this problem: "Even if your digestive system is in the optimum working condition, it isn't able to process all the raw food you need in a full day. The answer to this problem is to do the *first part* of the processing before consuming it—through juicing!"[36] Malkmus proposed that through juicing, living cells could gain direct access to the nourishment they needed.

In addition to the rules about raw food, there is a complete ban on animal products in the Hallelujah Diet. Malkmus was adamant that animal products are an unacceptable source of nourishment. "The single most destructive thing you can put into your body is something of an animal origin: beef, poultry, seafood, milk, cheese, and eggs—anything that comes from something with a face." Malkmus offered many reasons for human abstention from meat. First, meat is dead—and not just dead, but cooked and empty of the fiber that would allow it to be digested quickly. He referred to meat as "putrefied flesh" and explained that consuming meat causes an array of ailments, including body odor, stomach problems, irritable bowel syndrome, colitis, Crohn's disease, and cancer. Second, Malkmus proposed that humans are not the omnivores they claim to be. He offered detailed charts that showed humans to be closer physiologically to herbivores than carnivores. Finally, Malkmus informed his readers that the meat available to Americans is particularly unacceptable: "Diseased meats are everywhere in our mass-produced food supply." Meat production will be discussed at length in the next chapter, but about half of the videos we watched while at the health retreat dealt with the state of the modern meat and dairy industries and the health benefits that await those willing to forsake those industries. Finally, Malkmus also prohibited the consumption of white sugar, white salt, white flour, caffeine, alcohol, nicotine, and narcotics. The white foods are prohibited for the processed nature and the chemical additives that make them white. Malkmus explained, "To no great surprise, after years of consuming such 'Franken-foods,' our bodies react to all those chemicals by getting sick."[37] The prescribed solution, according to Malkmus, was to reject these foods and return to the plant-based, raw food diet of the Garden of Eden.

The Lake Lure Hallelujah Diet Health Retreat

Andrea and Tom purchased the Hallelujah Diet Health Retreat in Lake Lure and began operating retreats in October 2006.[38] Their son Robert shared the title of "head chef" with Tom. Together, the three of them ran weeklong programs like the one I attended, longer two-week programs, and the "Raw Gourmet Living Culinary Academy," a one-week program focused on culinary skills. Andrea learned about the Hallelujah Diet in 2002 while she was working in the marketing department of a Whole Foods Market in Florida. Part of her job was interviewing customers, but one of her customers began interviewing her instead and told her about the Hallelujah Diet. The customer told Andrea he had been diagnosed with terminal brain cancer and had been sent home to die. But this conversation took place six or seven years after that. Andrea told me that his testimony and the hundreds of others she found when she did research later at home convinced her to give the diet a try. Andrea had searched for the perfect diet for many years. She studied nutrition and fitness; spent many years teaching dance therapy, macrobiotic nutrition, and herbal remedies; and ran a natural foods restaurant on Long Island in New York. Yet, she hadn't found a diet worth sticking to until she learned about the Hallelujah Diet. Andrea explained, "I knew immediately that it was what I had been searching for. I have never doubted its tenets since then and have had the good fortune, the blessing, of being able to see by our experience here, the nine years practically that we've been here, that it works."[39]

Andrea and Tom started the diet soon after her conversation with that customer, and they both became health ministers in 2003. They were holding mini-retreats in their home in Boynton Beach, Florida, and searching online to find a place where they could start their own lifestyle center when they learned that the Hallelujah Diet lifestyle center in Lake Lure, North Carolina, was going to be sold. Andrea described her reaction when they got the phone call asking them to take over the center at Lake Lure: "It was an answer to prayer. We believe that God put us here. We're certainly glad and grateful that he has." By the time I visited in 2015, they had hosted about 1,400 guests at their center. Andrea and Tom taught classes throughout the week at the retreats and provided us with a wide array of resources in the form of handouts, PowerPoint slides, films, discussions, articles, and the information they had personally acquired through their years of experience. Despite the wealth of knowledge they dispensed, Andrea stressed that it was not important that people remember every detail but rather that they get the gist of it. Andrea recalled a story from when she and Tom attended the health minister training. Tom was standing onstage with George Malkmus, and in response to a question Malkmus posed, Tom replied, "It's really simple, folks. It's fruits and vegetables, seeds and nuts and some grains. That's it. Don't adulterate it. Eat as close to the garden and to the natural foods as you can."[40] Tom's overview of the diet was clear, but in practice, the diet was more complex.

Healing Bodies

The health retreat participants arrived with different goals in mind. Lori and Calvin, a married couple—and also the oldest participants in the retreat—decided to sign up for the health retreat after Lori was diagnosed with breast cancer. She told me that she was planning to go through with the lumpectomy her doctor had scheduled for the week after the retreat but had "determined years ago that if this should ever happen to me, that I would not take chemo."[41] Calvin had heart problems and recently had two stents put in. He was taking a blood thinner and had been told by his doctor that the medication was the only option.[42] The Hallelujah Diet was recommended to Lori by a friend, so she and Calvin decided to come and "learn how to eat the healthiest way possible."[43] They were both hoping that the diet would provide an alternative to the medical options they had been offered. Another participant, Danni, was a medical doctor and had been through a similar raw foods program before, but she had not been able to stick to the program. She explained, "I came to Hallelujah Acres to see if I could detox and transform my mind to be able to wrap around potentially eating better so that I could be healthier and have a body that was able to be functional to do all sorts of exciting things in my last half of my life."[44] Danni was in her fifties and had three children at home, so she was particularly interested in keeping her energy up for her kids and her patients.

Mike and Faith, another couple at the retreat, were also trained health ministers, and they were looking to get back on the Hallelujah Diet after some time away from it. They went on the diet in the 1990s after Faith had a lumpectomy for breast cancer. A nutritionist told her that George Malkmus was coming through town, so they went to see him. Faith remembered that they had decided quickly to try the diet and see whether it would work.⁴⁵ Her breast cancer had been in remission for twenty years, but they stopped following the diet about ten years ago and had recently noticed that "things started going south as far as our health was concerned." They were attending the retreat to "get kick-started."⁴⁶ Mike and Faith were enthusiastic participants and helpful resources for the rest of us throughout the week.

There were also a few people in our group who were interested in gathering the information not only for themselves but also for a loved one back home. One participant, Cathy, had traveled from the Midwest to learn more about the diet after her mother told her about it. Her family had some health issues and her mother had fought cancer with alternative treatments and was still living almost fifty years later. Cathy figured this was a sign that her mother was doing something right. Cathy, who was in her forties, thought she would come learn more about the diet to see whether she could prevent some of the health issues her family members were facing. She also hoped to bring the information home to her mother, who was not feeling well enough to travel.⁴⁷ Kendall came to the center after realizing that her and her husband's health and eating habits had gotten out of control due to job stress. Kendall had participated in a study conducted by the Hallelujah Diet's research director Michael Donaldson "many years ago" for people with fibromyalgia. Kendall was impressed with the results she saw in that study: "I have—had—very mild fibromyalgia, and the diet pretty much cleared it up."⁴⁸ Although Kendall was interested in going back on the diet herself, she was mostly looking to help her husband. We learned a lot about Kendall's husband throughout the week. He worked long hours in a quarry, blasting rocks. His workplace was very hot, he ate on his breaks standing up, and he commuted for hours a day.⁴⁹ Tom and Andrea worked with Kendall throughout the week to figure out creative ways to send him to work with Hallelujah Diet–approved foods.

The final participant was my roommate for the week, Erica. She was in her fifties and told me that she came because she was "very overweight" and had high blood pressure and high cholesterol. She started reading about the Hallelujah Diet about twenty years before the retreat and was pleased with the testimonies she read at that time. She was also very interested in the diet because her husband had been diagnosed with multiple sclerosis six years before, and she was hoping to learn about the diet and convince him to go on it as well.⁵⁰ The participants at the Hallelujah Diet Health Retreat were looking to improve their own health and the health of those around them, but only Lori was struggling with a life-threatening crisis like those I had read about in testimonials. Andrea informed me that this was fairly normal for their health retreats. They got a mix of people dealing with a serious illness, people just looking to improve their health, and people like Mike, Faith and Kendall who have experienced the diet but need a reminder. Andrea recalled guests who finished the retreat and got in touch with her later, after they were subsequently healed from cancer, diabetes, osteoporosis, and fibromyalgia. She also said that a lot of people who come don't have serious illnesses but simply wish to be healthier. She added that they got a lot of repeat customers who were hoping for a fresh start on the diet.[51] Tom suggested that people tend to get comfortable and eat what they like until something happens that forces them to consider a change. At that point, he said they often remember things they've heard before about juicing and raw food, and then they seek out a solution like the Hallelujah Diet.[52]

The relative health of the participants was not the only surprise I encountered at the retreat. Religious studies scholars tend to emphasize the theological and moral foundations of religious diets over the health and bodily aspects of those diets, but that is not what I experienced at the retreat. Rather, as evidenced above, what I found was a deep concern for physical health among the retreat participants. R. Marie Griffith brought bodies into the conversation in her book *Born Again Bodies*, where she detailed the complicated and intertwined history of body image in America and Protestant Christianity, but she identified bodily health as a means to an end. Griffith included the Hallelujah Diet along with other religious diets as she argued that these diets encourage people to strive toward ideal bodies as an act of devotional intimacy. Griffith saw religious diets mainly as an expression of the human dieter's relationship with God. She explained how "participants in devotional diet culture rarely imagine health and thinness as final ends; rather, they pursue bodily fitness as a vehicle for developing close, satisfying relationships with a beloved whom they aim to please through obedient self-discipline."[53] In all of my conversations with participants at the health retreat, I did not hear anyone connect their interest in the retreat or the diet with a desire for intimacy with the divine. The participants at the health retreat sought to enhance and extend their relationships with family and friends rather than with the divine. I heard about playing with children and grandchildren far more than I heard about devotion to God.

Religious studies scholar Annie Blazer conducted ethnographic research at the same Hallelujah Diet Health Retreat Center that I visited; "Hallelujah Acres: Christian Raw Foods and the Quest for Health" was the essay that resulted, included in the volume *Religion, Food, and Eating in North*

America. She also focused on the theological aspects of the diet as she asserted that it was representative of a broader trend among evangelicals to see themselves as morally superior to others. In her words, "For those who experience healing through changing their diet, belonging to the Hallelujah Acres community affirms a sense of distinction and moral superiority that resembles Evangelical ideology generally."[54] Though it is possible that practices changed between our visits, during the retreat I attended I heard very little conversation about how the diet would distinguish participants from their friends and family and almost nothing to suggest that participants saw themselves as morally superior. We did have plenty of discussions about how dieters would follow the diet while participating in their usual array of social events, including church potlucks, family weddings, and gatherings with friends. Our hosts also explicitly discouraged us from walking around trumpeting the superiority of the diet. The diet is promoted in books and online materials as the best option for humans, but Tom and Andrea suggested that we quietly live the diet, improve our health, and then tell people about it when they ask what we've been doing. During my time at the Hallelujah Diet Health Retreat, I did not observe the same motivational binary privileging theology and morality over health and body that Griffith did or the separation between Christians and the world that Blazer saw. The participants I met at the retreat *were* pursuing health and thinness as final ends; they wanted to live longer and healthier lives. They were doing so as part of their relationship with God, but they were not at the retreat primarily to improve or embody that relationship.

Both Griffith and Blazer suggested that the Hallelujah Diet requires a 100 percent commitment, but this claim was complicated by conversations the other participants and I had throughout our retreat about how to prioritize and maintain social and familial relationships. Griffith noted that "one either adopted the Hallelujah diet in all its entirety or not." She saw a parallel between how foods are described in diets like the Hallelujah Diet and other aspects of secular culture that were rejected by Christians: "The tensions among these programs over which foods to demarcate as 'good' or 'evil' represent, in a sense, larger disagreements over which parts of so-called secular culture to appropriate and which to reject." Griffith, speaking specifically about *The Hallelujah Diet*, found that dieters would have to overhaul their lives and accept the diet in full. "Making only a handful of doctor-recommended dietary changes—less red meat, more produce, reduced salt, and so forth—was too half hearted an effort to matter, leaving the dieter as reliant as ever on artificial, cooked and therefore 'dead' foods."[55] This certainly aligns with the ideals expressed in *The Hallelujah Diet*, but while at the retreat center, I did not get the sense my choice was an either/or in the way that Griffith described. This may come down to a difference in method. *The Hallelujah Diet* book and published testimonials of dieters in the book and on the website do present an all-or-nothing approach. But at the retreat, there was more flexibility. We were encouraged to follow the diet to the best of our ability and to try our best at least to eat vegan and mostly raw, but space was made for accommodations, especially if we were trying to participate in community and family events.

In fact, Tom and Andrea worked with us to think through solutions to the practical issues we might face at home. For example, a few days into the retreat I asked Andrea whether she had recommendations for juices that I could purchase from the store because I would be traveling after leaving Hallelujah Acres. She reminded me that juicing my own vegetables would be better, but then she brought me into the kitchen to show me a brand that cold-processes its juice. So, even if it wasn't ideal to purchase juice, I was offered an option to buy some that hadn't been pasteurized with heat (and is therefore not raw) in order to maintain the diet. In addition, the Hallelujah Diet literature stresses a very strict ratio of raw to cooked foods. In the literature the ratio is given as 85 percent raw and 15 percent cooked. As I mentioned above, at the Hallelujah Diet Health Retreat we were told to try to adhere to an 80 percent raw and 20 percent cooked food ratio. This was described and practiced as an estimate. We never actually calculated the percentages of the food we ate during the week and were not encouraged to do so when we returned home.

The descriptions of the Hallelujah Diet provided by both Griffith and Blazer—that the diet was primarily theological, intended to separate Christians from society, and strict—were incongruent with how the diet was practiced during my visit to the retreat center, where participants were seeking bodily health for longer lives to spend with Christians and non-Christians and dieters and nondieters alike. My fieldwork at the retreat revealed that people were seeking health, thinness, and happiness and were not there for theological, moral, or devotional reasons, even as they did appreciate the Christian foundations of the diet. The dieters were learning to eat living foods to be wholly alive and chose a religious diet center to avoid teachings that might have contradicted what they were hearing in church. In addition, despite the fact that there has been significant scholarly attention paid to Christian diets, very little work has been done to assess the actual eating plans or the people who follow them. As is the case with many aspects of religion, I found that the lived experience of following and even teaching the diet differed substantially from the prescriptive literature promoting it.

FREE-RANGE RELIGION AT THE HALLELUJAH DIET HEALTH RETREAT

There were twelve people total at the house during the retreat I attended, nine participants and three leaders, and as I mentioned above, only nine of those people identified as Christians. This complicates Annie Blazer's description of the diet and the retreat as evangelical. This is especially true because Tom and Andrea, who ran the retreat center and did most of the teaching, were not evangelical Christians.[56] Tom and Andrea both identified as Messianic Jews, and this affected the ways that the diet and religion were discussed during the retreats they hosted. My presence as both a researcher and a Reform Jew further complicated this picture and likely explains some of the differences between what Blazer and I observed. As a full quarter of the people present, including the two people in charge of running the retreat, did not identify as Christian, the Christian character of the retreat became a fascinating site for observing the differences between what the Hallelujah Diet was set up to do and what it was actually doing on the ground.

The fact that this diet is based on Genesis brings up interesting issues for the health retreat. Christians, Jews, Muslims, and others venerate figures, stories, and texts found in Genesis. For this reason, there are myriad interpretations, and when discussed in mixed company, these divergences become clear. The diet also engages with ideas and practices outside Christianity, including medical science and New Age spirituality, among others. There is also nothing in the diet itself that prevents non-Christians from participating. Tom asserted that this diet is important not only for Christians but for all people. "Even George, the founder of Hallelujah Acres, says that you can be an atheist and still heal yourself on the Hallelujah Diet, because it has nothing to do with your belief system. It has to do with how you're nourishing your body."[57] In other words, the practice of diet is more important than the beliefs of the dieter. Dieters do not need to read the Bible literally or believe that this was the original diet intended for humanity to decide it is the best plan for their own body. The Hallelujah Diet Health Retreat at Lake Lure was a site where religious, spiritual, and secular mixed and mingled, so I will discuss the diet in this section as the complex assemblage it was, rather than as a bounded Christian thing.[58] I will also discuss the ways that retreat leaders and participants navigated their interest in practices they often identified as "New Age," even as they distinguished their own religiosity from "New Age spirituality."

Messianic Judaism played a particularly important role at the Lake Lure retreat center, and it is a movement that is often misunderstood. Messianic Judaism began as a missionary effort in the nineteenth century in Europe and the United States, but today many Messianic Jews identify themselves as being both Messianic and Jewish. Yaakov Ariel, scholar and author of *Evangelizing the Chosen People*, suggests that modern post-1970 Messianic Judaism is the logical outcome of a century of missionary efforts to evangelize Jews through the use of Jewish symbols, language, and practices.[59] Or, as Messianic Jewish author David Stern wrote in his book *Messianic Judaism*, "The destiny of Messianic Judaism is to live out the fact that it is simultaneously 100% Messianic and 100% Jewish." Stern went on to argue that Messianic Jews reject the "'either-or' demanded by many Christians and Jews."[60] Messianic Jews complicate a boundary between Christians and Jews that stood firm for hundreds of years.

This hybrid identity is not synonymous with evangelical Christianity. Ariel explained that Messianic Jewish congregations have their own culture. They often engage evangelical Christian theology and political agendas, but they do so alongside the adoption of distinctly Jewish practices and rituals. These include the messianic bar mitzvah and the use of a distinctly Messianic Jewish vocabulary, as in the use of "Yeshua" instead of "Christ" or "Jesus."[61] Andrea and Tom exemplified this hybrid Messianic Jewish culture. Their home was decorated with Jewish symbols and art, and their teachings were filled with references to the Hebrew Bible and the Judean context of Jesus. Andrea and Tom told me that it is true that the majority of the retreat's guests are evangelical Christians, but they have had many other Christians at the center, a number of Messianic Jews, and even a few people who did not identify as religious at all.[62]

Andrea told me that she was raised as a secular Jew, became a Christian as part of the Worldwide Church of God, and then later became a Messianic Jew.[63] In our conversation about how her Judaism has impacted the retreat center, Andrea said that participants often felt that she and Tom were sent to the retreat center by God, in part to start discussions with Christians about "the importance of Israel in God's plan."[64] For Andrea, teaching people about the Hallelujah Diet offered an exciting opportunity to also teach them about Jews and Judaism, so she started sharing what she believes. She told me that she was careful to avoid proselytizing.[65] Andrea explained, "Since the program was already in operation, and devotions were a part of it, it gave us a floor for being able to do that in a gentle way." Andrea and Tom's messianic faith came up most often during the daily devotions. During my time at the retreat, they often offered information about the Jews who lived at the time of Yeshua (Jesus) or about Judaism in general to complement the biblical texts we were reading and discussing. Andrea used Hebrew words and explained their meaning to give the participants a sense of the texts as they would have been read in their original language.[66] Andrea noted that for the most part, this gentle introduction of Jewish concepts and ideas has worked well, but there have been a few challenges along the way.

Tom told me that George Malkmus had also faced challenges with spreading the word about the Hallelujah Diet to Christians and was at times ostracized by his peers. He described some of the challenges posed to Malkmus: It's "a bunch of New Age thinking," "It doesn't belong in the church," and "Other scriptures seem to indicate that you can eat whatever you want." Tom also explained that these challenges persist despite the success of the diet. He reflected that "there seems to be a good bit of resistance within the Christian church." He thought this might be due to the tendency of many churches to focus on the avoidance of sin as the most important aspect of Christianity. He told me that the diet is not a sin issue but a health issue. In his words, "You're not going to burn in hell if you eat meat." Tom thought that this was the piece the churches were missing: "The church looks at it solely as a spiritual matter and ignores the physical aspect."[67] For Christians who are more concerned with the next life than with their current one, the Hallelujah Diet is not a priority.

Somewhat contrary to Tom's interpretation, George Malkmus did spend some time in *The Hallelujah Diet* explaining the moral consequences of dietary choices, and Marie Griffith noted this tendency of Malkmus's to connect the consumption of good and bad foods to good and bad moral behavior.[68] Some dieters at the retreat center echoed this language and spoke to me about the damage they were doing to their God-given temples.[69] However, their conceptions of eating bad foods as morally wrong still related to their desire to be healthy in this life on earth. In general, this reflects the overall flexibility of the diet's precepts and the ways that dieters are empowered to make the eating plan work for their bodies and souls. Throughout the retreat, we were offered seemingly endless resources and were always encouraged to take it all home and figure out what would work best for us. Andrea stressed that the retreat center "is an education facility. It's not a clinic." She underlined the fact that she doesn't heal anyone. Instead, "People heal themselves by feeding their bodies correctly and their minds and all of that.

It's emotional, it's mental, and it's physical and spiritual. We try to address all of those issues."[70] Andrea touched on a key component of the Hallelujah Diet here. It is an individual effort. If you follow the proper diet, you will be healed. Andrea's statement also brings up another complicated aspect of the Hallelujah Diet—it is not a medical clinic. Authority at the Hallelujah Diet Health Retreat is sometimes offered to medical practitioners, but they are never seen as the sole arbiters of the diet or health.

"No New Age for Me"

I was congested the entire time I was at the Hallelujah Diet Health Retreat. Tom and Andrea thought I might be detoxing from dairy products. I thought I was experiencing allergies related to being in the mountains. Either way, my nose was running, my throat hurt, and I was not feeling well. After about a day with the cold, my roommate Erica asked me whether I wanted to use some of her essential oils. I was unfamiliar with essential oils, so she had to teach me how to use them. First, I was told to rub olive oil on the soles of my feet and under my nose. Then I was to apply thieves oil, a blend of essential oils. This particular blend was supposed to be good for my immune system. It contains clove and rosemary oils and apparently got its name from the thieves who used to wear it while they robbed dead bodies. The oils felt refreshing on my skin and smelled amazing. I applied the blend each night for the rest of the week. My congestion persisted, so Andrea offered colloidal silver. I was very wary of drinking silver, but Andrea was persuasive, and this was research, so I started taking a spoonful twice a day. Silver tastes exactly like I imagined: metallic, oddly cool, and like something that shouldn't be consumed. Toward the end of the week, Kendall and I began enjoying an evening cup of tea. I chose the immune support tea each evening. My detox/allergy symptoms went away after a few days. The various alternative remedies I was offered at the retreat to combat my congestion exemplified an interesting dynamic that persists there. Evidence was drawn from numerous sources for an array of health and nutrition-based issues, but authority was granted to only two sources—the Bible and certain types of science. Other sources were engaged informally even as they were explicitly dismissed as having no authority. The participants and our hosts referred to this broad range of practices and ideas as "New Age." Throughout the week, the specter of "New Age practices" was frequently invoked as the antithesis of the Hallelujah Diet. And yet, many practices used and prescribed at the health retreat, like essential oils, herbal teas, and colloidal silver, are common in the New

Age arenas the Hallelujah Diet strives to differentiate itself from. Similarly, science is sometimes acceptable, and at other times it is seen as the work of Satan. Authority within the Hallelujah Diet depends on whether the evidence in question works with the biblical text. It doesn't have to be mentioned explicitly in the Bible, but evidence cannot compete with the Bible.

At the Hallelujah Diet Health Retreat, there was an awareness that many of the practices incorporated into the diet and lifestyle are shared with those in the New Age movement, as they understood it. "New Age" for the Hallelujah Dieters is a combination of therapeutic practices like yoga, philosophies borrowed from Buddhism and Hinduism, and spiritual practices that have the potential to lead one away from Christianity. This fits with scholarly understandings of New Age. Janet Klippenstein argued that New Age is "comprised of an almost random collection of disparate practices, beliefs, and lifestyles," which she suggested makes it hard for scholars to define.[71] Sarah Pike, scholar and author of *New Age and Neopagan Religions in America*, similarly proposed that the lack of singular charismatic leaders and the fluidity between New Age people and practices and the rest of the world make the movements difficult to study.[72] Just as the New Age movement is difficult to pin down for study, it is difficult to separate the Hallelujah Dieters from New Agers when they share practices and ideas. Klippenstein pointed out that one of the main complications here is that many scholars have worked to define New Age in opposition to religion. Instead, she proposes understanding New Age as religion in order to "mutually unsettle" both categories.[73] This language of a mutual unsettling fits my experience with Hallelujah Dieters. They identify similar problems and draw on practices from other traditions, just as New Age practitioners do, but they make an effort to distance themselves from New Age. This is because the Hallelujah Dieters ascertain different underlying causes and solutions to their problems, which are mainly centered on bodily health. Pike finds two main theories of illness among New Agers and neopagans: Some see illness as the result of a blockage of the body's natural energy flow, while others see it as a symptom of "spiritual and emotional imbalance."[74] The Hallelujah Diet diverges from these New Age explanations of illness, as it proposes the simple suggestion that humans are eating the wrong food. Any blockage of energy flow or imbalance detected would be the result of an improper diet. And while the Hallelujah Diet solution may include the incorporation of New Age tools and practices, the key is a complete change in diet to align with the diet that God intended for human bodies.

The status of the Hallelujah Diet Health Retreat as an alternative to similar New Age centers came up frequently in interviews when I asked why people chose to come to Lake Lure. Erica told me that she knows "there's a lot of New Agers" in alternative health care and that she "wasn't interested in that." The fact that the Hallelujah Diet had a Christian background was really important to her.[75] Kendall had some previous experience with New Age trainings and chose the Hallelujah Diet for that reason. She said she would not have gone to a "New Age" center: "I get enough of that through my yoga. I just—I don't agree with the philosophy, so it would have been very uncomfortable for me." Kendall said that she put up with New Age places to get her yoga certifications, but for her a diet and lifestyle change was too important to deal with at a New Age place.[76]

Danni chose the Hallelujah Diet Health Retreat both because it was in driving distance and because being at a Christian place would allow her to relax. She explained, "At a New Age place, then I have to think about whether this is something I want to participate with or something I want to go do something else with." Danni had been to another raw food retreat that she had not found very relaxing. "They claimed to be Christian, and they used scriptures, but they taught about all the New Age practices. In a sense that was a good thing for me to learn about and be exposed to, but I want to cleanse my spirit as much as my body."[77] Both Danni and Kendall felt that they would be more comfortable at the Lake Lure retreat because it was Christian and that they would be better able to work on their bodies and spirits.

So, what is the difference between candles and booklets about New Age philosophies and essential oils and colloidal silver remedies? The practices that were acceptable within the framework of the Hallelujah Diet were those that could be interpreted as biblical. As Hallelujah Dieters saw it, a raw and vegan diet was justified by the book of Genesis, and essential oils were used throughout the Old and New Testaments. Young Living Essential Oils, the multilevel marketing company that produces the oils that both Erica and Andrea used and sold, offers an "Oils of the Ancient Scripture" set on its website.[78] Tom offered a simple way to think about the New Age issue in relation to veganism: "It's not a New Age concept. It's an 'Old Age' concept. It was in the Bible originally. And it's OK."[79] Tom's clarification sums up the incorporation of New Age practices at the Hallelujah Diet Health Retreat quite well. Those that are in the Bible are OK. Those that espouse a different philosophy or encourage practices that cannot be found in the Bible were not acceptable for Hallelujah Dieters.

Science and the Bible

George Malkmus and our retreat leaders dealt with science in a similar way. If the science aligned with biblical precepts, then it was acceptable and was often utilized to bolster the evidence of the Bible for the importance and effectiveness of the Hallelujah Diet. During our week at the retreat, we watched at least one film a day. We often viewed these films in the evening, curled up in blankets on the couches in the living room. All the films featured medical doctors, either as the main speaker giving a lecture or as interpolated talking heads who were there to lend authority and scientific proof to informational videos about juicing, fighting cancer, or the dangers of dairy and meat. As we watched these films, the other participants would often take notes, chat with each other about facts that were raised by the videos, and exclaim "yes" or "mm hmm" when they agreed with the speaker. One evening we were watching a particularly long film about the dangers of eating meat. Everyone was interested, and a few people were writing down key facts to bring home to their families. Toward the end of the film, there was a section about the environmental effects of the meat industry. To introduce this section, the narrator said something about how the earth had been around for billions of years. There were audible gasps. The atmosphere in the room shifted, and the group ended up turning off the film before it ended. As we gathered our binders and water bottles to head to our bedrooms, I asked Erica what she thought of the film. She said she thought it was interesting but that she wasn't so sure how true it all was. It seems that the mere mention that the earth has been around longer than 6,000 years was enough to call the authority of this film into question. This speaks to a pattern I saw throughout the retreat. Participants chose the diet because it aligned with their current worldview, and they approached views that differed from their own with caution and suspicion.

Blazer suggested that moments like the conversation I had with Erica characterize the Hallelujah Diet. "This use of secular materials demonstrates a central tension within Hallelujah Acres's reeducation: Hallelujah Acres presents doctors in general as ignorant or blatantly evil yet relies on credentialed experts to support its dietary recommendations."[80] Rather than viewing this as a tension, I preferred to approach this interplay of religion and science at the Hallelujah Diet Health Retreat as an entanglement common in religious alternative food movements. George Malkmus, the retreat leaders, and the participants were all working through a process wherein they were culling evidence from different sources and seeing what worked well together and what might not. Films and materials used throughout the week featured medical doctors and researchers. This relationship between religion and science is a key example of the effects of the liminal spaces that groups like the Hallelujah Diet movement occupy. There are aspects of medical science that were abhorrent to George Malkmus, as was the case with traditional cancer treatment practices. However, we watched an entire film about the evils of the "cancer industry," and the alternatives presented were also authenticated by medical professionals who were utilizing nutritional approaches to treating cancer. So, it wasn't medical professionals who were the issue; it was the particular solutions that the medical professionals were promoting. And the tension wasn't between the Hallelujah Diet and science, but rather between science that supported the diet and science that didn't.

The Hallelujah Diet is generally disapproving of medical science that involves the addition of certain chemicals into the body but permits and promotes medical professionals and treatments that are understood to have an herbal or nutritional basis. In addition, as I saw with Lori and Faith, the dieters often come to some individual compromise between the diet and science that works for them. After their cancer diagnoses, they both had lumpectomies but refused chemotherapy and radiation. Lori described her approach to making medical decisions: "We're afraid of medicine and what it does to our bodies. I've been taking lisinopril for my blood pressure for years now, and I even wonder if it had some effect on my body, the toxin from that that's gone to my breast and done that."[81] Lori was wary of medicine but had decided to accept blood pressure medication from her doctor. When she found out that she had a tumor, she wondered whether the medication she had agreed to take was what made her sick. Lori's example offers us a window into how complicated medical decisions can be. Even when dieters didn't want to take medicine or have surgery, there were moments when a compromise was made. The status of medical science in the Hallelujah Diet is complex and situational and can't be categorized with a generalized claim.

Malkmus actually addressed this issue in *The Hallelujah Diet*: "As a preacher, I have learned to weigh the council I get from science against the wisdom from another, even higher source."[82] The higher source here is God and the Bible. And once Malkmus verified the science using his higher sources, he proclaimed that science across the Hallelujah Diet platforms. One example was his cross-promotion of Dr. T. Colin Campbell's China study, which was conducted in rural China and indicated a correlation between plant-based diets and lower rates of heart disease and some cancers, in *The Hallelujah Diet*. Campbell also wrote a foreword to *The Hallelujah Diet*. In this foreword, Campbell acknowledged that he and Malkmus were not always on the same page: "On the more specific points, I am not sure our research has arrived at exactly the same nuances—specific ratios of raw vs. cooked vegan foods, for example." However, Campbell and Malkmus had enough in common to work together. Campbell explained, "I agree that a diet that emphasizes a trend toward raw foods is in the right direction."[83] I include all of this because it further complicates the black-and-white approach others have assumed creates tension within the Hallelujah Diet. In reality, even the approved medical professionals had points of disagreement with Malkmus, but they were still able to work together. For Campbell, only the science was necessary, and he promoted a vegan diet because he felt his study had proved that it is better for human beings. Malkmus reviewed the evidence offered by Campbell and others alongside the evidence offered by God in Genesis and then decided what he thought humans should eat. Campbell and Malkmus arrived at similar answers, even as their path to those answers differed.

The Biblical Difference

It is also not as simple as it would appear to say that the biblical text is universally authoritative within the Hallelujah Diet. The diet is based on one verse from Genesis, but a few chapters later God instructs Noah that he may eat the meat of clean animals. So, even with the biblical evidence, Malkmus weighed his higher source material with what he found to be true in practice when he cured his own health ailments. Malkmus shared his reasons for seeking nutritional advice in the Bible with his readers: "The Bible is a complete guide for life. It not only deals with the spiritual; it also deals with the physical. *But most people look to the Bible as only a spiritual book, and then look to the medical world for the answers to physical ills.* My friends, we are suffering terribly because we are not taking into account God's intelligent design for perfect health." The "intelligent design" aspect of this quote is key to understanding why Malkmus chose to base his diet on Genesis 1:29: He felt it was the diet that the humans originally created by God were meant to follow. Malkmus explained, "In Genesis 1:29, God told Adam that these fruits, vegetables, seeds, and nuts, in the garden, that He had previously created, were to be Adam's food. Who would know better what Adam's physical body had been designed to be nourished with, than the very Creator of that physical body?"[84] For Malkmus, no doctors or scientists could possibly understand as much about human bodies as God, but when their work aligned with what he understood about humans from the Bible, he touted their support.

Malkmus further supported the idea that the Genesis 1:29 diet is the best diet for humans by offering an explanation of what happened after humans turned away from that diet. Malkmus argued that humans followed this "pure raw vegan diet" for 1,700 years, from creation to the flood, and that during those years humans lived to an average age of 912, "without a single recorded instance of sickness." Malkmus continued with his analysis of the post-flood situation: "Within ten generations, the average lifespan of 912 years on the pure Genesis 1:29 diet before the flood, fell to 110 years on a cooked, meat-based diet after the flood."[85] This explanation resonated with the participants at the retreat center. When asked why he started to follow the Hallelujah Diet twenty years ago, Mike said, "It's just that it made sense. It really did. I mean, it's that simple. You go to Genesis 1:29 and it's very simply and plainly stated in a few words what God intended us to eat."[86] Kendall echoed Mike's explanation. "It's biblical, so it's God's instruction to us, so I know it's true and right and I know it will work if you do it."[87] Cathy mentioned that she thought about the place in the Bible "where God talks about how we're supposed to treat our bodies like a temple and we're not supposed—it's almost like a sin if we mistreat ourselves."[88] For the participants, the biblical support for the diet was important. They chose to come to the Hallelujah Diet Health Retreat for health reasons, but they were also convinced that this diet would work and help them fight or prevent disease because it was right there in the Bible.

CONCLUSION

On Wednesday morning during our week at the Hallelujah Diet Health Retreat, a miracle occurred during our walk. We walked every morning during the retreat. Prior to Wednesday, we had split up into two groups. The five "single ladies"—Danni, Kendall, Erica, Cathy, and I—would walk together in a mile-long loop on the road around the retreat center. The loop involved some hills, and the heat was often already fairly intense on those June mornings. On Wednesday, we had finally persuaded Tom and Andrea to switch the times of our devotion and the walk so that we could walk earlier when it was (slightly) cooler. So, that morning, the couples—Lori and Calvin and Mike and Faith—joined us at the start of our walk with the intention of turning around on the road and heading back when they got tired. Instead, Lori and Calvin stayed with us for the whole walk. We took a break about halfway, because Danni had brought containers from the kitchen so we could collect the wild blackberries that lined the path. After the break, we checked with Calvin to make sure he was doing OK. He was excited and said he could make it. We had already completed the uphill portion of the walk, so he was sure he could finish. And finish he did! Calvin referred to this walk as a miracle from that point forward. He had been in physical therapy after his stents were put in, and he hadn't progressed very far. He told me he could walk on the treadmill only for about ten minutes and that when he tried out the small track inside the physical therapy building, which he was supposed to walk around three times, he could barely make it around twice. This walk was a turning point for Calvin and for the rest of us. When I interviewed Calvin later that day, he was still glowing when he smiled and said, "I am delighted to see the results so far."[89] The walk also encouraged Lori: "I know I'm in the Lord's hands. I'm just so overjoyed with what he has already done for Calvin. I know it's a miracle, what's took place with him. I expect a miracle in my life, too."[90] Lori and Calvin planned to go home and follow the diet, and they did so with the understanding that their lives were in God's hands and the expectation that miracles were not only possible but probable.

Upon returning home, the communications between participants switched to email. We got a few reports of progress. Mike and Faith were sticking to the diet despite a refrigerator failure that claimed a fair amount of their stored produce.[91] Erica reported weight loss, the lifting of her "brain fog," and some extra energy.[92] The diet seemed to be working for people. They were sticking to it and feeling better. If the Hallelujah Diet truly represented a complete commitment, Mike and Faith might have quit the day they lost their produce. Instead, they improvised for a few days and ate some more cooked food than planned while they worked on restocking. The Hallelujah Diet alternative food system is flexible and multifaceted, so dieters have the space to make the diet work for them. The Hallelujah Diet Health Retreat I attended was a space where religions, food studies, science, medicine, and alternative remedies were all entangled together. *The Hallelujah Diet* was written as prescriptive, but in the lived reality of the diet, there is room for individuals and groups to make the diet their own. Above all else, the Hallelujah Diet infrastructure enables its success. The Hallelujah Diet has established an alternative food system through its website, books, retail store, lectures, and health retreats. And this system has provided inspiration, evidence, and a basic framework for religious people to feel comfortable adopting a diet of raw vegan food. As Tom proclaimed, "You don't have to be a Christian to be a vegan."[93]

CHAPTER THREE

Cows, Chickens, and Certifications at Baldwin Family Farms

Beloved, I pray that all may go well with you and that you may be in good health, as it goes well with your soul.

3 JOHN 1:2 (ENGLISH STANDARD VERSION)

I arrived at Baldwin Family Farms on a chilly June morning as an unannounced visitor. After a few emails and phone calls had gone unanswered, I decided to drive the hour or so from where I lived in Durham to Yanceyville, North Carolina. It was drizzling when I got out of the car outside the On-Farm Beef Outlet. The sign at the store was lit up, but no one was around. There was a list of phone numbers on the door for the office, V. Mac Baldwin, and Peggy Baldwin. I called the office number and a woman picked up, so I asked whether anyone was available. She said someone would be right out, and V. Mac emerged from the house a few minutes later. I introduced myself as he opened up the store and we headed inside. He never introduced himself, but I recognized him from the Baldwin Beef website. He told me later that the "V" in V. Mac stands for Von and the "Mac" for MacLloyd. He shortened the names to V. Mac because he found it was easier for people to remember and explained that this is especially important when one is in the direct marketing business.[1] At Baldwin Family Farms, the Baldwins and their workers raise Charolais beef cattle entirely on grass.[2] Charolais is a French breed, and V. Mac explained, "They're white, they're lean, and they're excellent grazers."[3] He also told me that their white coloring is particularly well suited for hot North Carolina summers.

The pastures at Baldwin Family Farms appear idyllic at first glance. White cows graze in shady areas on rolling, picturesque hills. The eight large industrial barns in the distance disrupt this scene even as they contain the secret to Baldwin Beef's success. Grass-fed beef is resource-intensive, and the breeding hens in those barns provide both nutrient-rich fertilizer as they defecate and supplemental income as they lay eggs. I argue in this chapter that V. Mac's religious beliefs form the basis for his alternative food system and that those beliefs guide his approach to the land, the cows, and the chickens on-site. V. Mac's approach to animal husbandry is best understood in the context of broader conversations about human-animal relationships, so after a brief overview of Baldwin Family Farms, this chapter will begin there, followed by an in-depth analysis of the Baldwin Beef alternative food system. I'll next describe the complex religiosity of Baldwin Beef, because while the cattle are raised in accordance with V. Mac's Christian beliefs, they are then processed in either a halal or a secular slaughterhouse, and the resulting meat is sold to multiple publics via the on-site store, nearby farmers' markets, and large-scale chain grocery stores like Whole Foods and Kroger. The differences between V. Mac's overt expressions of Christian faith on the farm and the secularized marketing materials and packaging used to sell the meat exemplify a tension between religious participants in the alternative food movement and the consumers who support that industry.

BALDWIN FAMILY FARMS

V. Mac didn't intend to go into the cattle business. He bought his first calf when he was ten and dreamed of raising cattle, but after high school he joined the navy and then went to college, earning degrees in electrical engineering. He worked as an engineer but retained his passion for cattle. In 1969, he bought a couple of heifers. V. Mac recalled those early years and told me that he had to learn quickly about the resources available to farmers in North Carolina. V. Mac was especially grateful to the local cooperative extension. Cooperative extensions are remote locations run by land-grant universities, which in this case was North Carolina State University.⁴ V. Mac remembered relying on the experts at his local cooperative extension quite a bit during the first twelve years. By 1981, V. Mac had thirty-five "real good Charolais mama cows," and his young son, who loved working with the cows, was getting antsy. V. Mac laughed as he recounted his son's urgent plea, "Dad, let's go, let's go, let's go." So, later that year, V. Mac and Peggy Baldwin bought the 331-acre farm they currently own and operate. They expanded the farm gradually, and the family now owns over 800 acres in Yanceyville, with an additional 2,000 acres of leased pastures in other parts of North Carolina and Virginia.⁵

The Baldwins initially sold their meat through other companies. They began direct-marketing their beef in 2002 under the Baldwin Charolais Beef label. They opened the On-Farm Beef Outlet in 2003. The Baldwin Family Farms mission statement is "to produce chemical-free, all-natural grass-fed lean beef with superior health benefits, quality and flavor utilizing old-fashioned, sustainable techniques—Our farm to your family."⁶ On the Baldwin Beef website, this mission is listed next to an image of the family's cows with the following text, attributed to "V. Mac and Peggy": "To the GLORY of GOD—'Our purpose is to be good stewards of all things held in trust from God the Creator, Maker of Heaven and Earth.'"⁷

V. Mac is in the beef business, but he also frequently described himself to me as a grass farmer, a land clearer and preserver, and a chicken breeder. In 2015, the Baldwins had eight large "hen houses" on their property. V. Mac told me that each house initially cost $200,000–$250,000 and that two were owned by V. Mac's son. At that time, each house generated about $700,000 per year. I will discuss this income in detail later in this chapter. V. Mac told me that all eight houses would be paid off in the subsequent five years, so the money generated by the henhouses after that would be pure profit. V. Mac excitedly reported that beyond producing all the fertilizer he needed to grow grass and cows, "these breeder houses are my social security."⁸ The chickens are the linchpin of the entire operation. Chicken waste has fertilized the grass for twenty years, and it allows the Baldwins to grow both grass and cattle without chemical fertilizers and pesticides. The income generated by the henhouses allowed V. Mac to continue purchasing land around his farm and increasing his herd. I will discuss V. Mac's approach to raising cows and chickens in-depth later in this chapter.

In addition to V. Mac's engagements with land, grass, and chickens, meat production has also required the devout Christian to engage with secular government agencies in order to make his products appealing to secular consumers and supermarket chains. V. Mac has worked hard to please his customers, and his Christianity has played a vital role in that process. And, though it hasn't always been overt, V. Mac sees missionary potential in his meat business. He feels his business enables him to connect with customers who have not accepted Jesus, and it also brings him into regular contact with his Muslim meat processor, Abdul Chaudhry. Because he participates in the meat industry and sells his product widely, V. Mac has to work outside the protective world of religious idealists. V. Mac raises his cows and chickens in accordance with his Christian beliefs and values, but he has also met Christians, non-Christians, and nonbelievers in the public sphere where he processes and sells his meat, and his faith similarly informs those encounters. Later in this chapter, Baldwin Family Farms will serve as the focal point for an exploration of the encounter between religious food reformers and the secular alternative food industry.

This chapter relies on interviews and on-site experiences with V. Mac Baldwin because my access to other interlocutors at this site was limited. In 2015, Baldwin Family Farms had seventeen staff members, and many members of the Baldwin family are also involved in the business, but I was able to interview only V. Mac, who determined that he was the best spokesperson for both the farm and the family. I used the Baldwin Beef website, participant observation on the farm, and secondary sources to supplement the interviews with V. Mac. Initially, I was also hoping to interview employees at Chaudhry Halal Meats. Unfortunately, as I was preparing to do the fieldwork for this book in the spring of 2015, a bill was working its way through the North Carolina House, which sought to prevent undercover investigations of workplaces, including agricultural workplaces.[9] This bill, House Bill 405, known as the "Property Protection Act," was ratified by the North Carolina General Assembly in May 2015.[10] I was concerned about the potential legal ramifications of interviews in a slaughterhouse at that time and decided not to pursue those interviews as part of this project. Though the analysis of this particular slaughterhouse would have made this study more robust, I was able to incorporate secondary literature about contemporary slaughterhouses and halal slaughter to provide a window into those aspects of beef production.

HISTORICAL CONTEXT FOR BALDWIN FAMILY FARMS

My first visit included a guided tour of the on-site store with V. Mac. There were two large refrigerator cases of meat displayed at the front; in the back was a large storage room. On a side table near the entrance were informational brochures about Baldwin Beef. The walls were decorated with newspaper articles about the farm, the Whole Foods marketing poster about V. Mac, and information about the beef's many certifications. As V. Mac began explaining his beef business, we were interrupted repeatedly, often by his cell phone, which mooed to let V. Mac know someone was calling. I took notes by hand, scribbling down everything V. Mac said as quickly as possible. He stopped often to clarify or to make sure I had written down exactly what he had said.[11] V. Mac started by telling me that he was a Gideon. He belonged to the Gideons International, which is "an Association of Christian business and professional men and their wives dedicated to telling people about Jesus through associating together for service, sharing personal testimony, and by providing Bibles and New Testaments."[12] During our conversations, V. Mac frequently mentioned the value and transformative power of scripture. He told stories of sharing "the Word" with customers and colleagues he met through his business, and he cited Bible verses often as he spoke. After about an hour of talking with brief interludes of mooing phone calls, two of V. Mac's grandchildren came home after a day at Bible camp. His granddaughter was dressed similarly to her grandfather—they both wore jeans, cowboy boots, and straw cowboy hats. However, his granddaughter's boots were pink, and, as she proudly pointed out to me, her red T-shirt bore the Baldwin Family Farms logo. Direct marketing, the Bible, cows, and family—these elements recurred throughout my conversations with V. Mac in the visits that followed.[13] The Baldwin family's Christian approach to animal husbandry and land management are best understood in the context of a long history of Christians wrestling with their relationship with animals and the land.

Christianity, Animals, and Meat

Christianity has, at times, been associated with the apathetic approach to animal welfare that has enabled the contemporary system of factory farms and mass slaughter. Scholars like Margaret Adam, David Clough, and David Grumett complicate this understanding and argue that while Christianity has been used to justify these systems that exploit animals, Christians actually hold a wide range of opinions on animal welfare, from indifference to advocacy.[14] In the ninth chapter of Genesis, humans were granted permission to consume meat after the great flood that wiped out all humans and animals except for Noah, his family, and all the pairs of animals he fit on his ark. This is often interpreted as a concession meant to alleviate some of the violent tendencies of humanity, but there are other interpretations as well. Norman Wirzba has suggested that Noah's sacrificial offering showed that all animal life is precious and comes from God.[15] Adam, Clough, and Grumett argue that when read in the context of other stories related to animal welfare in the Old Testament, a general theme of concern for animal welfare emerges.[16] As these differing approaches suggest, there is no unified Christian understanding of meat eating, and the production and consumption of meat has a rather complicated history in Christianity.

In "Practicing the Presence of God: A Christian Approach to Animals," Jay McDaniel divides Christian approaches to animal welfare into what he calls "The Negative Traditions" and "The Positive Traditions," arguing that the negative traditions formed the dominant approach to animals in Christianity.[17] He lists five teachings that scholars have pointed to that, he maintains, have contributed to this approach to animals: (1) Animals were put on earth for humans, (2) some animals are unclean, (3) some animals are meant to be sacrificed for rituals, (4) animals are slaves to human needs, and (5) animals have no rational mind, soul, or sentience.[18] McDaniel and other scholars, including Andrew Linzey and David Clough, have pointed to these themes as they recur throughout the history of Christian theology, including in the works of Augustine of Hippo, Thomas Aquinas, Martin Luther, and John Calvin.[19] McDaniel uses this example from Aquinas: "There is no sin in using a thing for the purpose for which it is. Now the order of things is such that the imperfect are for the perfect. . . . It is not unlawful if man uses plants for the good of animals, and animals for the good of man as the Philosopher [Aristotle] states." This quote, in which Aquinas cites the Greek philosopher Aristotle, exemplifies this strain of thought within Christianity. These Christians believed that God created plants, humans, and animals so that each serves the other in perfect order; in this system, animals exist for the good of man. McDaniel argues that this has led to a system in which animals are treated as machines. He continues to note that this tendency was "intensified by consumerist habits," which often "reduce all living beings—plants as well as animals—into commodities for exchange in the marketplace."[20] This understanding of animals existing as commodities for human use undergirds the contemporary meat industry.[21]

McDaniel's fifth point, the belief that animals lack such fundamental qualities as language and morals, which separate them from humans, was particularly essential to the development of the modern meat industry. The question of animal sentience and souls has both created and reinforced a human/animal binary that plays a central role in animal welfare conversations. Many scholars have argued that religion bears the brunt of the blame for the endurance of this binary. In *Animal Liberation*, Peter Singer argued that the attitudes of Westerners toward animals have roots in Judaism and Greek philosophy. He explained that these two separate roots came together in Christianity, and through Christianity they came to prevail in Europe and the West. Singer suggested that Jewish tradition put forward the idea of the uniqueness of the human species but that Christianity put a greater emphasis on this concept when it was combined with the notion of an immortal soul.[22] Adam, Clough, and Grumett complicated this picture within Christianity, noting that several saints, Christian leaders, and Christian movements across the centuries incorporated animal advocacy into their Christianity.[23]

Despite historical efforts to the contrary, the idea that animals lacked a soul persisted within Christianity. In the seventeenth century, René Descartes incorporated this Christian understanding of animals as he observed the motion of animals and reported his findings, noting that animal movement could originate from basic mechanics and that the presence of a thinking soul could not be proved.[24] For centuries, the idea that animals lacked souls and were thus inferior to humans pervaded literature in science, philosophy, and theology. In the nineteenth century, Charles Darwin placed humans alongside nonhuman animals in his theory of evolution but incorporated religion in his framework, suggesting that belief in God distinguished humans from "lower animals."[25] Despite periodic attempts to remind humans of their place among the nonhuman animals, the human/animal binary perseveres in and outside Christianity. The meat industry has reinforced this dichotomy between humans and animals. Singer proposed that contemporary Americans experience "the most direct form of contact with non-human animals . . . at mealtime," when he concluded, "we eat them."[26] In the end, while there have been many attempts to realign the human/animal relationship, Christianity has more often reinforced not just the human/animal binary but a human/animal hierarchy wherein humans are seen as superior to animals.

The human/animal hierarchy has enabled a level of detachment from nonhuman animals that has proved to be detrimental to domesticated cattle, pigs, chickens, and turkeys in the United States. This detachment has two key components. Humans imagine themselves as being different from animals, but in the United States, most humans are also physically separated from the animals they eat. Baldwin Family Farms illustrates this well. The meat is sold in urban areas of North Carolina, but the cows are raised and slaughtered in less-trafficked rural areas. Driving on a major highway through North Carolina in 2015, drivers would have seen a billboard advertising Baldwin Beef but none of the actual cows. In *Every Twelve Seconds*, Timothy Pachirat argued that the combination of distance and concealment enables American slaughterhouses to kill tens of millions of cattle and billions of other animals each year for meat.[27] The distance and concealment also allow people to imagine cows grazing on grassy hills instead of the reality for most cattle, which entails many months in crowded feedlots. David Kirby, author of *Animal Factory*, explained that the US government and the meat industry call the feedlots "confined [or concentrated] animal feeding operations," or CAFOs, though they are also commonly known as "factory farms." Both the number of cattle and the confinement of those cattle characterize CAFOs, with the term usually reserved for operations where more than 1,000 "animal units" are confined.[28] In 2015, the Baldwins had 750 cows, but even if they ended up with more than 1,000, their farm would not be designated as a CAFO because their cows were not confined. In the United States, CAFOs are seen by those in the meat industry as an innovative method for producing meat faster and with less land. Cattle that eat grain on feedlots reach their slaughter weight much faster than those who remain on pasture, and the resulting meat has a higher fat content, which is seen by many as desirable and results in higher USDA-quality grades.[29] As I will discuss below, alternative food movement consumers tend to prioritize animal welfare and lean meat over the efficiency that CAFOs provide.

In nonacademic literature, descriptions of factory farming are far less clinical. In *Eating Animals*, Jonathan Safran Foer argued, "We have waged war, or rather let a war be waged, against all of the animals we eat. This war is new and has a name: factory farming."[30] Whether it is framed as a war or a technological innovation, factory farming dominates the meat industry in the United States. Kirby explained that "two percent of U.S. livestock facilities now raise 40 percent of all animals, and the vast majority of pigs, chickens, and dairy cows are produced inside animal factories."[31] A USDA report from 2013 noted that beef from alternative production systems, including natural, organic, and grass- or forage-fed, accounted for only 3 percent of the US beef market. However, the report also pointed out that these alternative production systems "have grown about 20 percent in recent years."[32] Baldwin Family Farms is one of these alternative production systems, though V. Mac didn't set out to oppose factory farming when he bought his first heifers. In our conversations, he never explicitly articulated an opposition to factory farming. Instead, he framed his work in relation to his views on the role of humans in the world he believed was created by God.

The scholar David Fraser described what he calls a "pastoralist ethic," which he argued pervades the Bible and shapes how many religious people approach animal agriculture. Fraser suggested that a pastoralist ethic approach allows animals to be used for certain purposes as long as certain conventions were observed and that this ethic attaches high value to diligent care of animals. Fraser saw this ethic as one that is evidenced in the Bible, and those who adhere to it cite passages from the Bible related to the proper treatment and care of animals.[33] Fraser lamented the fact that this pastoralist ethic "has been largely ignored by most of the philosophers and social critics who have contributed to modern animal ethics." He suggested that a return to this pastoralist ethic could provide "an alternative philosophy that would give practical guidance on farm animal welfare."[34] In V. Mac's case, his devotion to the Bible as a Gideon shaped his approach to raising animals because it shaped his worldview. In my conversations with V. Mac, he turned frequently to scripture for answers and told me that he did the same when he started raising cows. In those early days, he read the Bible and determined that God loved grass and saw a system within creation for raising animals. V. Mac felt that adopting that system would lead to better treatment of the land and benefit human health. He adopted a pastoralist ethic, though he never referred to it as such, because that was the ethic that he found in scripture. V. Mac told me that he is reminded daily when he looks out as his pastures of the fact that "the Lord says he owns the cattle on a thousand hills."[35] In addition to his stewardship of the cattle, V. Mac also approaches his "thousand hills" through his Christian faith and his readings of the Bible.

Christianity and Land Stewardship

After my first visit and impromptu interview, V. Mac and I decided to plan a visit when I could get a tour of the farm. V. Mac thought it would be best if I came on a day when he had to collect soil samples around the farm. That way I could see the whole property and help him out. When I arrived a few days later, I found V. Mac in the On-Farm Beef Outlet. After he finished up a project in the freezer, we grabbed a bucket, the boxes for the soil, and the soil sample probe. We said a quick hello to V. Mac's wife, Peggy, and headed out to the fields on an ATV. We started in the closest field to the house, where some "mama cows," as V. Mac called them, were grazing with baby calves that had been born in April and May. V. Mac collected samples from the ground using the soil sample probe, and I broke up the soil in the bucket. When we had enough soil to fill the box, we would empty the bucket into the box. When I asked V. Mac why we were collecting soil, he told me that he needed to send it out as part of the process of being certified as sustainable in order to get the land designated as "farmland in perpetuity." This is a legal designation granted through North Carolina's Article 61, "Agricultural Development and Preservation of Farmland," which permits landowners to enter into perpetual conservation agreements with the state to restrict land for agricultural use.[36] V. Mac explained that he would pay 25 percent of the initial purchase value of the development rights, North Carolina would pay 25 percent, and the federal government would pay 50 percent to keep the land farmland. He told me that he's not really worried about the farm for the next few generations because he was leaving it to his son and then it would hopefully pass on to his grandsons, but he wasn't sure what would happen after that. He was concerned that without designating the land as farmland in perpetuity, it may end up with condos on it someday.[37] V. Mac felt that the land would be in the best possible hands with farmers like him, who prioritized sustainability. He believed that he was on the earth for a short time, and in that time he was meant to be a steward of the land God gave his family. So, he planned to leave the family's land in better shape than when they purchased it.[38] A lot of V. Mac's land had previously been used to grow tobacco, so his shift to grass was already an improvement.[39]

V. Mac is part of a growing movement of Christians who are motivated by their faith to approach agriculture with sustainability and care for creation in mind. Todd LeVasseur argues in his introduction to the book *Religion and Sustainable Agriculture: World Spiritual Traditions and Food Ethics* that agriculture itself is "an act of faith and an embodied expression of what people care most about."[40] This broad perspective on religion and agriculture applies to many of the religious alternative food groups in this book, and there are also particularly Christian expressions of agriculture as an expression of faith. Wendell Berry is frequently invoked as a source of inspiration for Christians engaged in sustainable agriculture. In his 1977 book *The Unsettling of America: Culture and Agriculture*, Berry contrasts industrial agriculturalists, whom he calls "exploiters," with the nurturer, whose "goal is health—his land's health, his own, his family's, his community's, his country's." Berry promotes this kind of nurturing, small-scale agriculture throughout his work.[41] Norman Wirzba calls for the addition of theological depth to eating in his book *Food and Faith: A Theology of Eating*, arguing that this kind of theological attention is necessary because food, which "has its source in God," is "precious." For Wirzba, "eating as a spiritual exercise" includes a shift away from industrial agriculture and toward the kind of sustainable agriculture that God intended.[42] As I will discuss later in this chapter, the Baldwins see their work as an expression of their Christian faith and consider God to be the source of their land and their cows. In her book *Food, Farming and Religion: Emerging Ethical Perspectives*, scholar Gretel Van Wieren builds on the work of Berry and Wirzba, among others, as she analyzes religious people's engagements with small-scale sustainable agriculture, which she calls "restorative agriculture." She explains that the religious people engaged in this form of agriculture see their work as being "good for the Earth and good for the human soul." She notes that restorative agriculture "serves to promote the flourishing of natural processes and systems while connecting people to particular landed places."[43] Van Wieren's restorative agriculture model certainly aligns with the Baldwins' approach. In my discussions with V. Mac and in Baldwin Beef's marketing materials, the idea of nature and the natural was invoked frequently.

V. Mac saw land stewardship as part of his larger goal of approaching agriculture "in a spirit of praise and adoration for the Lord."[44] This aligns with what scholar Jay McDaniel has identified as an eco-justice perspective, which he argued has recently taken root in Christianity. He relied on Dieter Hessel's work to lay out four basic principles of Christian eco-justice: (1) solidarity with other peoples and creatures, (2) ecological sustainability, (3) sufficiency as a standard for organized sharing, and (4) working for the good of the commons.[45] V. Mac did not mention concerns related to sufficiency or hunger when we spoke, but the other three principles came through clearly in every conversation we had. V. Mac saw himself as part of creation. During one of our conversations, he reflected on his dependence on the rest of creation: "We depend on rain, we depend on sunshine, we depend on good health to be able to do what we do physically, we're entirely dependent on God in our life because the resources that we have are his providence in our life."[46] In this reflection, V. Mac articulated a deep solidarity with his grass and his cows. They all depend on God and God's rain, sun, and good fortune.

In line with Van Wieren's suggestion that religious people engaged in restorative agriculture are often connected to particular places, V. Mac was invested in encouraging ecological sustainability in Caswell County and in the state of North Carolina. When I asked about his motivations for working with the state to preserve his farmland, he started with a definitive statement: "The Lord loves grass." He continued, noting that if you look at the creation story in the Bible, God created grass very early.[47] Given his sense that grass was an important component of creation, V. Mac was concerned about the loss of grassland in North Carolina and beyond. He committed himself to rectifying this loss: "The rest of my years here on earth, I'm devoted to making more grassland and to having it available for my family, my children, my grandchildren, my great-grandchildren."[48] V. Mac told me that he and his staff put in countless hours to restore and retain the grassland that V. Mac believes God loves. This relates to the fourth principle of eco-justice—working for the good of the commons. V. Mac wanted to provide his customers with a superior product and to keep the land in good shape for the future generations. He did this by leaving portions of his land alone so that wildlife systems would remain intact and waterways would be left untouched. According to the Baldwin Beef website, "Ponds and streams are fenced to exclude cattle entry. Habitat and woodlands breaks are managed and protected to encourage wildlife."[49] As I toured the farm with V. Mac, it was clear that this was true. The grassy pastures were bordered by forests, ponds, lakes, streams, and in some cases fences and roads.

V. Mac frequently identified himself as a grass farmer, and land stewardship is a key aspect of his grass farming. V. Mac told me he's always been "nuts about grass," and that is why he decided to raise grass-fed cattle. He informed me that you have to be a grass expert to raise cattle. And in my experience, V. Mac was definitely a grass expert. He explained that most grass in North Carolina was Kentucky 31 fescue. This is an annual grass that is not generally used to graze cattle. At Baldwin they use a combination of cereal ryegrass in the winter and crabgrass in the summer. V. Mac told me that rye and crabgrass are not annual grasses, so they don't need to expend energy on their root systems. He explained that there is more sugar in the grass, so when the cattle eat it, their meat tastes better.[50] V. Mac was adamant that grass-fed beef tastes better than grain-fed beef, or even beef from cows that were grass-fed and grain-finished.[51] Though the market for this higher-priced beef suggests V. Mac is correct, there is some evidence that consumer preference for grass-fed beef may be due at least in part to a halo effect, which means consumers may think products are better or safer than they really are because they are marketed under an eco-label like organic or grass-fed.[52] As I mentioned above, it takes longer to raise cattle on grass. According to the Baldwin website, the twenty-four months it usually takes for the farm's steers to reach their finishing weight of 1,250–1,300 pounds is about 50 percent slower than cattle raised on commercial feedlots.[53] However, the Baldwins considered this extra time worth it. They advertised their beef saying that customers would get "the best protein benefits that Nature has to offer," including being rich in omega-3 essential fatty acids, vitamins A, B, and E, and zinc and iron. They also noted that the beef was free of preservatives, antibiotics, and hormones, which are all common in factory-farmed meat.[54] The Baldwins were raising cattle on grass, in accordance with their beliefs, and they felt their meat was a better product as a result.

BALDWIN FAMILY FARMS' ALTERNATIVE FOOD SYSTEM

V. Mac informed me that three issues drove his business: (1) People do not trust the USDA; (2) people can use the Internet to do their own research about meat, and when they do the research, they end up wanting to eat grass-fed beef; and (3) people are concerned about animal welfare—did the animal have an enjoyable life? Was the animal harvested in a way that did not cause it to suffer?[55] These three aspects of alternative food movements shaped V. Mac's approach to raising cows and producing meat, which I'll describe in detail in this section. The Baldwins' agriculture model was informed by their Christianity, but in this section, it will become clear that they have found success in large part because their approach to producing meat aligns with the interests of alternative food movement consumers. I'll begin with the alternative certifications V. Mac pursued because of his contention that people do not trust the USDA, followed by a discussion related to the health benefits that V. Mac believed his consumers were seeking in grass-fed beef. I will conclude this section with an examination of animal welfare at Baldwin Family Farms, paying particular attention to breeding practices and the ways that the welfare of cows and chickens were determined separately.

Certifications and the USDA

In 2013, the national supermarket chain Whole Foods Market announced that it was committed to providing full genetically modified organism (GMO) transparency to its customers by 2018.[56] The term "GMO" generally refers to products that contain ingredients that were subject to genetic modification or engineering, often for the purposes of favoring a desirable trait. GMO corn, for example, is often modified to help plants resist pests or tolerate specific herbicides. GMO corn is much more common than non-GMO corn; 92 percent of all the corn planted in the United States in 2020 was GMO corn, and most of that was used to feed livestock, like cattle.[57] V. Mac's cows ate only non-GMO grass, but in order to continue selling his beef at Whole Foods Markets, V. Mac needed to pursue a third-party certification to verify that Baldwin Beef was a non-GMO product. In 2015, he told me he had already lost business because of this requirement. A Whole Foods Market in Virginia had recently stopped carrying Baldwin Beef in favor of another farm that was already non-GMO certified so it could compete with the Publix across the street. V. Mac stressed that he did not want to lose any more stores, so he was trying to get certified as soon as possible. He had spoken with a few different non-GMO certifiers to get his beef certified, but there were high costs associated with this certification.[58] During a visit six months after our first conversation, I asked about the non-GMO certification, and V. Mac was still looking for an agency that would be an affordable option.

The non-GMO certification exemplifies the increasing need for third-party certifications in the alternative food system to satisfy consumers who do not trust the USDA. V. Mac had made many difficult decisions related to certification over the years and frequently found himself explaining his certifications or lack of them to customers. Baldwin Beef was sold in stores under two different labels because it was processed in two different plants. The beef that was processed at Chaudhry Halal Meats bore a simple black-and-white label. Large print marked the beef as "Baldwin Charolais Beef, Grass-Fed, All-Natural." Smaller text indicated that the meal was halal. This beef was sold in Whole Foods Markets, where it was often displayed in cases with Whole Foods labeling. The beef that came out of a processing plant in Piedmont was more intricate. On the front label the Baldwin logo was in color (blue and red), and the back label had two stamps that read "Got to be NC Beef" and "Animal Welfare Approved." There was also a blurb about Baldwin Family Farms related to its animal welfare practices and the better-tasting meat that results from the farm's attention to animal welfare. This beef was sold at Kroger stores.

A stamp at the bottom of the Chaudhry label had a USDA certification number. The mooing phone calls V. Mac had answered during our first conversation that weren't about the non-GMO certification were about that USDA number. All of the Baldwins' certifications at that point were through Chaudhry Halal Meats. A USDA inspector at the Piedmont plant that processed the rest of Baldwin Beef had recently noticed that V. Mac did not have USDA certification through that plant. The inspector stopped the processing of Baldwin Beef at that plant because the farm was "non-compliant"; this inspector determined that processing could not continue until Baldwin Beef was "certified through the USDA to use Piedmont."[59] V. Mac had to pursue separate certification through the USDA to use this second plant. To be clear, both plants are certified independently to operate through the USDA. But V. Mac also needed certification through the USDA to send his cows to the plants for processing. The USDA's system of regulations and certifications

Baldwin Grass-Fed Beef display at Whole Foods in Chapel Hill, North Carolina, January 2016.

is complex and difficult for producers to navigate, and the resulting labels often go unnoticed by consumers. In addition, the actual effectiveness of these certifications for ensuring animal welfare standards has been called into question on numerous occasions.[60] During all of my visits with V. Mac, we ended up talking about certifications because they make up the bulk of the administrative tasks that occupy V. Mac's time.

The Baldwin Beef website clarified the certifications and labels the Baldwins used to market their beef. They used the phrase "all-natural" and explained what they meant by that: "It means we have attempted to do everything according to the laws of nature. We don't use pesticides or chemical fertilizers on our pastures because we want our grass to grow chemical free. We also do not use any hormones (most of which are estrogen-based) or antibiotics on our steers. Should any steers get sick and require treatment to recover, they are removed from our direct marketing program."[61] "All-natural" required explanation because it was used on so many products with varying meanings, and that terminology is not regulated. The Baldwins defined the term in regard to their approach to growing grass and steers in particular. Subsumed under "all-natural" was their additional dedication to animals that were "antibiotic-free" and "hormone-free." Antibiotics are generally used prophylactically in CAFOs due to the crowded living conditions that animals are subjected to in those spaces. When the Baldwins claimed that Baldwin Beef was antibiotic-free, they were positioning themselves against the factory farms that did use antibiotics. At Baldwin Family Farms, the cows had room to move around and sick cows were removed from the herd and placed in separate areas, so prophylactic antibiotics were not necessary. The Baldwins used "hormone-free" for similar reasons. Hormones are used in CAFOs to increase growth in cattle. Baldwin cattle did not grow particularly fast—it took them eight to ten months longer to reach slaughter weight than a CAFO steer—because V. Mac decided to prioritize the health of his herd over speed. His concerns were shared by alternative food system consumers, many of whom believed that humans who eat meat from animals treated with antibiotics and hormones were ingesting them as well, which may affect human health.

Baldwin Beef was not USDA-certified organic, so the Baldwins could not label their beef organic. However, their cows ate grass that was not treated with chemical fertilizers, pesticides, or herbicides. V. Mac had strong feelings about this. He told me that you can feed cattle organic grains instead of grass and obtain a USDA organic certification. V. Mac was not against organic certification, but he did think his beef was superior to the grain-fed beef that bore the USDA organic label, so he wasn't particularly motivated to pursue that certification, especially because the third-party organic certifications can be expensive. Instead, the Baldwins preferred to use "all-natural" and other indicators that let their customers know that their cows ate chemical-free grass. As it said at the time on the Baldwin Beef website, "We think our beef is beyond organic."[62] Baldwin Beef was also "Animal Welfare Approved," and this certification did not cost V. Mac anything. All that was required for the animal welfare certification was a regular audit of the farm and the animals who live there. I asked V. Mac about this certification, and he said that "people want to make sure that if they eat meat, the animal was raised well. People want animals to receive the best care." He also let me know that Whole Foods uses Global Animal Partnership to stress its own dedication to animal welfare, so Baldwin Beef was also "Global Animal Partnership Approved."[63] Over time, V. Mac has sought out certifications, rejected certifications, and been required to obtain certifications. Selling meat as part of the American meat industry, and especially as part of the alternative market within that industry, requires dedication to learning the terminology, selecting the certifications that consumers are willing to trust and identifying those that they do not, and investing in the selected certifications.

Meat and Human Health

V. Mac often stressed the health benefits of his grass-fed beef. He didn't mention frequently cited benefits like lower saturated fat or increased beta-carotene in our conversations; rather, he emphasized a different health benefit, "the omega-3," which he referred to as "beautiful." I asked him to tell me more about this, and he let me know that Peggy had cancer in the past but didn't have it any more. He said that part of what they learned when they started raising grass-fed cattle is that grass-fed beef is high in omega-3s. V. Mac told me that omega-3 is "an awesome antioxidant that fights radical cells in your body." Since cancer is a radical cell, omega-3s are important when "cancer is running rampant."[64] V. Mac stressed that "we need his solution"—that is, God's solution—to fight cancer, and omega-3s are one way to do that. The Baldwin Beef website contained additional promotional information about omega-3s, noting that they improve cholesterol by increasing the "good" HDL cholesterol and decreasing the "bad" LDL cholesterol.[65] It also pointed out that omega-3s are anti-inflammatory.[66] Finally, the Baldwin Beef website stressed that grain-fed meats add to an imbalance between omega-3s and omega-6s that is common among Americans and emphasized that grass-fed beef could help balance out the omega-6s coming from grains. The website also included a section where the Baldwins addressed a common concern—that red meat is not healthy—by explaining that the unhealthy red meat was the factory-farmed red meat. They suggested that the issue was not the meat itself but the way the animals were raised: "Red meat, when it's raised the proper way—Nature's Way—is a superior source of nutrition! It's great for your health!"[67] The "Nature's Way" language here is reminiscent of the language of the Hallelujah Diet. In fact, the Baldwins put their faith in a different diet: "We are especially impressed with God's Biblical health plan as it is presented in Dr. Jordan S. Rubin's bestselling book *The Maker's Diet.*"[68] This biblical diet differs from the Hallelujah Diet in that it allows for the consumption of meat—especially meat raised "Nature's Way." V. Mac told me they have also been hearing from more doctors and customers that grass-fed cattle bones have medicinal value when they are used to make bone broth. V. Mac let me know that they were shipping bones "all across the country," and there was a recipe for bone broth on their website from a registered dietician.[69]

The health benefits from grass-fed beef make the extra time and resources it took to raise cattle on grass worth it to the Baldwins. They had to clear a lot of land to have enough pasture for their growing herds, so V. Mac often felt that he was in "the land-clearing business." V. Mac wasn't in the business of clearing just any land, though. He informed me that they are serious about buying land only when it borders their property. Over the span of a few visits, I saw this land clearing in process. The Baldwins often purchase forestland, which means the first step is clearing out the trees and selling the lumber. They had recently acquired a stump remover to assist them with this difficult process. They also hired temporary workers to help clear out land. When the land was cleared, they spread a bright turquoise mixture of grass seed and newspaper pulp. When I commented on the color, V. Mac smiled and told me that "God made it look good."[70] Once the grass was planted, it needed fertilizer to thrive. The Baldwins didn't use chemical fertilizer, so over time they have developed a secondary venture to provide the fertilizer they needed. This secondary venture—a hen breeding operation—was the true heart of their farm.

V. Mac explained that they realized plant food was going to be a major expense early on, so he and his workers started "hauling poultry litter to this farm and spreading it." V. Mac was impressed with the litter, so when he was offered an opportunity to add two poultry houses to the farm in 1995, he jumped at the chance. The houses were finished in 1996, and he and Peggy liked them so much they built two more a few years later. When I asked why the litter was so exciting, V. Mac launched into a detailed exposition of chicken poop. He explained that the chicken poop contains significant amounts of nitrogen, phosphorus, and potassium, which are the elements required to grow "good grass." Each henhouse produces 300 tons of poop each year. When the benefits of the plant food are combined with the income from the breeding operation itself, V. Mac was clear that on his cattle farm, it was the henhouses that were the real "cash cow."[71]

Breeding: A Tale of Two Species

The fieldwork for this book required me to visit a number of different farms in the same summer. This was working well, but I hadn't yet come up against the regulations required for large-scale operations like the Baldwin Family Farms henhouses. During my second visit to Baldwin Family Farms in June 2015, while V. Mac and I were out on the ATV collecting soil samples, I noticed the rows of giant white buildings with metal roofs and asked V. Mac what they were. When he said that the chickens lived there, I asked what the chickens were for—eggs or meat? He told me that they were breeding chickens for meat. The breeder chickens laid one fertilized egg per day. For every egg that was sent to be raised for meat at Allen Harim in Delaware, Baldwin Family Farms received five cents. That didn't seem like a lot, but there were about 10,000 breeder hens in each of the eight houses that worked together to produce about 2 million eggs per year.[72]

Sensing my interest in the henhouses, V. Mac offered to show me one. We drove over a bridge to the henhouses, and V. Mac started explaining that the area was bio-secure. We would need to wash our feet and the ATV to enter the area where the breeder houses stood. As we pulled up to the biosecurity station, V. Mac remembered that I mentioned something about witnessing a chicken slaughter recently and asked when that had happened.[73] I told him it had been two days prior and I was wearing different shoes, clothes, and everything, which didn't assuage him at all. He turned the ATV around and drove away from the henhouses. As he drove, he told me that there was an avian flu scare in the Midwest and he couldn't take any chances that I might carry something into the bio-secure area. The biosecurity is regulated by the FDA and Allen Harim, the company that purchases the eggs.[74] I never did get to go into the henhouses, but their role in the grass-fed beef operation had captured my interest. The Baldwins dedicated a significant amount of time, land, and money to raising their cattle on pasture, but their chickens were kept indoors in cages. To me, it seemed that the Baldwins had an incongruous approach to animal welfare because they raised their chickens quite differently than their cows, but as with everything else on his farm, V. Mac was intentional about his approach to welfare in both cases.

During my subsequent visits, I asked more questions about the chickens and their relationship to the cows. V. Mac explained: "Everything on the farm relates to multiplicity. Each cow has to have a calf every year. The hens have to lay an egg every day to be profitable. It's a sex farm." V. Mac bred chickens to buy land to plant grass, which he fertilized with chicken litter, all in an effort to raise cows. For V. Mac, there was no issue with the henhouses. I had visited other farms that benefited from chicken litter but did so by letting their chickens roam, so I asked why the chickens didn't go outside to fertilize the grass themselves. V. Mac reminded me that his operation was not small—he could not fertilize thousands of acres of land by letting chickens roam around. He also showed me the turf they stood on to emphasize that each chicken got about a square foot of space, which he felt was enough room for them to move around. He also explained that the turf sat slanted in the cages so the eggs rolled right down the production line. My question was really about why cows were able to graze on open pastures while chickens lived in crowded houses, so I rephrased the question and asked why the chickens didn't get the same access to the outdoors that he granted the cows. V. Mac, now understanding my question, amended his answer. He told me that chickens, like pigs, were "corn eaters." He said they balanced the corn they fed the chickens with some soymeal to provide them with extra protein, and they did this because what the chickens needed was "concentrated energy." V. Mac continued, explaining that chickens were not ruminants like cows, so they could only eat so much in a day and they needed as much energy as they could get from their food.[75] In keeping with V. Mac's attention to "Nature's Way," his chickens ate corn and soymeal because that was what he felt the chickens needed to eat for energy. On the contrary, eating grass would not help the chickens, and certainly would not enable them to lay an egg per day, so the chickens did not need to be outdoors.

V. Mac maintained that his breeder houses were much cleaner and safer than the broiler houses, where chickens are grown for meat. He told me that whereas there were about 10,000 hens in each of his houses, around 80,000 chickens could occupy a broiler house. This was true, but the breeder houses were part of the same system, so the eggs hatched at Baldwin Beef ended up as chickens in those broiler houses. As V. Mac and I talked about chickens, it became clear that for him, animal welfare was contextual and relative. V. Mac conceptualized the needs of chickens differently than those of the cows. He also valued them differently. He told me that whereas the beef raised on the farm had those valuable omega-3 fatty acids, chicken did not.[76] For V. Mac, chicken was not as valuable a commodity and the henhouses were not related to the animal welfare certifications for the beef, so they were not handled the same way. V. Mac, who saw himself primarily as a grass farmer, bred the chickens to provide fertilizer for his grass operation. The chickens were valuable as a source of fertilizer and their eggs were valuable as a source of income, but the chickens themselves were seen primarily as a means to those ends.

As V. Mac and I continued our tour of the farm and soil sample collecting, he detailed the breeding procedure that he uses with the cows. He bred the cows in August each year. This was one of the major reasons that he valued the Charolais breed—their white coloring kept them cooler, which meant they were willing to breed during the hottest days of the North Carolina summers. V. Mac found the Charolais heifers to be quite fertile. He bred two-year-old virgin heifers with Charolais semen purchased from the American Breeder Service. This is fairly standard practice in the meat industry and involves a human inseminating the cows by hand. For the experienced heifers, V. Mac moved his own breeding bulls around the farm, and the breeding happened without human intervention. V. Mac brought a veterinarian out to test the semen of his bulls before he bred them. That year, of his fifty-nine bulls, only two were "shooting blanks." V. Mac was pleased with that percentage. He also told me that the two "shooting blanks" would be transitioned from breeding to beef. These breeding procedures were part of what V. Mac referred to when he called Baldwin Family Farms a "sex farm."[77] But the sex that happened among animals on the farm was organized and sometimes even performed by humans. And in cases where the animals acted outside that system, issues arose.

V. Mac shared a story about some of his cows that lived on Baldwin land in Virginia. When the heifers were in heat, a black Angus bull from a neighboring farm jumped a fence two fields away and bred half of the heifers before anyone noticed. V. Mac hadn't quite decided what to do with the mixed-breed calves that resulted from this incident. He usually kept a close eye on his mama cows and their calves. All the calves were tagged at birth. Female cows and calves had two tags, one in each ear. Male steers and calves had one tag. Male calves were grown for beef unless they showed promise as a breeding bull. Female calves were kept mostly on-site, though they were used for beef if they needed the supply. When females failed to breed or nurse or carry calves to term, they were moved to the beef side.[78] V. Mac spoke matter-of-factly about both the chicken and cow breeding procedures. He clarified that he did what he could to utilize natural processes and filled in with human intervention as necessary. His approach to animal husbandry took the needs of both the farm and the animals into account, but in the end, the needs of the farm triumphed over the needs of individual animals.

FREE-RANGE RELIGION AT BALDWIN FAMILY FARMS

In the end, all the cattle V. Mac raised ended up as beef. He reflected on his role as a meat producer, noting that "people forget that animals have to die" in order for them "to eat meat." He experienced those animal deaths regularly, but some of his customers struggled with the concept. He told a story about a woman who once called his phone. She asked how the cows die—and, according to V. Mac, she lowered her voice and whispered "die" in hushed tones. V. Mac told her that his animals died in a humane way. He gave her the details—they were rendered unconscious and then their throats were slit and they bled out. He told her that this process helped them die without suffering. The woman was shocked. She told V. Mac she didn't think she could keep eating meat. This is not the conclusion he imagined when he started the conversation. V. Mac stressed to his customers that he had chosen a good processor whom he trusted and who treated his animals well.[79] He didn't always tell them that the processor was a Muslim.

I asked V. Mac how his relationship with Abdul Chaudhry began.[80] He explained that because large processing plants had taken over the industry, it was difficult to find processors willing to do small custom jobs. It happened that Chaudhry Halal Meat Co. Inc., in Siler City, North Carolina, was the closest small-scale processor. V. Mac met with Abdul and recalled his thoughts from that initial meeting. V. Mac remembered learning that Abdul was Muslim and having some initial concerns, but then he met Abdul's family and determined that he was "number one, an honest man, and number two, capable of doing a good job." Abdul knew that the Baldwins were Christian and the Baldwins knew that the Chaudhrys were Muslim, but they "respected each other," V. Mac recalled, which enabled them to be in "an ongoing relationship now for twelve going on fifteen years."[81] This is not to say their relationship isn't complicated, and from V. Mac's perspective, most of the complications are related to their religious differences.

V. Mac considered Abdul a personal friend. One of the first times I asked about his relationship with Chaudhry, V. Mac told me that he was the best processor and that he was honest. Then he continued, "Sadly, he's going to miss heaven." V. Mac has been doing business with Abdul for years, and through that time, he told me he had often viewed this relationship as an opportunity to talk to Abdul about Jesus. He had many stories about his conversations with Abdul about Muhammad, Jesus, and sin.[82] V. Mac let me know that he received many emails from people whom he identified as "fundamentalist Christians" who were upset about the halal slaughter, noting that "they badmouthed him pretty bad." I asked V. Mac how he responded to them, and he replied, "I say I'm doing missionary work. They have to accept that."[83] He told me that Abdul is exposed to the gospel of Jesus Christ every time V. Mac sees him, and that was what he told these customers. My own conversations with V. Mac, who knew from the start that I am Jewish, validate this claim. He frequently raised theological points and practical questions intended to get me thinking about Jesus during my visits, so I have some sense of what those exchanges might have been like for Abdul.[84]

Beyond this missionary impulse, V. Mac also seemed to view his partnership with Chaudhry as a service to his friend. V. Mac had some very specific ideas about how the slaughter functioned for Abdul. The first day I met V. Mac, he cited John 19:30: "When Jesus had received the sour wine, he said, It is finished, and he bowed his head, and gave up his spirit" (ESV). He told me that these were the last words of Jesus and then continued with his exegesis. "'It is finished.' What is finished? The atoning system for sin was finished. Christians believe it and receive it by faith and their sins are atoned through this process."[85] V. Mac and I had a similar conversation on this topic a few times during my visits. On each occasion, he stressed to me that Christians do not need to sacrifice animals to atone for their sins because Jesus died for their sins. And V. Mac believed that both kosher and halal slaughter are used by Jews and Muslims to atone for their sins.[86] However, his thinking was based on an outdated understanding of kosher and halal slaughter as a sacrificial act. He told me that "blood is appropriated for [Muslims'] sins" and that they sacrifice animals to pay their "sin debt" and argued that Christians don't have to deal with "the sin problem" because "Jesus was the sacrifice for sin."[87] This explanation, which reflects a very Christian understanding of both sin and slaughter, makes for a particularly interesting interreligious encounter. Halal slaughter is not understood by Muslims to be related to releasing sin debts.[88] Rather, it is connected to the belief that Allah created animals, so permission and proper procedures are required to kill animals.[89] So in the end, Chaudhry Halal Meats was slaughtering the Baldwin Beef, but it seemed that V. Mac and the team at Chaudhry held very different ideas about what was actually happening at the moment of slaughter and how it was best understood from a religious standpoint.

The halal Baldwin Beef was sold at Whole Foods Markets to customers who were often unaware and likely uninterested in the theological explanations that the farmers and slaughterers attached to the life and death of the animal they planned to eat, which added another level of complexity to the situation. I visited the two Whole Foods stores that were closest to me at the time in Durham and Chapel Hill, North Carolina, and the packaged Baldwin Beef was not identified as halal at either store. V. Mac's Christianity was also absent from Whole Foods marketing materials. In 2015, the Baldwin Beef website banner contained a citation for a Bible verse, "III John 2," in red letters.[90] This verse, which was meant for all customers visiting the Baldwin Beef website to learn more about the farm or to order meat, reads, "Beloved, I pray that all may go well with you and that you may be in good health, as it goes well with your soul" (ESV). In November 2015, V. Mac partnered with Whole Foods Markets to put up a forty-by-sixty billboard on I-85/I-40, a busy thoroughfare where two major highways overlap in North Carolina. The billboard image became the banner image on the Baldwin Beef website at that time, and the Bible verse was removed. V. Mac hinted at his reason for this change when he told me about the customers he was trying to reach through Whole Foods. He mentioned that the farm is in Caswell County, an hour and twenty minutes from the heart of the Research Triangle, an area that includes the cities of Raleigh, Durham, and Chapel Hill, three major research universities, and an ever-increasing number of tech companies, which V. Mac said meant "lots of people that love to eat healthy, and they have above-average incomes." In addition to eating healthy, Whole Foods customers were often seeking local food and food that was produced with environmental sustainability and animal welfare in mind. Interested in appealing to this growing consumer market, V. Mac said he and his business "try to make them our friends and invite them up here and get to know them and get acquainted through the internet."[91] In other words, according to V. Mac, the Whole Foods customers were not in search of meat raised with a biblical pastoralist ethic or meat that was certified halal, so Baldwin Family Farms was not highlighting those attributes of the meat in its advertising materials or package labels. V. Mac told me that the billboard had been a success and beamed as he said, "That part of the operation is growing like gangbusters."[92]

When I asked V. Mac about the relationships he forged with a Muslim processor, secular markets and grocery stores, and Christian and non-Christian customers, he told me that food systems are all intertwined like this and everyone gets mixed up with different people in the process. V. Mac's livelihood depended on his customers, so he was not always able to use his meat to minister to customers as he might have liked. He had also faced harsh criticism from Christians for his partnerships with non-Christians. However, V. Mac was not deterred. On my second visit to the farm, V. Mac explained a recent complication on the farm and asked me to recite Matthew 11:28–30 for him, because those are the verses that get him through difficult days on the farm. He was disappointed to learn that I did not know those verses off the top of my head and recited them for me: "Come to me, all who labor and are heavy laden, and I will give you rest. Take my yoke upon you, and learn from me, for I am gentle and lowly in heart, and you will find rest for your souls. For my yoke is easy, and my burden is light" (ESV). Through every tough decision V. Mac made on the farm and in his business, he found comfort in the knowledge that he shared those burdens with Jesus.

CONCLUSION

Religion played a key role in the production of Baldwin Beef, but that role was downplayed for consumers, which speaks to the frequent invisibility of religion in alternative food movements. Customers, who are often secular, enable alternative food producers like Baldwin Family Farms to exist and thrive. In fact, the reason Whole Foods carries Baldwin Beef was because the customers demanded it. V. Mac told me that when he first started selling his meat, he began with a booth at the Carrboro Farmers' Market. The customers liked the beef so much that they wanted to be able to buy it all the time and not just on farmers' market days. These customers started a conversation with the team leader at the Chapel Hill Whole Foods at that time. Eventually, the team leader came out to the market and asked V. Mac what was so good about his beef. V. Mac told him to try it because he wanted to "let the beef speak for itself."[93] V. Mac reported that not long after that, Whole Foods decided to start carrying Baldwin Beef. In 2015, Baldwin Family Farms supplied its beef to nine Whole Foods stores and a number of Kroger stores, but it still went to the Carrboro Farmers' Market every Sunday because the venue provided the Baldwins with an opportunity to meet and talk to the customers. V. Mac stressed the importance of his customer: "So basically, our market is the consumer. And she's driving this bus. If she didn't like our beef, we'd be out of business." Recognizing this dynamic, V. Mac said he and his workers did everything they could to figure out how to package their meat so the customer would like it, which he explained meant clear labels and high-quality vacuum seals that allowed customers to freeze the meat and find it later. V. Mac pointed out that this packaging also allowed his customers to purchase their meat in large quantities.[94]

V. Mac did everything he could to please the customers. He always urged them to try his grass-fed beef so they could taste the difference, as he did with the Whole Foods team leader. At the farmers' market, he told me he answered all of their questions about how the animals were treated and dealt with their questions and complaints about his partnership with Chaudhry Halal Meats. The Baldwin Beef website in 2015 listed a set of principles that drove the company's interactions with customers:

> OUR CUSTOMERS are the most important people in our business.
> OUR CUSTOMERS are not dependent on us . . . we are dependent on them.
> OUR CUSTOMERS are not an interruption of our work . . . they are the purpose of our work.
> OUR CUSTOMERS do us a favor when they call . . . we are not doing them a favor by serving them.
> OUR CUSTOMERS are of our business . . . not an outsider.

Cows, Chickens, and Certifications

OUR CUSTOMERS have feelings and emotions just like our own.

OUR CUSTOMERS are not someone with which to argue.

OUR CUSTOMERS are deserving of the most courteous and attentive treatment we can give them.

OUR CUSTOMERS are the lifeblood of our business.[95]

The Baldwins were selling meat to customers whose values, ideas, and religious beliefs and practices frequently differed from their own. V. Mac engaged people in conversation about scripture when he could, but that was only possible when people were interested in his product. Christianity drove V. Mac, but customers drove his business. He offered me another Bible verse to explain the role of Christianity in his business: "And we know that for those who love God all things work together for good, for those who are called according to his purpose."[96] V. Mac loved God and felt that he was called to put scripture in people's hands. Baldwin's grass-fed, antibiotic-free, hormone-free, halal beef allowed him to minister to countless people, and he was hopeful that the beef would continue to provide those opportunities as his business grew.[97] V. Mac's Christian commitments and business acumen landed him in a broad entanglement of grass, chickens, cows, land, buildings, markets, regulations, retailers, processors, and customers. And in the middle was V. Mac, who sought to spread the gospel of Jesus to everyone he encountered in the alternative food system he had developed through his grass-fed beef. In an effort to meet the need of his customers and retailers, the Christian message was not coming through as overtly on packaging and marketing materials, but he was sure that his beliefs and his dedication to raising animals as he believed God intended was visible in the beef he produced and the land he stewarded.

CHAPTER FOUR

A Year of Rest and Restoration at Pearlstone Center

> *Six years you shall sow your land and gather in its yield; but in the seventh you shall let it rest and lie fallow. Let the needy among your people eat of it, and what they leave let the wild beasts eat. You shall do the same with your vineyards and your olive groves.*
>
> EXODUS 23:10–11 (JPS)

On a hot sunny day in June 2015, the farm at the Pearlstone Retreat Center in Reisterstown, Maryland, was relatively quiet.[1] A small group of volunteers was harvesting the last of the asparagus while another group was breaking down worn boards from the greenhouse beds. A Pearlstone staff member was cutting the lawn at the edge of the farm. I was sitting in a patch of chamomile harvesting the flowers with Sydney, a Chesapeake Conservation Corps volunteer who was assigned to Pearlstone for the year.[2] Eventually, the chamomile would be dried and used by the program staff for goat milk soap demonstrations. It was a calm task and one that contrasted drastically with the work I had done when I visited and volunteered on the farm for

Pearlstone Center farm, June 2013.

the first time in 2013.³ During that summer I worked with a group of farm apprentices planting, watering, weeding, pruning, hoeing, and harvesting produce for their community-supported agriculture program. In 2015, the four acres of land that were usually dedicated to raising vegetables and herbs for the CSA were in the midst of a year of release, and the apprentice program was suspended for the year. However, the fields were not barren. The two acres dedicated to perennial plants continued to produce. On the other two acres, the usual rows of squash, peppers, and tomatoes were absent, but the fields still abounded with vegetation. Buckwheat, barley, and oats grew in places of annual vegetables to nurture and rejuvenate the soil. These cover crops were preventing soil erosion and adding nitrogen to the earth. Under the surface, worms were moving through the soil, leaving nutrient-rich castings in their path. Networks of mycorrhizal fungi were expanding and reconnecting all the areas of the farm, fostering communication underground.

In 2015, I stood overlooking the land with Gabe, Pearlstone's farm director at the time, marveling at how the farm was simultaneously the same as it had been during my first visit in 2013 and yet completely different.⁴ Gabe agreed and commented that what we were looking at was "just one degree

Pearlstone Center farm, June 2015.

different than what we would be looking at any other year that you would be standing in this spot. Ninety-nine percent of this is the same, but the 1 percent difference is the *shmita* ingredient," which Gabe said was Pearlstone's aspiration for the year.[5] The "*shmita* ingredient" Gabe referenced was Pearlstone's interpretation of a set of biblical principles that were revived in the United States in the twenty-first century.[6] The literal meaning of *shmita* is "release," but it is more popularly translated as "sabbatical." As I mentioned in the introduction to this book, shmita is a Sabbath for the land. Similar to the weekly Sabbath, a day of rest after six days of work, shmita is a year of rest for the land after it has been worked for six years. A shmita year occurred in the Hebrew year 5775, which began on Rosh Hashanah in September 2014 and ended on the following Rosh Hashanah in September 2015.[7] Throughout that shmita year, a number of Jewish organizations in the United States, like Pearlstone, leaped into (in)action. The introduction of shmita to the United States was enabled by the Jewish agricultural spaces that grew within the Jewish environmentalist movement, as described in chapter 1 of this book.[8] The implementation of shmita at Pearlstone was part of a collaborative conversation about the sabbatical year within American Jewish environmentalist organizations. The leaders of the contemporary shmita movement in the

A Year of Rest and Restoration

United States consider both the history and textual traditions of shmita, even as they adapt their observance of shmita to the modern context.

In this chapter, I argue that when the leadership at Pearlstone implemented shmita, they introduced their community to an alternative food system that decenters the needs of humans and instead focuses on ecological restoration. They based their understanding of shmita on their interpretations of the relevant biblical and rabbinic texts and traditions, and their innovative approach was also shaped through collaboration with other Jewish organizations. In the second section of this chapter, I provide an overview of the textual basis for shmita and the movement to implement it in the United States. After that, I discuss the food system at Pearlstone during the shmita year and then describe the ways that Pearlstone's Jewish and non-Jewish staff worked together to implement shmita and provide environmental education experiences for Jewish and non-Jewish audiences in the Baltimore area throughout the sabbatical year. Shmita provides a particularly interesting example of how ancient Jewish traditions have been applied in the contemporary era and how they appeal to a wide audience because of their relevance in a time of environmental destruction and climate crisis.

PEARLSTONE CENTER

The Pearlstone Retreat Center was initially founded as the Jack Pearlstone Institute for Living Judaism in 1987 to honor its namesake, Jack Pearlstone, who was passionate about informal Jewish education and committed to ensuring a "bright Jewish future."[9] In 2001, Pearlstone became a retreat center when accommodations were added and "immersive Jewish experiences" were incorporated into the organization's mission.[10] In 2006, Jakir Manela, who trained as a Teva educator, started what was then called Kayam Farm at Pearlstone.[11] The farm was later integrated into Pearlstone and took on the Pearlstone name.[12] When I visited Pearlstone in 2015, it was a seven-acre property adjacent to Camp Milldale.[13] Both the Pearlstone farm and the conference center catered to Jewish and non-Jewish groups, and the staff at Pearlstone was mostly made up of people who identified as Jews, but there were many non-Jewish people on staff as well. As I mentioned above, prior to 2014–15, the farm had a CSA program, where people in the area could purchase a share of the farm's produce. The farm had an apprentice program, similar to the apprentice positions at Adamah described in chapter 1 of this book, and the apprentices provided most of the labor for the farm as well as assistance with educational programs for the retreat groups, schools, and camps that Pearlstone served. I will describe some of the educational programs that the program staff at Pearlstone ran during the shmita year in the third and fourth sections of this chapter.

I spent the majority of my time at Pearlstone in the summer of 2015 with the farm staff and the program staff. The farm staff included Gabe, the farm director, and Sydney, the Chesapeake Conservation Corps volunteer who was assigned to Pearlstone for the year. I spoke with the former farm director, Jake, and worked on the farm alongside volunteers from the Baltimore community throughout my time at Pearlstone. I also worked with the program staff at that time, which included program director Nora, lead educator Natalie, and program associates Daniel and Ava. In order to gain a better understanding of Pearlstone's work in the broader community, I additionally spoke with the director of community sustainability, Rachel. Jakir, who was the executive director of Pearlstone in 2015, was not available to meet during my visit, but I was able to interview him by phone after my visit. My experiences at Pearlstone and the interviews I conducted serve as the primary sources for this chapter alongside Pearlstone's public-facing website and social media pages and scholarship on Jewish environmentalism and shmita. In the conclusion to this chapter, I also provide some information on the plans that Pearlstone developed in 2014–15 for subsequent shmita years.[14] In my time at Pearlstone during shmita, I saw the potential for this practice to transform agricultural and other types of land, educational programs, workplaces, and communities. This transformative power is due, in large part, to the fact that shmita is not one law but a set of laws that address many aspects of social and economic life.

HISTORICAL CONTEXT FOR SHMITA AT PEARLSTONE

It's in the Torah, in the land of Israel
To create equality for me and you-oo-oo-oo
We let the livestock and the wild creatures
Eat from the land just like we do-oo-oo-oo
It's a reminder to help each other always
And let go, let go, let go of anything you're owed
And why oh why oh, why oh why oh why oh
Is there still hunger when we know that there's food out there
Shmita
    It's a chance for us to relax

A Year of Rest and Restoration

>Shmita
>>And take the load off our backs
>Shmita
>>It's an exciting opportunity
>Shmita
>>To help in our community[15]

The shmita spirit was in full swing at Pearlstone in 2014–15, as demonstrated by the song lyrics above, which were written by Pearlstone's lead educator at the time, Natalie, and set to the upbeat tune of "Hey Ya!" by OutKast. But outside of Jewish environmental spaces like Pearlstone and Adamah, most Jews in the United States didn't even know it *was* a shmita year. There are two primary reasons for this. First, as noted in the first line of the song lyrics, shmita is in the Torah, but it is not a required practice for Jews outside the land of Israel.[16] Second, farming has not been a common career path among Jews in the United States, particularly in the contemporary era, so most American Jews are not familiar with agriculture or the biblical agricultural laws.[17] Nora, who was the program director at Pearlstone in 2015, also emphasized the distance from agriculture among American Jews as she reflected, "I think we've become a very indoors people. We're 'People of the Book.' You read the book inside instead of outside."[18] Nora's observation speaks to a long history of Jews concentrating on the areas of Jewish law that were more applicable to their day-to-day lives over those that applied only in theory, especially for Jewish communities that were in the Diaspora and disengaged from agricultural work. For these reasons, shmita is discussed in Jewish texts relatively infrequently, and there isn't a historical record of Jewish communities observing shmita in full. The song lyrics offer some clues as to why shmita exists more as an ideal in the Jewish imaginary than as a practice in reality. As I will discuss below, shmita is not one law but rather a set of laws, which taken together make for a rather arduous year and include leaving the land fallow while simultaneously ensuring that there is still enough food to sustain all humans and animals. Despite the difficulty of shmita, these laws have garnered interest among contemporary Jews amid the environmental and climate crises.

The Textual Basis for Shmita

In order to understand the intricacies of Pearlstone's implementation of shmita, it helps to begin with a foundation in the key texts and traditions.[19]

The first mention of the laws of shmita in the Bible was in the book of Exodus: "Six years you shall sow your land and gather in its yield; but in the seventh you shall let it rest and lie fallow. Let the needy among your people eat of it, and what they leave let the wild beasts eat. You shall do the same with your vineyards and your olive groves."[20] These verses form the basis for shmita's Sabbath for the land. Most importantly, the ancient Israelites were commanded to let their land "rest and lie fallow." This meant they could not seed, plant, or plow their land during the shmita years. Perennial plants, like fruit trees and wild edibles, would still produce food without human intervention during the shmita year, so they were meant to serve as the primary food source for the entire community and the wild beasts at that time. The verse "Let the needy among your people eat of it" points to the justice-oriented qualities of shmita that tend to appeal to contemporary Jews. Even during the shmita years when food was going to be harder to access than usual, the laws required Jews to ensure that everyone—humans and animals—had enough to eat.

In the book of Leviticus, these laws were repeated, but additional details were added: "But in the seventh year the land shall have a sabbath of complete rest, a sabbath of the Lord: you shall not sow your field or prune your vineyard. You shall not reap the aftergrowth of your harvest or gather the grapes of your untrimmed vines; it shall be a year of complete rest for the land."[21] This verse explicates the previous instruction to leave the land fallow and makes it clear that activities like sowing, pruning, reaping, and gathering were forbidden during the shmita year because "it shall be a year of complete rest for the land." Louis Newman, author of *The Sanctity of the Seventh Year: A Study of Mishnah Tractate Shebiit*, noted that "implicit in this view is the notion that the Land of Israel has human qualities and needs," and because the land has these needs, it requires a sanctified rest, just as humans do.[22] Though Newman's argument leaned on anthropocentrism, he was clear that the laws of shmita put forward the radical idea that the land works, and every seven years it is granted time to rest.

The text of Leviticus also offered more information about what the Israelites were meant to eat during that year. This section began with a question: "And should you ask, 'What are we to eat in the seventh year, if we may neither sow nor gather in our crops?'" This question was followed by an answer: "I will ordain My blessing for you in the sixth year, so that it shall yield a crop sufficient for three years. When you sow in the eighth year, you will still be eating old grain of that crop; you will be eating the old until the ninth year, until its crops come in."[23] These verses served as a reminder to the ancient

Israelites that God was commanding them to let their land lie fallow but was also promising to provide enough perennial crops to last them for three years (the sixth year, seventh year, and eighth/first year in the sabbatical cycle).[24] Newman argued that this is also why the shmita laws were restricted to the land of Israel: "Israelites must observe the restrictions of the seventh year as an affirmation of the unique bond between God's holy land and his chosen people."[25] All the laws of shmita are based on the understanding that the land was a vital actor in the covenant between the Israelites and their God, and because of this role, the land required a Sabbath.

There are additional references to shmita throughout the Hebrew Bible in the books of Deuteronomy, 2 Kings, Jeremiah, Nehemiah, and 2 Chronicles.[26] These texts expanded on the agricultural restrictions and added economic and cultural elements to shmita, including a debt relief requirement and a prescribed public Torah reading during the shmita years. These texts also described both the timing and requirements of the *yovel* ("jubilee") year. The *yovel* year occurs after seven shmita cycles of seven years, in the fiftieth year.[27] According to Leviticus, in the *yovel* year slaves and prisoners had to be set free, land had to be released from ownership and redistributed, and debts were forgiven.[28] After the destruction of the Second Temple, as the rabbis interpreted the laws for a new era of Judaism that was suddenly without its sacrificial system, the sabbatical cycle was discussed but rarely enforced. Shmita is the topic of the fifth tractate of Seder Zeraim (Order of Seeds) of the Mishnah, which was compiled by the early rabbis in the second century of the Common Era. Newman identified a shift in the Mishnah, wherein the rabbis increasingly saw the Jewish people themselves as the source of sanctification in the land of Israel, and the responsibility for maintaining that sanctification without a temple was accomplished by adhering to laws like the shmita laws.[29] However, even as the rabbis continued to deliberate topics like the geographical boundaries of shmita, they were reticent to enforce the laws in full. In *The Way into Judaism and the Environment*, Jeremy Benstein pointed out that the redactor of the Mishnah, Rabbi Judah the Prince, "called for the annulment of the *shmitah* year because its implementation was so arduous."[30] The scholar Gerald Blidstein suggested this is representative of "the commonplace struggle between a radical religious demand and an un-consenting world." Blidstein argued that the power of shmita to disrupt social and economic patterns was the cause of its descent into relative obscurity within the Jewish tradition.[31] Beyond the challenges associated with shmita, the laws also applied to a limited number of Jews, as the majority of the Jewish population was located outside the land of Israel. Interestingly, it was both the power and the challenge of shmita that attracted attention in the modern era, even in the Diaspora.³²

Shmita in the United States

The 2014–15 shmita year was the first time the staff at the farm at Pearlstone observed the sabbatical year. In the previous shmita year, in 2007–8, Jakir had just started Kayam Farm at Pearlstone, and when someone asked him what they were going to do about shmita, he recalled being unfamiliar with it beyond recognizing the term from Jewish sources. In the winter of 2007, Jakir heard Nati Passow speak at the Hazon Food Conference.³³ Passow, who was director of the Jewish Farm School at the time, was an early leader in the shmita movement.³⁴ He published an article about shmita in 2008 that contained many of the ideas he shared at the Hazon Food Conference. He urged Jews in the United States to learn about and consider shmita, even if the laws didn't apply outside the borders of the biblical land of Israel. He wrote that "there is so much potential to use the *shemita* year as a foundation for renewed Jewish ecological education around the world, for *shemita* requires of us a humility and reverence for that which is greater than any one person."³⁵ As I discussed in chapter 1, Jewish environmentalism was growing in the early years of the twenty-first century, and shmita presented an opportunity to address the environmental crises of that time with Jewish resources.

In the same article, Passow laid out three main ideas that he found in shmita after he analyzed the relevant texts. The first idea he identified was a "need to rethink our concepts of ownership and the inherent entitlement we assume to exploit our natural resources for our benefit alone." The second idea was "to cultivate a sense of empathy and compassion for the less fortunate and more vulnerable members of our society." The third and final idea that Passow discussed was an overall goal for the Jewish community—"to create systems that benefit the whole rather than encourage the accumulation of material wealth among a minority of individuals."³⁶ Jakir was inspired by the speech and by the concept of shmita. He recalled that it struck him "how powerful this paradigm is, to commit to think in long term holistic ecological cycles, social cycles, social community life beyond . . . industrial food and industrial society, industrial culture." Jakir was so enthusiastic about the potential of shmita that he talked to Nati after the speech and committed to bringing shmita to the farm at Pearlstone, even though he and the farm had been there for only a year at that point. Jakir and Nati became close friends and continued to research shmita together for the next seven years.³⁷ During that time, shmita began to gain traction in the United States. When I attended the Teva Seminar on Jewish Outdoor, Food and Environmental Education in 2013, Nati led sessions on shmita to prepare Jewish leaders for the upcoming shmita year. In those sessions we talked about the agricultural practices, but we also spent a great deal of time discussing debt release and communal responsibility. At that same seminar, I attended a session led by Yigal Deutscher, author of *Envisioning Sabbatical Culture: A Shmita Manifesto*, which I discuss below. Both Yigal and Nati went on to manage the collaborative Shmita Project.

Jews in the environmental movement in the United States felt that shmita had the potential to reinforce both the importance and the sacred qualities attributed to land in Judaism, even outside the land of Israel. A movement of Jews seeking to reimagine the practices of the sabbatical year came together under the umbrella of the Shmita Project, which was administered by the Jewish environmental organization Hazon.[38] The Shmita Project sought "to expand awareness about the biblical Sabbatical tradition, and to bring the values of this practice to life today to support healthier, more sustainable Jewish communities."[39] The project was based primarily on the foundational work of Passow, as described above, and Deutscher's *Envisioning Sabbatical Culture: A Shmita Manifesto*, which was published in 2013.[40] In Deutscher's slim book, he described shmita as more than a calendar year and instead as "a way of being, a blueprint for a sacred, whole-systems culture, one grounded in vibrant, healthy and diverse relations between self, community, ecology, economy & spirit." Deutscher went on to argue for the implementation of a "sabbatical food system," which he explained should be focused on land stewardship because shmita is meant to encourage rest and restoration for the land. Deutscher suggested that a year focused on the needs of the land and alternative food sources provided "a direct challenge to re-enter the sacred relationship with food production, distribution, and consumption." He offered numerous ideas for people interested in engaging in a sabbatical food system, including establishing personal and communal gardens; learning about wild edibles; purchasing local, organic, and seasonal produce; and hosting harvest and canning parties.[41] As I will describe below, Pearlstone hosted educational experiences like those proposed by Deutscher during the shmita year to inspire both Jews and non-Jews to engage in land stewardship and sabbatical food system practices.

Many ideas from *Envisioning Sabbatical Culture* were incorporated into the *Hazon Shmita שמיטה Sourcebook*, which was developed by Deutscher and Anna Hanau and Nigel Savage from Hazon and published in 2013.[42] This sourcebook included over a hundred pages of biblical and rabbinic texts intended for Jewish education related to shmita with suggestions for Jews interested in enacting shmita in their own homes or communities. The authors of the sourcebook asked readers to "meet this ancient tradition anew, ripe and fresh, to harvest her lessons for today, and begin a conversation which will ripple into years to come, many generations ahead."[43] These texts and the Shmita Project were the first efforts to implement shmita in the United States, but previous generations had also found inspiration in shmita. Arthur Waskow, Renewal rabbi and founding director of the Shalom Center, began discussing the sabbatical year in the 1990s "as a way to enforce cessation of economic activity and promote reflection concerning the effects of our work and economy on the earth and each other."[44] Jeremy Benstein was similarly motivated by the model of shmita as an alternative to capitalism, arguing that "the biblical *shmitah* is a stirring example of an entire society choosing to live at a significantly lower material standard for a year in order to devote itself to more spiritual pursuits than the daily grind."[45] These shmita enthusiasts highlighted these elements, which they felt were particularly pertinent in the modern era and provided an opportunity for the shmita year to transform not just the Jewish community but perhaps even society as a whole.

As the example of Pearlstone will show, shmita impacts the entire ecosystem, not just humans, and the central principles of shmita have the potential to appeal to both Jews and non-Jews. Whereas many biblical laws related to the earth are anthropocentric, prioritizing the needs of humans, shmita prioritizes the land and its need for rest. This presented a challenge for places like Pearlstone, where implementing shmita required a real shift in organizational structure at every level. As I will discuss in the next section, leaders changed their entire approach to their on-site farm, implemented new programs for employees, and refocused their environmental education curriculum on shmita principles. As I discussed in chapter 1 of this book, the leadership team at the Adamah Farm Fellowship also incorporated shmita into their work as they rotated their crop production through seven fields with one field always at rest, donated at least one-seventh of their produce to charitable organizations, and established a shmita garden in 2014–15.[46] The spring 2014 fellows at Adamah also recorded and produced a digital album inspired by the shmita year.[47] These creative interpretations of shmita enabled Adamah to continue its CSA program and the farm fellowship during the shmita year while observing shmita in spirit.[48] At Pearlstone, the timing of the shmita year and its identity as a site for innovative Judaism in the Baltimore area allowed Pearlstone to bring that spirit, along with some of the more traditional aspects of shmita, to life in Maryland.

PEARLSTONE'S SHMITA YEAR ALTERNATIVE FOOD SYSTEM

When the program staff at Pearlstone received a shmita-themed game that had been developed by a former coworker, they decided to adapt it so they could use it in their environmental education programming. They ended up using their version countless times throughout the shmita year.[49] Daniel, who was a program associate at Pearlstone at the time, described the shmita simulation game to me. Each player was allotted a set amount of food and assigned a biblical-era persona—a servant, farmer, or stonemason, for example. Then participants played through rounds that represented the six years leading up to shmita. They drew cards that allowed them to accumulate blankets and food for themselves, and because the game was based on the biblical texts, they were also meant to gather supplies for the servants in their home. When the shmita year came around in the game, all servants and debts were freed, and players had to take stock of their supplies to see if they had enough food and blankets to get through the year. Daniel explained, "People who get the game will share."[50] The program staff said the game worked quite well as an educational tool about the biblical laws related to shmita.[51] The simulation also highlighted one of the most important aspects of shmita —creativity. Just as players may have needed to improvise during the shmita year when they found themselves without enough food, Pearlstone's implementation of shmita also required a bit of imaginative thinking and collaboration.

Innovation and Environmentalism at Pearlstone

At Pearlstone, creativity was central to its identity. Pearlstone was located just fifteen minutes from the main building of the Baltimore Jewish Community Center. However, Jakir explained that this short drive takes people through about five minutes of cornfields, which gives Pearlstone the feel of being far away.[52] Nora, who was the program director at Pearlstone during the shmita year in 2014–15, echoed this sentiment: "When you're here, you don't feel like you're part of a city. You do feel like you're fully engulfed in nature. We have great trails and woods and land to really feel away."[53] Jakir saw this distance and their location outside the city as "a priceless gift" that allowed Pearlstone to be "the innovator, the incubator, the experimental," and "the living laboratory for what Jewish life can be." Jakir continued to extol the benefits of a place like Pearlstone: "It's subversive, and it's hands-on, and it's young, and it's earth-based."[54] Pearlstone was located close enough to urban and suburban Baltimore for it to be a central institution in that Jewish community, while its identity as a different kind of Jewish space allowed for some flexibility with participants' interpretation of Judaism. Pearlstone was not a legacy Jewish institution: It was not a synagogue, a Jewish community center, or a Jewish federation, though it was supported by the local federation. It was not bound within a formal national network of institutions, it was not tied to a single Jewish movement, and it was not indebted to honor a particular history.

Pearlstone's identity as a Jewish space outside the Jewish mainstream enabled staff members' work, as put forth in the organization's mission statement: "The Pearlstone Retreat Center ignites Jewish passion."[55] The mission statement went on to list the four core values that shaped everything that staff and visitors participated in: warm hospitality, immersive experiences, living Judaism, and stewardship of the earth.[56] The farm was only part of how the staff at Pearlstone acted as good stewards of the earth. Rachel, the director of community sustainability, helped Pearlstone become a Maryland Green Center.[57] A geothermal heat pump helped decrease the site's energy use, and the retreat center also installed energy-efficient lighting.[58] Staffers served sustainable fair-trade food in their dining hall and recycled and composted waste. Rachel also worked with organizations and schools in the greater Baltimore Jewish community on their greening efforts. At Pearlstone, staff were able to experiment with Judaism and bring new, revitalized, and reimagined Jewish experiences to retreat center visitors and to the surrounding community.

The program staff at Pearlstone worked to reconnect Jews to the agricultural traditions present in Jewish texts and history. Nora pointed out that they saw holidays as great occasions for Jews to rediscover their literal and figurative roots. She explained, "Any holiday in [the Jewish] calendar has nature-based, land-based connecting points." She felt that many Jews had lost touch with those aspects of the holidays and that often "they've become part of the history of the holiday as opposed to part of our current contemporary celebration." Nora offered an example of how the staff at Pearlstone reimagined the celebration of Jewish holidays. Tu B'Shevat, the "New Year for the Trees," provided many Jewish organizations with an opportunity to talk about the importance of trees and nature in Jewish tradition. All over the country, Jews attend Tu B'Shevat celebrations at their local synagogues and Jewish community centers, where they plant trees, eat fruits and nuts, and sing songs about trees. So Pearlstone had to do something different, or in Nora's words, it "had to bump it up a notch." The staff learned how to tap their maple trees and turn the sap into maple syrup over an open flame in the Pearlstone firepit. They used their newfound skills and created programs for families and other community groups to celebrate Tu B'Shevat with tree-centered programming.[59] Nora stressed that these types of creative programs offered at Pearlstone were not necessarily new; rather, they were "just reclaiming a connection that North American Jews have lost." Shmita provided an opportunity to expand Pearlstone's experiential, nature-based Judaism programs because it was an entire year dedicated to stewardship and sustainability.

Shmita at Pearlstone

"How the hell did we get to a point that only professors and clergy get sabbaticals?" Jakir posed this provocative question in a phone conversation. I was a graduate student at the time with mere dreams of sabbaticals, so I sympathized with his point. Unsurprisingly, given his thoughts on the matter, when Jakir and his staff implemented shmita at Pearlstone, they ensured that sabbaticals were offered to land, animals, and humans. Jakir explained that he "tried to bring sustainability, balance, not just environmental sustainability, but work-life balance, workplace sustainability, organizational culture to the whole institution."[60] The farm staff worked toward environmental sustainability by using the year to deal with invasive species control and repairing and restoring the wooded areas that surrounded the farm. The leadership worked on a financial plan to carry them forward to the next shmita year and reimagined the role of the farm on the Pearlstone campus. The idea behind these initiatives was to revive not just Pearlstone's land but the organization itself. I will describe the land restoration efforts in this section and will cover the organizational efforts in the fourth and final sections of this chapter.

Prior to the shmita year in 2014–15, annual crops were usually grown on just under two acres of land at Pearlstone.[61] The farm was not certified organic, but the methods used on the farm aligned with organic principles.[62] Just over two acres of land were dedicated to perennial crops, including fruit orchards, herbs, asparagus, and mushrooms.[63] There was a one-acre animal pasture that usually housed seven goats and almost a hundred laying hens.[64] In preparation for the shmita year, the staff at Pearlstone learned about shmita, talked to other organizations, and brainstormed for about a year to figure out what to do with their farm during the sabbatical year. About four months before shmita was set to start, when Jakir remembers them having "many ideas and very few plans," he was approached by his perennials manager, Penny. She asked to work part-time during the shmita year so she could focus on restoring abandoned lots in Baltimore, and she urged Jakir to do shmita "all the way" on the farm.[65] After some quick planning, the staff decided to suspend the CSA and apprenticeship programs for the year.

Jake, who was the farm-to-table specialist during the shmita year and had previously been the farm director during the shmita planning process, recalled that he and the other staff saw this as a way to enact an idea that would be "really true to the meaning of shmita." Jake continued, explaining that they viewed it as "an ideal time to take a step back . . . from the kind of merciless grind of production."[66] They also decided to make changes to their animal program. Ava, who was a program associate in 2015, told me that the animal flock was cut down to four goats and eighteen hens in accordance with the shmita principle related to animal care and letting animals roam free.[67] Sydney started before the beginning of the shmita year and remembered the amount of work required when the animal program was at its peak, particularly in the spring when the goat kids were born. She also made the retreat center's goat milk soap and recalled the process being rewarding. She reflected that it was really interesting "to know the goats, feed the goats, milk the goats, process the milk, and then use the milk to make soap, and then sell the soap," and she enjoyed being part of "every step of that process."[68] Visitors to Pearlstone also appreciated the ability to get to know the goats and the hens. Natalie explained that they kept some animals because they had become part of Pearlstone's identity in the Baltimore community. Natalie also assured me that the animals they didn't keep were sold, not eaten.[69] Changes were made in staffing to accommodate the changes to the animal pastures and the farm. This included hiring Gabe as farm director; he came to Pearlstone in February 2015 and took charge of the agricultural aspects of shmita.

Gabe estimated that 90 percent of the production spaces on the farm were in a healing process during the shmita year in an effort to achieve a maximum restoration. He was hoping that the year of healing would ensure the success of the farm in future years. Gabe pointed out that in all cases, Jewish or secular or industrial, agriculture is a product of more than just human planning. He explained that farmers "do the labor of organizing it and timing it to our satisfaction" but that this actually isn't necessary "for that plant to grow and be successful as an organism." He knew from his own experiences that once you start growing things, "it occurs to you fairly early on that green thumbs are not that relevant." Gabe also felt that the more time he spent in agriculture, "exposed to rain and heat and around insects," the more appreciation he had for the resilience and abundance of nature itself.[70]

In Gabe's view, human skills and planning were helpful in agriculture only up to a point, and then nature would take its course. So, healthy soil was more of an indicator of the success or failure of food production than anything the farmers might do. During the shmita year at Pearlstone, staffers decided to rest their soil by cover-cropping it so that the period of rest would also rebuild and strengthen the soil.

Gabe and Sydney both compared their agricultural methods to those of the conventional farms that surrounded Pearlstone. Gabe pointed out that even though the neighboring farms were "spraying every chemical we can devise," there were still resistant weeds. He saw in this the power of nature, as he marveled at the "basic ability of the earth to grow and thrive," which he felt was "really profound."[71] Sydney noted that conventional agriculture upsets the natural balance and that approaches like growing in polyculture can help restore that balance. So, "instead of having to fertilize your particular crop, the other plants will do it for you." Sydney suggested that this would fill a "niche that conventional agriculture takes away."[72] This was the goal of the restorative work at Pearlstone during the shmita year—to restore some of the balance that had been lost on the center's land and in their soil. So, with the soil at rest, the farmers were hard at work restoring the rest of Pearlstone's land. This suited them well, because, as Ava pointed out, "farmers don't rest."[73]

I learned more about Sydney's work that year as we hung lavender we had harvested a few days before to dry. She explained that her work on the farm during the shmita year was divided so that she spent 20 percent of her time in programs, 30 percent on the farm, and 50 percent in restoration, which she found the most interesting of the three. By the time I arrived that summer, she had been hard at work restoring Pearlstone's riparian zone—a wooded streamside area at the boundary between the farm and the woods. We had worked in the riparian zone the day before, and that hot afternoon of hard labor was the main reason why Sydney had assigned us our lavender task indoors that day. In the riparian zone, we had worked alongside a group of volunteers from an AmeriCorps program to clear out invasive species. Though clearing out invasive species was an important part of Sydney's restoration work, she clarified that she did not think invasive species were objectively bad. Instead, she offered her definition of invasive: "a non-native plant, meaning it didn't evolve here, that has the capacity to outcompete native plants and take over biodiversity."[74] Our restoration work was focused on reviving local biodiversity, so it necessarily involved the removal of the invasive plants. Our tasks the previous day included pruning thistles, removing honeysuckle that had overrun a hillside area, and cutting back invasive vines from indigenous trees planted in the zone. We also kept a careful eye on the spread of a parasitic species that Sydney had tentatively identified as Japanese dodder, which involved walking carefully to avoid stepping on it and removing remnants from our shoes by hand if we did step on it to avoid spreading the potential dodder elsewhere. At the end of the day, we were all scratched up, sunburned, and exhausted. A number of the volunteers reported back the next morning sporting inflamed poison ivy rashes, but I heard very few complaints.[75]

A few minutes spent with Sydney were enough to convince me that battling invasive species was important work. She explained that most of the invasive species she dealt with on a daily basis came to North America a few centuries ago, at a time when people weren't "thinking about the ecological ramifications." She didn't blame those historical plant lovers, but their actions had significant consequences. She told me that once invasive species take hold, they outcompete native plants and disrupt local ecologies. It was also very hard to get rid of them without herbicides, which Sydney clarified was a solution that was neither sustainable nor particularly effective. Sydney described herbicides as a "Band-Aid for a bullet wound" and suggested that what we really needed was "a dramatic change in thinking and behavior around our ecosystems." And for that to happen, we're going to need more people who care about this issue. Sydney argued that "it's a kind of ecological danger that people don't pay as much attention to as they should." She continued, "There's a real danger there and no one's really doing anything about it, or not doing enough, anyway."[76] Sydney's work at Pearlstone fit neatly within her twofold solution. She was working to restore native plants and the local ecology on-site, and she was also educating others on the threat of invasive species.

Sydney also completed a restoration project before my arrival. She had designed and planted a model edible forest garden. She acquired permissions from the Baltimore County Department of Environmental Protection and Sustainability and began a partnership between Pearlstone and the Alliance for the Chesapeake Bay for the Trees. Bolstered by a mini-grant she was awarded by the Chesapeake Bay Trust, she was able to set up a garden that showcased Baltimore's indigenous plants and told their stories.[77] She also ensured that the garden was ecologically healthy and sustainable. Sydney explained that she set up the garden with "little pockets of polyculture where the tree was the nucleus and then there were things surrounding it." As an example, she told me that Pearlstone had a problem with Japanese stiltgrass, an invasive grass that takes over and doesn't let anything else grow, and this had endangered their native pawpaw trees.[78] So, Sydney set up the pawpaws with plants indigenous to the area surrounding them in her garden. Sydney described an example wherein a pawpaw tree was circled by blue wild indigo (*Baptisia australis*), which converts atmospheric nitrogen into forms that can be used by plants to aid growth. This was surrounded by another ring of green-headed coneflower (*Rudbeckia laciniata*) as ground cover; Sydney said that as it spread out, it was able to compete with the invasive stiltgrass. Then there were aster flowers, which Sydney explained would "harbor beneficial insects" like pollinators, which would help the tree to remain healthy.[79]

Planting with a polyculture method, as shown in Sydney's pawpaw example, protects native trees from invasive plants, adds usable nitrogen to the soil, and attracts beneficial insects, all without the use of herbicides, pesticides, and fertilizers. And Sydney noted that this method is "just mirroring the way nature works, but kind of taking a hold of it." All of these projects were part of Sydney's work to offset something she was studying at the time, which she called the nature-agriculture continuum. She explained that with conventional agriculture, "you're forcing nature to go in a direction that it doesn't want to go, so you need to supplement those actions with an input of energy."[80] In conventional agriculture, humans have to intercede and put in labor and time to deal with issues that nature had already developed solutions to combat. Sydney was working to lessen the need for human energy input. The polyculture plantings would establish a healthier local ecology, which aligned with Pearlstone's general focus on ecological restoration during the shmita year. This kind of work was not possible during the pre-shmita CSA years, when the farm staff had to focus their energy on growing and harvesting annual crops. The shmita year provided an opportunity for Pearlstone staff to repair some of the damage to the soil in their fields done by their annual planting and to their wooded areas done by the land's previous owners and by invasive species. And though this work was based in Judaism, it was carried out by a staff of Jews and non-Jews in collaboration with Jewish and non-Jewish organizations.

FREE-RANGE RELIGION AT PEARLSTONE

Shmita at Pearlstone included many elements that were not prescribed by the Hebrew Bible, and the flexibility of not having to adhere to all the shmita restrictions required in the land of Israel gave Pearlstone staff some flexibility to teach their community about the sabbatical year even as they continued to provide environmental education programs to the Jewish and non-Jewish communities in the Baltimore area. In this section, I'll describe the ways that Pearlstone's Jewish and non-Jewish staff implemented shmita practices and education and found ways to introduce shmita to diverse audiences. For example, in keeping with his belief that "everyone needs a sabbatical" and with Pearlstone's focus on community outreach, Jakir also implemented shmita days for the staff. Employees each got one extra vacation day and six additional days to use for community service during the shmita year. Jakir wanted "to give folks a few days to do something meaningful to contribute to the broader community." During my visit in the summer of 2015, Jakir and staff members I spoke with mentioned that many people had not yet used their shmita days. However, Jakir noted that some people had already done great things and that the shmita days were something he planned to keep even when the shmita year ended. He mentioned that carrying the days forward and continuing to call them shmita days was in keeping with the Jewish traditions related to Shabbat: "Just like you should bring Shabbat into the rest of the week, you should do the same with shmita and the rest of the years."[81] He thought the days might change a bit in structure and that they might try to organize one or two whole staff volunteer days in future years. This wasn't quite the year of rest that many saw in the biblical vision of shmita, but as Daniel noted, "Shmita looks different in late capitalism than it does in ancient Israel."[82] The shmita days were an innovative way to allow staff to get some extra time away from their jobs and invest in the community around them. The shmita days also demonstrate the ways that Pearlstone embodied and modeled Jewish values beyond the boundaries of the campus.

Throughout the shmita year, a few areas of the farm, including the Hebrew calendar garden and the greenhouse, were still being used for annual crops during the shmita year, which again speaks to the flexibility that observance of shmita outside the biblical land of Israel permits.[83] With these areas in use, the Pearlstone staff were able to continue their educational programs for school and camp groups throughout the year. Nora explained that they approached shmita-year programs in two ways: They created some new ones with shmita themes and framed some of their existing programs through the lens of shmita. Nora offered an example, explaining that they "do pickling workshops all the time," but during the shmita year, they framed those workshops with discussions about how preserving fresh vegetables would be important preparation for a shmita year.[84] This kind of creativity allowed the staff to run programs that had been successful in the past even as they prioritized shmita education throughout the year.

The staff also decided to hold a big community event, Shmita Fest, in June. Nora said the idea was to put on an event at the time of the year when the farm would usually be starting to produce and staff and visitors might begin to feel something was missing.[85] The morning of Shmita Fest, the staff set up canning and preservation workshops, art projects, an edible plant walk, a worm-composting demonstration, a text study, and the shmita simulation game.[86] In the end, the staff felt that the event was not very well attended, but as with all things shmita, this was an experiment, and the staff would have six years to figure out how to rework Shmita Fest to entice more of the community into participating in the future. The program staff also continued to run programs where groups could choose to visit the animals or the orchard, because those aspects of the farm hadn't changed much during the shmita year.[87] Jake emphasized that because Pearlstone is a Jewish educational farm, staff wanted to showcase shmita in their work throughout the year and teach people about it.[88] Many of the visitors to Pearlstone were not Jewish but were able to learn about Judaism through this kind of shmita education. Many of the educators were also not Jewish, and those who were had diverse backgrounds and relationships with their Judaism.

Before he started as farm director at Pearlstone in February 2015, Gabe ran an educational farm for the Baltimore City Public Schools for seven years. He was drawn to Pearlstone because it was similar work with "mission-based agriculture," and he liked that the job would blend familiar work with new things. Gabe observed that most farms where he had worked were driven by a common purpose, and at Pearlstone he had identified spirituality at the core of its mission. The spirituality Gabe noticed and incorporated into his own work was Jewish in nature, but employees from all backgrounds learned to incorporate Jewish values and teaching into their work. In Gabe's case, he was raised Roman Catholic but no longer identified as a Catholic. He and his family had practiced at a meditation center associated with Shambhala Buddhism for about a decade. He explained that he had learned a lot about Judaism during his time at Pearlstone but not through formal education. He said he was picking it up "relationally" through conversations with employees and visitors and compared his experience to learning a foreign language.[89]

Gabe observed that "Judaism influences people in their own way of living and relating to people," and one of the things he enjoyed most about the Judaism at Pearlstone was the singing. He appreciated being able to walk around and hear a visiting cantor. He liked the songs that the program staff incorporated into educational programs and the prayers that were commonly heard around the campus. He talked about the singing as something that wove the aspirations of Pearlstone into practice as a form of communication, pausing thoughtfully before saying, "I really love that." Gabe noted how the Jewishness of Pearlstone meant there was a different texture to the work because there were different stories as well as different permissions and taboos. And during the shmita year, in particular, Gabe appreciated the ways that Jewish stories and ideas were woven into the work as a priority, even when they weren't convenient. He compared this to his work with plants and animals, noting in those cases that one also has to do things when they aren't necessarily convenient because plants and animals "don't care what you think."[90] Gabe found things in the Jewish traditions around shmita and agriculture that connected both to his previous work on farms and practices like singing that made his work more enjoyable.

Sydney grew up in a Christian home. Her family was Lutheran, but she told me she didn't identify with a particular denomination as an adult. And though Pearlstone is a Jewish organization, she chose it for other reasons. Sydney went through a ranking process that each Chesapeake Corps volunteer goes through and chose Pearlstone because of the breadth of experience it offered. She remembered, "It just seemed like I would be learning a lot of skills and kind of get a more well-rounded experience here than I would have gotten anywhere else." Though she was acquiring a lot of experience, she found that the people were the best thing about her appointment "in a list of a lot of good things." And she learned a lot about Judaism but didn't feel pressured to do so. She explained that it was helpful for her job to understand shmita and Jewish terminology and beliefs so she could have conversations with the Jewish guests at Pearlstone about what they were doing and why they were doing it. She offered an example from before the shmita year started when she was working the CSA table "and someone comes up and says, 'Can I sign up for the CSA next year?' and I say, 'No' and they say, 'Why?' I have to have an answer for that." Sydney learned enough to explain the basics of shmita to answer those questions, but she said no one ever sat her down to explain the rules of shmita. Like Gabe, she picked up most of her Jewish knowledge through her relationships with her Jewish colleagues: "You just kind of have to learn through the atmosphere and listening to what other people are saying." This speaks to the power of the informal Jewish education that occurs at Pearlstone, even when programs and retreats are not in session. And although no one pressured her to do anything, she told me she had participated in almost every Jewish holiday that year with her coworkers and friends out of her own volition.[91]

One of the things Sydney noticed about Judaism at Pearlstone was the organization's "respect for the earth," which she described as a "commitment to understanding what's going on rather than trying to do what we do with no regard for the earth." In her time at Pearlstone, she also began to see religions beyond Judaism differently as well. She reflected that this probably happens "any time you immerse yourself in a new culture, a religion, or any kind of way of life that hasn't been known to you before." Interestingly, she saw the most change in her attitude toward Islam. Pearlstone hosts numerous Muslim groups throughout the year, so she had interacted with many Muslim guests through those programs. She reflected, "I think being here as someone that was raised Christian, working in a Jewish environment, and then hosting an Islamic group has made me more aware of the judgments that I would have been prone to, having not gained that kind of experience and perspective." Perhaps unsurprisingly, Sydney compared her experience working at Pearlstone to the plants she knew and loved. She told me that acquiring a "little seed of knowledge" can "grow into something bigger" and "bring something to light."[92] Sydney had certainly learned about ecological conservation while working at Pearlstone, but the little seeds of Judaism and Islam that she picked up along the way had also changed her worldview.

Some of the Jewish employees at Pearlstone also found that their relationships with Judaism changed or perhaps stayed the same but became a more active presence in their worlds. Daniel connected with Judaism by seeing himself as part of the Jewish people. He cited Benedict Anderson and told me that for him, being Jewish was about being part of a nation, an imagined community.[93] And Daniel found that the Jewish community was still really strong in the United States and in the Baltimore region, where he felt that strong communities were otherwise uncommon. He also appreciated that questioning was central to Judaism, and the practice that most resonated for Daniel was Shabbat. He told me he liked sharing food and singing together with people at Shabbat meals and that he even liked praying with other people, even though he didn't connect with Jewish theology. He explained, "I don't really believe that anyone's listening, but I think that other people in the room are listening."[94] Daniel's identification with the Jewish community aligned with his work at Pearlstone, where it was his job to engage that community in questioning, in Shabbat practices, and perhaps even in prayer.

Ava also mentioned Shabbat as a central aspect of her Jewish identity, and she told me that working at Pearlstone led her to observing Shabbat more often. But again, this shift was more about the people than the ritual elements of Shabbat. Prior to working at Pearlstone, she recalled that her friends either weren't Jewish or were Jewish but didn't practice Judaism. But at Pearlstone she had Jewish friends and coworkers, and they were able to practice Judaism together. That said, for Ava, the biggest change was less about practicing Judaism and more about prioritizing Judaism. She reflected, "Being Jewish became important to me." She recalled that in high school, her attitude had been "Yeah, I'm Jewish, but so what?" But at this point in her life, she was able to talk at length about Judaism and her own Jewish values. She also found that this increased attention to her Jewish identity was shaping what she wanted in a future partner and her plans for raising her future children.[95] For Jewish and non-Jewish employees, being part of Pearlstone's Jewish community shaped their work and, in many cases, altered their worldviews. The immersive experience of the employees was harder to replicate in shorter-term visits and retreats, but Pearlstone staff were doing their best to create meaningful Jewish and environmental experiences for the wider Jewish and non-Jewish communities.

Many of the groups that visit Pearlstone are not Jewish groups, including school groups from Baltimore that visit the farm annually. I asked Natalie how they explain shmita to non-Jewish groups. She said that they tell them, "We're taking a year off; just like on every seventh day God said we're supposed to rest, every seventh year we're also supposed to rest." She wasn't sure that many of the visitors even understood what it meant that Pearlstone "is a Jewish farm."[96] As Natalie noted, the religious identity of the farm seemed to play an especially interesting role during the shmita year. In other years, the farm looked like a farm. Perhaps the non-Jewish visiting groups were aware that the signage was in Hebrew or that the farm was located at a Jewish conference center, or maybe they just saw a farm. But during the shmita year, they saw a farm without vegetables and heard explanations about the land taking a sabbatical. The Jewish staff at Pearlstone had to figure out how to explain a relatively obscure Jewish concept to Jews and non-Jews, and the non-Jewish staff at Pearlstone also had to learn about shmita so they could answer questions posed by curious visitors.

Daniel mentioned that whether he was working with Jewish or non-Jewish students, his job was to connect them "with their natural environment and with the food that they eat" with the goal of helping them think about living a more sustainable life. He explained that a lot of this education was farm-based. Students engaged with the animals and learned about growing food. But he also did a lot of what he classified as "outdoor education," which most often involved him taking students into the woods to identify wild edibles and learn about ecology. He appreciated this approach to Jewish and non-Jewish education and thought that engaging students with different modalities was a good pedagogical method.[97] The farm and the forested areas at Pearlstone enabled students from urban environments to experience and appreciate the natural world. For Jewish groups, that was often framed as a Jewish value. With non-Jewish groups, staff members didn't go into detail on those values but did tell those groups that Jewish people value a connection with their food and with the natural world.

The shmita year offered the Jewish and non-Jewish staff at Pearlstone an opportunity to learn about an ancient textual tradition and reimagine and implement those traditions in the twenty-first century as a model for how Jews should engage with their land and their community. In addition to broader environmental education, the program staff worked hard to bring shmita to the rest of the Baltimore Jewish community through work on and off their own campus. Natalie and Daniel worked with a religious school group that visited once a month, and Natalie also visited area preschools throughout the year. Through these programs they taught young Jews from all over the Baltimore area about the environment, sustainability, and shmita. Pearlstone staff also did a lot of work to educate their fellow Jewish professionals in the Baltimore area. Jakir taught a shmita session for the Jewish professional development agency in Baltimore, which has between 500 and 1,000 members, and another shmita session for all the agency CEOs working under The Associated: Jewish Federation of Baltimore. His goal in these professional development sessions with Jewish professionals was to use the model of shmita to get them thinking about the effects of industrial food and industrial culture and the ways that long-term shifts toward more holistic ecological and social cycles could improve lives in their community.[98]

In another effort to provide education off their campus, Pearlstone staffers also launched ten Jewish community gardens in the Baltimore Jewish community. Jakir called these gardens a "micro-opportunity" and noted that they often measured ten-by-ten feet or less. These gardens were built at diverse Jewish institutions, including early childhood centers, synagogues, day schools, a college Hillel (a Jewish campus organization), and a senior center. Jakir told me that these gardens had worked well as an engagement tool and that they were giving Jews of all ages a direct experience with food and growing things that they might not otherwise have.[99] In all of these efforts throughout the shmita year, the Jewish and non-Jewish staff at Pearlstone worked together to enact a meaningful and educational sabbatical year. As they engaged both Jews and non-Jews in environmental education based on the principles of the shmita year, many people learned more about this ancient practice and the ways that it offers a glimpse into a world where community; connection to the land, food, and animals; rest; and release are the most important things in life.

CONCLUSION

Shmita came at a good time for Pearlstone in many ways. The ability to take a break and re-vision its food system was particularly useful for the Pearlstone Retreat Center farm. Jake emphasized that shmita, which centers sustainability as a Jewish value, was a good fit for the organization "in a time of environmental degradation and destruction." He also told me that the farm had been struggling financially on a few levels leading up to shmita. He felt the timing was ideal for the farm and that its needs were "really true to the meaning of shmita."[100] Jakir suggested that responding to challenges like these were why shmita is important, because it was "a useful and real rhythm that allows release of people, of land, of things that need to be released."[101] Gabe expressed an admiration for the precedent that shmita had set, which allowed Pearlstone to take this year to rebuild. He elaborated, "There's no way that you stop, basically, and focus on fundamentals for a year in the middle of your eighth year unless you have something that gives you some type of permission, like cultural currency to do that."[102] The cultural precedence of shmita allowed the staff to take a crucial break and enabled them to move forward with a clear idea of where they were going. Jake added that shmita would allow them to "take a year to really bring in new people, do market research, [and] craft a farm business plan that was going to hold water financially." Jake also found the shmita year personally fulfilling as he shifted to part-time work at Pearlstone during that time, which allowed him to start his own business installing and maintaining gardens for families, businesses, and schools.[103]

As Jake stepped back, Gabe stepped into the farm director role and began working on a seven-year shmita cycle business plan that would guide the farm through to the next shmita year. Part of that plan included getting more of the food grown on the farm into Pearlstone's kitchen. Gabe was working with Pearlstone's head chef on a plan to bring more of the food from the farm into Pearlstone's dining room.[104] Jakir was excited about this development and felt that this shift would transform Pearlstone into "a one-of-a-kind kosher farm-to-table establishment." He also felt that the shmita year had set the organization up well to thrive on its seven acres of land.[105] This was a particularly interesting reflection in 2015, given that in 2017, Pearlstone acquired the Camp Milldale property next to Pearlstone.[106] After that acquisition, Pearlstone engaged in a master planning process to develop a vision for its expanded footprint of 180 acres. As I walked the larger property with Jakir in 2018, he emphasized that ecological restoration and reforestation were still central components of Pearlstone's strategy for stewarding its land.[107]

In 2016, Pearlstone was awarded one of the first Lippman Kanfer Prizes for Applied Jewish Wisdom in recognition of its farm-based Jewish education, food justice teaching, and implementation of shmita.[108] Shmita was good for the land, the animals, and the people at Pearlstone. The staff tried a lot of new things, and some of them worked and some of them needed retooling, but on the whole, the staff considered the year a success. Gabe found the year rejuvenating and reflected, "It's quiet, we're all hearing the birds, we're all regaining our energy."[109] Jakir felt that the year "certainly resonated on the deep level of what is shmita supposed to mean, how is it supposed to feel, and then what are you supposed to come out of it with?" He continued, "Agriculturally it feels like very, very much an A+."[110] The staff also felt that there was potential in shmita for more innovation and restoration in the years to come. There were aspects of shmita that seemed out of reach in a time when Jews and their foodways, social lives, and finances were as deeply intertwined as they were in the contemporary United States. Nora addressed this: "It takes a community saying yes, we are all going to do this, because it doesn't work if not everybody is doing it." Without complete community participation, complete land and debt release are not possible. In a fully implemented shmita year, people would need to work together, share food, and agree to release debts. In Nora's words, "This whole structure has to move and shift."[111] Ava marveled at the power of some of these aspects of shmita that Pearlstone was not in the position to apply, like forgiving debt: "I think as an idea it's great. Just imagining the way that would change society now is crazy."[112] Ava's enthusiasm about debt release is a good example of how aspects of shmita invigorated Jews in the United States who were facing issues that shmita was well-positioned to address. There was a deep sense, at Pearlstone and in the broader Jewish community, that the world was in need of repair.

Because Pearlstone had already established an alternative food system on-site, staffers were able to engage shmita on multiple levels and relate their work to other Jewish traditions. Jake described his feelings about the industrial food system in relation to kashrut, the kosher food system. He defined kosher as "food that is pure" or "food that is fit to eat," explaining that the idea of kosher "juxtaposed with our planet-crushing, soul-crushing industrial food system and the political and financial systems that make it so incredibly dysfunctional and hypocritical." He finished this thought by stressing to me that he felt this, "as we say in Hebrew, *al-bisari*, in my flesh."[113] Jake felt that shmita was one of the Jewish concepts that could help realign kosher food with food that is sustainable. Jakir asserted that shmita was "certainly a deep value-based response . . . or alternative to industrial food."[114] Pearlstone and the other organizations and individuals united by the Shmita Project used the year to reimagine and reinvigorate shmita. They encouraged Jews to consider an environmentally sustainable agricultural model and a diet based on ethical food production, conscious consumption, and food security. Pearlstone provided a model for the Jewish community with its unprecedented agricultural observance of the shmita year in the Diaspora. Other organizations like the Jewish Farm School and Adamah introduced Jews to shmita in other ways, through text studies focused on shmita, skill-acquisition workshops, and creative innovations like Adamah's community shmita garden.

As the subsequent shmita year began in September 2021, Pearlstone merged with Hazon and the Isabella Freedman Jewish Retreat Center, making this collective, renamed Adamah, not just the largest Jewish environmental organization in the United States but the largest religious environmental organization in the United States.[115] Shmita remains a central part of the organization's work. The Shmita Project, housed under the Hazon brand, has offered accessible educational resources and a new program, Shmita Prizes, which focused on the arts as a way to explore the values of shmita in the 2021–22 sabbatical year.[116] This analysis of shmita at Pearlstone in 2014–15 provides a glimpse into one version of how this vision for a revitalized shmita practice was both practical and possible in the United States and how it might appeal to Jews and non-Jews alike.[117] It is unlikely that Jews will ever manage to fully implement shmita in the United States, but awareness and observance of shmita has grown in each of the last three shmita years, so perhaps time will continue to reveal the potential power of shmita.

Conclusion

The stone that the builders rejected has become the chief cornerstone.

PSALMS 118:22 (JPS)

INTRODUCTION: "FEED ME"

Each morning after Avodat Lev, the morning "Service of the Heart," the Adamah fellows did morning chores. During my second week at Adamah, I joined Rose and Debby for the compost chore, which Rose enjoyed and Debby hated. It was the most physically challenging assignment, and that, combined with the sights and smells that accompany compost, made it the least desirable. However, all of the fellows rotated through all of the chores. So, every morning that week at seven o'clock, the three of us put on our rain boots and walked down to the area outside the Isabella Freedman Jewish Retreat Center kitchen. Inside this fenced-in outdoor space were about fifteen bins filled with food waste and compostable tableware. The smell of food in various states of decay overwhelmed us as we stepped in to gather bins, some of which were so heavy that it took two of us to lift them. Each day that week, Debby, Rose, and I struggled to move a meager four to six bins up Beebe Hill with our wooden pushcart, although they told me that the staff was also able to move the bins with trucks. Later in my visit, I assisted the manager at Adamah's cultural center with its compost, and it took the two of us about a quarter of the time it had taken Rose, Debby and me and was far less strenuous because we were able to transport the bins in a pickup truck. However, the point of the compost chore isn't really to move compost from one place to another; it is about understanding compost. On foot, we felt the weight and smelled the decomposing food waste and were meant to gain an appreciation for the role that compost plays in Adamah's sustainable agriculture program.

After our arduous walk up the hill, we'd arrive at the compost yard, which also housed Adamah's chickens. Rose and I would climb up on a large pile, which was marked "Feed me!" with a hand-painted sign, and we would empty the bins as our boots sank into the soft mound. Then we would gather wood chips from a pile at the edge of the compost area to cover the fresh food waste. The wood chips added carbon to the pile, which is a necessary ingredient for balanced compost, and eventually soil. While we emptied the bins, Debby would turn on the hose and wash out the empty bins. We often chatted with Sam, who was assigned to the chicken chores and worked alongside us as he opened the coop to let the chickens out and then gathered the eggs they left behind. As we loaded the empty bins onto the carts and headed back down the hill, the chickens began their daily routine, which involved walking through the compost yard, eating the food waste, and donating their nitrogen-rich poop to the piles.[1]

There were always four piles in the compost yard, sorted according to their state of decay. "Feed me!" was the first pile, and as described above, it comprised recognizable fresh food waste, wood chips, and weeds from the farm. Some food items were also still visible in the next pile, which was marked "Are we there yet?" Only compostable utensils were still visible in the third pile labeled "Still cookin'." The final pile bore a sign that read "The good stuff," and that pile contained dark and rich soil that was ready for the fields. The signs moved as the piles decomposed. Through a process called thermophilic composting, the heat in the piles breaks the food waste down into forms more suitable for application onto soil. The result of this carefully regulated process is an ideal organic fertilizer.[2] Put another way, composting is the process of bringing diverse waste materials together and transforming them into a valuable and usable product. This process requires chicken labor,

Compost piles at the Adamah Farm Fellowship, July 2015.

"The good stuff" compost pile at the Adamah
Farm Fellowship, December 2015.

as they pick through the piles and keep the compost aerated, and human labor, including moving bins of food waste up the hill, turning the piles, and checking the compost temperature in all weather. This human-chicken compost collaboration was quite efficient. When I returned to the Isabella Freedman Jewish Retreat Center six months later, the pile where we had added fresh food waste during those morning trips was now marked with "The good stuff" sign.[3]

The compost yard is not unlike the history of religious alternative food systems in the United States. For the last two centuries, people have been motivated by their religious beliefs, texts, and traditions to try to transform the food system from what they see as a wasteland of inedible food into "the good stuff," or perhaps at least better stuff. These transformations involve collaborations between humans, animals, and land and draw on systems that worked in the past in an effort to engender a different future. In this concluding chapter, I'll use the compost pile labels as markers as I consider the past, present, and future of religious alternative food movements.

Each chapter of *Free-Range Religion* has offered a glimpse into a group of religious people who, for various reasons, considered the food available on supermarket shelves inadequate and came together outside traditional institutional religious spaces and worked to grow, process, prepare, and consume food that they felt was more sustainable, healthier, and in line with their religious values. At Adamah, the farm fellows grew vegetables, cared for animals, and learned more about Judaism, social justice, and themselves. The Hallelujah Diet appealed to a diverse audience of Christians who sought to improve their physical health by realigning their dietary habits with the biblical diet they believed God intended for them, and they encountered non-Christians and non-Christian practices as they participated in the Hallelujah Diet Health Retreat and the broader diet culture in the United States. V. Mac Baldwin raised his cattle on pasture in accordance with his Christian beliefs, but his business thrived because he partnered with a Muslim slaughterhouse and secular grocery stores to process and sell his product. The non-Jewish farm director at Pearlstone Center implemented ancient Jewish agricultural practices, like shmita, the biblical agricultural sabbatical year, while the program staff developed programming to teach Jews and non-Jews of Baltimore about agriculture, nature, and Judaism. In each of these case studies, creative collaborations between people with diverse religiosities resulted in alternative systems to produce and consume food that was conceived of as "better." The designation of "better" varied depending on the context: At Adamah it was sustainable, at the Hallelujah Diet Health

Retreat it was alive, at Baldwin Family Farms it was humane, at Pearlstone it was restorative—and these are just four examples of the many communities and companies in the alternative food movement. However, the religious ideologies that pervaded each group described here altered the ways that participants and employees conceived of the foods they were producing and consuming. The foods produced and consumed at Adamah, the Hallelujah Diet Health Retreat, Baldwin Family Farms, and Pearlstone Center were sustainable, alive, humane, and restorative, but they also acquired sacrality as a result of their production and consumption within broader religious systems.

The case studies demonstrated that people have been motivated by their religious beliefs and traditions to oppose the American industrial food system through the establishment of religious alternative food systems. As these groups engaged in what I've called free-range religion, they worked outside traditional religious institutions and in partnership with coreligionists, people from other religious groups, and people with no religious affiliation at all. Up to this point, I have focused on the people in these religious alternative food movements. In the next section of this concluding chapter, I will reflect on the food itself and the conceptualization of food in the history of the religious alternative food movements in the United States. As these groups turned their attention to food, they often shifted from understanding food as profane to seeing food as a sacred and vital component of their relationship with the divine. In the section after that, I'll focus on the religious alternative food movement groups described in this book and on others that developed alongside these groups over the last decade. In the final section, I'll reflect on the future potential of this movement and also on the ways that free-range religion thinking has been and could be applied in religious studies more broadly.

FOOD AS SACRED: "ARE WE THERE YET?"

In the mid-twentieth century, the anthropologist Mary Douglas theorized that purity is a central concern in human societies and that people were especially prone to distinguish between clean and unclean in their sacred spaces. The food laws of Leviticus were a key example in her analysis.[4] These laws, as they were formulated in the Hebrew Bible, were meant to ensure the purity of the sacrifices offered in the First and Second Temples of the ancient Israelites. These laws became the basis for the kosher food laws, and rabbis in every era of Judaism have turned to the laws to figure out what was "fit to eat" for their communities and what was not. As Christianity and Christian theology developed, it was determined that the food laws no longer applied, and other than particular foods used for rituals, food was generally desacralized.[5] A similar shift occurred in Judaism in the nineteenth century, as the rise of Reform Judaism brought with it a resistance to kashrut as the movement worked to adapt Judaism to the modern world. While Orthodox and other observant Jews contributed to the rise of the kosher industry in the United States, their liberal Jewish counterparts more often eschewed kashrut and its associated taboos.[6] As food in the United States became increasingly industrialized in the twentieth century and the distance between consumers and producers increased, religious people started seeing that food as impure and decided to seek out alternatives. The religious alternative food movements in the United States in every era represent a multifaceted effort to re-sacralize food.

As I discussed throughout the book, early religious alternative food movements in the United States involved efforts to label industrial food as "unclean" and encourage religious people to seek out "clean" or "pure" foods instead. Sylvester Graham prompted his followers to make their own bread at home instead of purchasing "adulterated" bread from bakeries; Zalman Schachter-Shalomi and Arthur Waskow exhorted Jews to incorporate environmental thinking into their observance of kashrut; Wendell Berry promoted a faith-infused form of agrarianism; and Nati Passow and Yigal Deutscher argued for the reintegration of shmita into Jewish communities in the United States. All of these individuals preceded the groups described in this book, and their work made space for ongoing innovation as people in the United States continued to seek out and establish alternative food systems based on their religious beliefs and traditions.

The religious alternative food movement groups discussed here approached food with the basic assumption that most of the food available for purchase in the United States was impure and unfit to eat. Each group had its own understanding of why the food in the United States was a problem. At Adamah and Pearlstone, participants were deeply concerned about the climate crisis, the environmental degradation caused by industrial monoculture farming, increased use of pesticides, and the alienation of American Jews from nature. They worked to repair the land, grow produce using sustainable and organic methods, and educate Jews of all ages and denominations about the agrarian context of the Bible and to provide Jewish alternatives to industrial agriculture. Their teaching materials and programs were not about kashrut as such, but they did encourage American Jews to work within a similar framework as they thought about what foods were fit to eat in the twenty-first century. George Malkmus, author of *The Hallelujah Diet*, and V. Mac Baldwin both considered the human body as a sacred entity created by God, which they believed functioned better on foods consumed closer to their natural state, as described in the Bible. The Hallelujah Dieters ate their vegetables and fruits raw and used juicing to increase their intake of vitamins and minerals. V. Mac raised his cows on pastureland, ensuring that the resulting beef products were filled with the omega-3s that he thought were a priority in a healthy diet. In each of these cases, the foods that were considered clean or fit were redefined in accordance with specific ideologies and theologies. In other words, within these groups, processed, factory-farmed food was rejected as taboo, while organic produce, raw fruits and vegetables, pasture-raised beef, and food grown in properly rested soil were seen as acceptable and even sacred, because these were the foods that these groups believed they were meant to consume according to their religious texts and traditions. There was an underlying assumption that all of the land, plants, animals, and humans on earth were created by God, and an attention to the relationships between these living entities was required to ensure the health and survival of them all.

As the title of this section suggests, the sacralization of food is by no means complete, even within the groups described in this book. Each religious alternative food movement group described here was encouraging people to approach food with new eyes, and at the sites I visited, people were engaging with food differently than they normally did. They learned more about agriculture, food preparation, animal welfare, and land restoration. But even the most enthusiastic visitors to these sites probably didn't alter their diets completely or in perpetuity. In the United States, people are used to food being convenient and cheap. The foods produced by the groups in this book rarely fell into these categories. For example, as I discussed in chapter 2, juicing was an inconvenient, time-consuming, and expensive process. However, the fact that these practices were unlikely to be adapted wholly or widely does not diminish their importance. These groups reconnected people to food systems and urged them, as consumers, to seek alternatives that were sustainable, humane, and organic. The four groups discussed here do not make up the entirety of the religious alternative food movement; they are joined by many others in this work, and this movement has only grown since I completed the fieldwork for this book in 2015.

Sign on the Adamah Farm Fellowship compost yard gate, July 2015.

RELIGIOUS ALTERNATIVE FOOD MOVEMENTS IN THE UNITED STATES: "STILL COOKIN'"

The sign that hung on the gate to the compost yard at Adamah contained a verse from Psalms: "The stone that the builders rejected will be the cornerstone."[7] In the compost yard, food scraps were turned into compost, an invaluable and necessary resource for organic farms like Adamah. However, composting is a slow process. Even in optimal conditions, decomposition of food waste is slow, and it takes even longer for compostable utensils, cups, and plates to break down. As humans, chickens, and microorganisms worked together to aid the process, it still took months for a pile to look like a cohesive whole instead of an amalgamation of apple cores, compostable forks, weeds, wood chips, and chicken poop. Similarly, the contemporary religious alternative food movements in the United States are diffuse and diverse. They have different goals, attract different audiences, and incorporate different religious traditions, beliefs, and practices.

The humans in each group described here were reconceptualizing their place in the world in relation to the animals and plants that they depended on for survival. Through their work, they came to see themselves as one piece of an entanglement of living things. The communities described here focused on food system change through agriculture and the consumption of minimally processed foods. They grew cucumbers and raised chickens, goats, and cows. They ate raw fruits and vegetables and gave the land a restorative Sabbath. The underlying assumption of all of these groups was that the current methods of food production, especially factory farming and industrial monoculture farming, were unsustainable. In response, these religious alternative food movement groups grew food using sustainable methods that prioritized soil health, which would enable them to continue growing food for many years to come. The Hallelujah Diet encouraged people to change their diets to improve their bodily health and lengthen their lives. At Baldwin Family Farms, V. Mac revitalized his farmland and worked to ensure its status as agricultural land in perpetuity as he raised cows on pasture to increase the nutrient content of their meat. In each of these groups, environmental sustainability was prioritized as part of a larger effort to sustain human bodies. All of these efforts were motivated and bolstered by the religious context in which they were developed. Close readings of biblical sources and other religious traditions engendered new perspectives on human-animal and human-land relationships as these groups established systems that produced food they wanted to eat.

The religious alternative food movement also continues to grow. Though I discussed only the Adamah Farm Fellowship and Pearlstone here, there is an ever-expanding network of Jewish community farming organizations with locations in the United States, Australia, Canada, Israel, and the United Kingdom. There are countless raw vegan restaurants in cities across the country, and new diet books and programs aimed at Christians in the United States are launched every year. The increasing demand for Baldwin Beef kept V. Mac and his staff busy clearing land so they could grow more grass and feed more cows. Research into alternatives like cultured meat has grown, and new plant-based meat alternatives appear on supermarket shelves regularly.[8] These movements have also expanded their reach through social media, and some of the ideas that were developed in these movements have gained traction among increasingly powerful people. The ideologies that undergird the Hallelujah Diet, especially those that suggest avoiding modern medicine in favor of dietary changes, are not dissimilar from those that convince people to avoid life-saving vaccines or pasteurized milk. If scholars continue to pay close attention to the history of religious alternative food movements and the food systems that were developed and promoted by groups like those in this book, we will be better equipped to navigate a world where ideas based in these lineages are becoming more mainstream.

Religious food justice activism is a growing sector of the broader food justice movement in the United States. These religious communities, which are most often also communities of color, are working to establish alternative food systems that address not only issues within the food system but broader social justice issues as well. Christopher Carter analyzes this movement in his book *The Spirit of Soul Food*, where he argues that "food justice should be significant to Black people due to the negative impact the US food system has on Black people and Black communities." Carter identifies historical movements like Fannie Lou Hamer's Freedom Farm Cooperative and more recent efforts like Heber Brown's Black Church Food Security Network and Leah Penniman's Soul Fire Farm, all of which have worked to address food insecurity in Black communities as well as racial, food, and environmental justice.[9] Penniman, whose work is informed by her own multireligious identity, provides a particularly interesting example of the ways that religion shapes food justice work in communities of color. As she wrote in her book *Farming While Black*, she initially thought she "was alone in identifying with Earth as Sacred Mother" but came to find that her "African ancestors were transmitting their cosmology" to her, "whispering across time, 'Hold on daughter—we won't let you fall.'"[10] For Penniman and many others in the food justice movement, religion is part of their work, even if it is not the focus of it. As work expands in this area, scholarship will hopefully follow and continue to illuminate the ways that people have been and continue to be motivated by their religious beliefs and principles to change the food system and make it more just for all the humans, animals, plants, and lands involved.

CONCLUSION: "THE GOOD STUFF"

The increased visibility of the climate crisis has drawn more attention from religious communities to the environment in recent years, even from the late Pope Francis, who dedicated an encyclical to the topic.[11] As interest and advocacy around environmental issues has grown, so has interest and advocacy around food and food justice. There is also work happening in areas that are directly related to food production and consumption, including industrial agriculture, animal welfare, food insecurity, migrant labor, and land sovereignty. This book touched on just four examples of an ever-expanding web of religious alternative food movements, and these burgeoning movements require sustained scholarly attention.

This book is also about studying religion as it happens outside long-established institutions. Religion in the United States is a dynamic phenomenon, and attention to its less-formal manifestations is essential for a holistic understanding of the role of religion in historical and contemporary lives. The examples here demonstrate that what appear to be Jewish farms, Christian diets, and Christian farms on the surface are more complicated than they initially appear. Participants in these sites and groups drew on a diverse array of religious and secular sources as they developed their alternative food systems and provided education, food, and experiences to a wide audience. These collaborative efforts are not easy to categorize, but that doesn't mean they shouldn't be studied. In the case of the religious alternative food movement groups and beyond, if we find that religious activities or people are difficult to categorize, it's probably a good sign to rethink our categories. This book is not about Jewish farms or Christian diets. *Free-Range Religion* is about a multireligious movement of people who didn't just change what they ate. They were inspired by their religious values and traditions to transform the food system in the United States. They have different ideas of what the food system should look like, and there are many other dedicated activists and communities working in the alternative food movement space, sometimes together and sometimes in opposition. Whatever successes or failures the alternative movement faces in the coming years, religious people will be there, working to enact their visions of a better food future for their communities—and for us all.

NOTES

INTRODUCTION

1. Matthew 11:28 (English Standard Version).

2. Alkon and Agyeman, "Introduction," 2–3. Alkon and Agyeman's critiques of the food movement's lack of attention to race, class, and gender are essential, even if they did miss religion, and their critiques will be discussed in more detail below.

3. Participant observation, Baldwin Family Farms, June 9, 2015.

4. In 2015, when I did the fieldwork for this book, Adamah was a farm fellowship program at the Isabella Freedman Jewish Retreat Center, which was at that time part of Hazon and most often referred to simply as "Adamah." Hazon later merged with Pearlstone Center, another field site for this book, and the merged organization was renamed Adamah. Under the merger, Adamah is now called the Adamah Farm Fellowship, and Pearlstone Center is now the Pearlstone Campus of Adamah. For the purposes of this book, I will generally refer to the Adamah Farm Fellowship as Adamah and to the Pearlstone Center as Pearlstone Center or Pearlstone.

5. Both the West Virginia and North Carolina retreat centers have ceased operations. The Hallelujah Diet currently operates one retreat center in Kingston, Georgia.

6. Sack, *Whitebread Protestants*, 190–91.

7. Weisenfeld, *New World a-Coming*.

8. For an in-depth analysis of a vertically integrated pork operation, see Blanchette, *Porkopolis*.

9. Gottlieb and Joshi, *Food Justice*, x, xi.

10. Alkon and Agyeman, "Introduction," 2, 4.

11. Broad, *More Than Just Food*, 7.

12. Schorsch, *Food Movement, Culture, and Religion*, 3.

13. LeVasseur, *Religious Agrarianism*, 1.

14. Van Wieren, *Food, Farming and Religion*, 14–15.

15. Imhoff, *Lives of Jessie Sampter*, 60.

16. These are industry standard definitions used by the United States Department of Agriculture (USDA) and by animal welfare organizations, like Global Animal Partnership, which certifies Baldwin Beef.

17. Mercadante, *Belief without Borders*, 4.

18. Fuller and Parsons, "Spiritual but Not Religious," 15–16.

19. Pew Research Center, *Jewish Americans in 2020*, May 11, 2021, www.pewresearch.org/religion/2021/05/11/jewish-americans-in-2020/.

20. Pew Research Center, *Jewish Americans in 2020*.

21. R. Gross, *Beyond the Synagogue*, 5.

22. Jain, *Peace Love Yoga*, 2, 6.

23. Lofton, *Consuming Religion*; McDannell, *Material Christianity*; Schmidt, *Consumer Rites*.

24. Hulsether, *Capitalist Humanitarianism*.

25. Orsi, *Between Heaven and Earth*, 190.

26. Orsi, *Between Heaven and Earth*, 2.

27. Jain, *Peace Love Yoga*, 22.

28. Lucia, *White Utopias*, 5.

29. Douglas, *Purity and Danger*.

30. Orsi, *Between Heaven and Earth*, 185.

31. Griffith, *Born Again Bodies*; Bender, *Heaven's Kitchen*; Mehta, "'I Chose Judaism.'"

32. See Haraway, *Staying with the Trouble*; Hodder, *Entangled*; Morton, *Hyperobjects*; and Tsing, *Mushroom at the End of the World*.

33. Hodder, *Entangled*, 5–6.

34. In rabbinic Judaism, matrilineal descent is the traditional indicator of Jewish identity. The Reform movement began to recognize patrilineal descent in the early 1980s and accepts people like me who have a Jewish father and a non-Jewish mother as Jewish. But the contemporary Orthodox and Conservative movements continue to recognize only matrilineal descent. I discuss the ways that these decisions affected the pluralism of Adamah in the first chapter of this book.

35. It also helped that all of the fieldwork for this book was conducted prior to the particularly divisive political era that began with the presidential election in 2016.

CHAPTER 1

1. When I was at Adamah in 2015, the fellowship program and the farm were most often simply referred to as "Adamah." Adamah and its umbrella organization, Hazon, finalized a merger with Pearlstone (the subject of chapter 4) in 2023, and the entire organization is now called Adamah, the farm is the Adamah Farm, and the fellowship is the Adamah Farm Fellowship. I use "Adamah Farm" and "Adamah Farm Fellowship"

here to refer to those specific programs, but I also use "Adamah" as a general term for both, as it was used in 2015.

2. All of the names of the Adamah Farm fellows, Adamah apprentices, and former Isabella Freedman employees have been changed to protect their privacy. However, I did not change the names of the Adamah staff, because their names and photographs appear on the Adamah website and social media pages, which are freely accessible to the public.

3. The text of this blessing relates to the distinction between the sacred (Shabbat) and the profane (the rest of the week).

4. Participant observation, Adamah Farm Fellowship, July 4, 2015. All participant observations in this chapter refer to specific locations within the Adamah Farm Fellowship.

5. This is a reference to Genesis 2:7: "God formed the Human [*adam*] from the soil's humus [*adamah*], blowing into his nostrils the breath of life: the Human [*adam*] became a living being." This is the Jewish Publication Society's most recent translation, though it notes that a more precise definition would be "loose dirt from the soil," and a previous JPS version translated *adamah* as "dust of the earth." I use "earth" and "earthling" both for simplicity and to align with common use at Adamah, where the organization often uses the terms "earth" and "earth-based Judaism," in particular. It also translates *adam* and *adamah* as "people & planet" (Adamah website, accessed April 22, 2025, https://adamah.org/about-adamah/). It should further be noted that *adam* is a masculine noun, so it is often translated using gendered terms for humanity like "man" or "mankind." The organization Adamah and the Adamah Farm and Adamah Farm Fellowship are intentional about avoiding that kind of gendered terminology.

6. "Adamah Farm Fellowship," Adamah website, accessed July 31, 2024, https://adamah.org/for-teens-youth-adults/adamah-farming-fellowship/.

7. Shamu Sadeh has had a number of titles over the years. In 2015 when I was at Adamah, he was director. More recently, in 2024, his title was managing director of education.

8. The fellows have the option to sleep outside in tents in a different area of the retreat center, but those fellows still participate in homesteading chores and eat meals in the Beit Adamah.

9. The fellows often refer to themselves as fellows, but they also use the Yiddishized monikers Adamaniks, Springniks, Summerniks, and Fallniks. I use "fellows" here because in my experience, "niks" nicknames are insider language usually reserved for participants and alumni of the Adamah Farm Fellowship program. I use "fellows" to mean "those in the fellowship" and not as a colloquial gendered term for men.

10. The daily schedule I experienced was very similar to that described in "A Typical Adamah Farm Fellowship Day" on the Adamah website, accessed June 20, 2024, https://adamah.org/wp-content/uploads/A-Typical-Adamah-Farm-Fellowship-New.pdf.

11. The Topsy Turvy Bus is a small yellow school bus with another small yellow school bus on top; the vehicle runs on vegetable oil.

12. For more information about the fellows' experiences with the demonstration and their subsequent decision-making around meat-eating, see my chapter, "Opening the Tent," in the edited volume *Jewish Veganism and Vegetarianism*.

13. "Rayna" interview. Dates of interviews in this chapter are found in the Adamah Farm Fellowship section of the bibliography.

14. "Sam" interview. The "Adamah-y thing" Sam references is Sadeh Farm (https://sadehfarm.co.uk/), which started in 2017.

15. The ADVA network comprises Adamah alumni and the alumni of Teva.

16. The farm at Pearlstone, discussed in detail in chapter 4, was started by Adamah and Teva alumni. I have also written about the broader Jewish community farming movement in a number of places, including an overview chapter, "Growing Food," in the edited volume *Feasting and Fasting*.

17. There were ten fellows when I arrived in mid-June 2015, but two left to pursue other opportunities while I was at Adamah. These departures were uncharacteristic of the program, so I do not delve into them here. Both of the fellows who departed show up in vignettes here, with pseudonyms (Leah and Shana), though they were not interviewed. Another fellow chose not to be interviewed and also shows up in vignettes with a pseudonym (Andie).

18. Janna Siller interview.

19. I'm borrowing "Judaisms" from Aaron Hahn Tapper, who argues that there have always been multiple forms of Judaism. See Tapper, *Judaisms*.

20. Janna interview.

21. אשרי יושבי ביתך עוד יהללוך סלה.

22. "Avodat Lev: Service of the Heart," Adamah binder, summer 2015, 22, digital images in author's possession.

23. The first line of the Shema, with gender-neutral language to mirror the language used at Adamah, is "Hear, O Israel, the Eternal is our God, the Eternal is one."

24. Participant observation, Avodat Lev, Beebe Hill, July 7, 2015.

25. Shamu Sadeh interview.

26. Participant observation, compost class, Kaplan Family Farm, July 8, 2015.

27. Herscher, *Jewish Agricultural Utopias in America*, 109–11.

28. Many individual Jews did settle as farmers during this period, but most of the philanthropic efforts emphasized communal settlement.

29. See Kranson, *Ambivalent Embrace*.

30. In one case, there is a direct link between a contemporary Jewish community farm and a historical one. William Levin, cofounder of the Alliance Community Reboot (ACRe) in Elmer, New Jersey, is the great-great-grandson of Moses Bayuk, one of the founders of the original Alliance Colony founded in Pittsgrove Township, New Jersey, in 1882. ACRe is rebuilding a modern collective Jewish farming community on land that was passed down through generations of Moses Bayuk's family through to the present.

31. LeVasseur, *Religious Agrarianism*, 83–84, 40. As mentioned previously, both the Adamah Farm Fellowship and the organization formerly known as Hazon are now part of an organization called Adamah.

32. For a more thorough overview of Jewish environmentalism, see my article "Judaism and Climate Change."

33. Tirosh-Samuelson, *Judaism and Ecology*, xxxiii.

34. Arthur Waskow is also a frequent visitor and speaker at various events at the Isabella Freedman Jewish Retreat Center, where Adamah is located. See Waskow, *Down to Earth Judaism*, for details on Schachter-Shalomi's eco-kosher ideas and their influence

on Waskow, and see Waskow, *Seasons of Our Joy*, for Waskow's discussion of environmentalism and Jewish holidays.

35. Ellen Bernstein had an extraordinary influence on Adamah. When she died in February 2024, the Adamah umbrella organization sent an email to all of its constituents with the subject line "Remembering Rabbi Ellen Bernstein, Jewish environmental matriarch," which speaks to her legacy (Adamah, email correspondence, March 1, 2024). Her most relevant work is Bernstein, *Splendor of Creation*, but all of her work is used throughout the Jewish environmental world.

36. Jacobs, "Jewish Environmentalism."

37. For an in-depth discussion of Jewish environmental ideas about creation, see my article "Judaism and Climate Change."

38. Bernstein, *Splendor of Creation*, 104.

39. Fenyvesi, "Befriending the Desert Owl," 30. Sometime between the publication of this article and my time at Adamah, Shamu shifted to primarily using Sadeh as a surname instead of Fenyvesi and sometimes using both together.

40. Fenyvesi, "Befriending the Desert Owl," 31.

41. Adamah binder, summer 2015, digital images in author's possession.

42. Aaron Gross defines *tza'ar ba'alei chayim* as "compassion for animals" in his book, which also provides a thorough discussion of the Jewish interpretations of this principle as well as Jewish responses to factory farming. See A. Gross, *Question of the Animal and Religion*.

43. Wertheimer, *New American Judaism*, 7.

44. Magid, *American Post-Judaism*, 1, 7, 8.

45. Wertheimer, *New American Judaism*, 17, 7.

46. Janna Siller, email correspondence with author, December 23, 2015.

47. Rebecca Bloomfield interview.

48. "Debby" interview.

49. "Elisa" interview.

50. "Zack" interview.

51. "Ari" interview.

52. "Sam" interview.

53. Mauss, "Techniques of the Body."

54. "Rose" interview. I actually met Rose prior to our encounter at Adamah. We were both participants at the Teva Seminar in 2012, but this prior encounter did not influence my work at Adamah.

55. Marx, *Economic and Philosophic Manuscripts of 1844*.

56. "Shira" interview.

57. "Amy" interview.

58. The album is titled *Release: Songs for Shmita*. It is available at https://hazon.bandcamp.com/album/release-songs-for-shmita.

59. During some retreats, the fellows ate in the dining hall with guests. During others, either because of the size of the group or the particular conditions the group set for their meals, the fellows ate at the BA.

60. Participant observation and photo, Beit Adamah, June 30, 2015.

61. Zeller, "Quasi-Religious American Foodways," 294, 302.

62. I measured this distance using Google Maps. It is an estimate.

63. These verses are cited on the sign as "Kohelet 3:1–2." Kohelet is the Hebrew title of Ecclesiastes. A slightly different translation of these verses inspired the Byrds' popular song "Turn! Turn! Turn! (To Everything There Is a Season)."

64. "Shira" interview.

65. "Max" interview.

66. "Shira" interview.

67. Participant observation, compost class, Kaplan Family Farm, July 8, 2015.

68. "Kitchen and Dining Policies and Procedures," Adamah binder, summer 2015, 14, digital images in author's possession.

69. "Debby" interview.

70. The Avodat Lev songs are popular enough that Adamah sells a CD compilation of the songs, recorded by Adamah fellows in 2007. It is available online as well (https://hazon.bandcamp.com/album/avodat-lev).

71. Participant observation, Isabella Freedman synagogue, July 1, 2015.

72. "Amy" interview.

73. "Rayna" interview.

74. "Zack" interview.

75. "Amy" interview.

76. Often non-Jewish milkers will be brought in to milk animals on Shabbat to avoid causing pain and working on Shabbat.

77. Participant observation, Adamah barnyard, July 1, 2015.

78. Participant observation, Beit Adamah, July 3, 2015.

79. "Elisa" interview.

80. Participant observation, Adamah Cultural Center, July 1, 2015.

81. Janna Siller interview.

82. "Elisa" interview.

83. "Miri" interview.

84. Minyans are counted differently in each movement of Judaism. In the liberal Conservative, Reform, Reconstructionist, and Renewal movements, Jewish men and women count. Conservative Judaism counts only those who converted or were born to Jewish mothers. Reform, Reconstructionist, and Renewal Jews count those who converted or were born to one Jewish parent.

85. Bahnson dedicates a chapter of his memoir, "Surpassing Civilization: Sukkot, Adamah Farm, Connecticut," to his experience at Adamah at Sukkot in Bahnson, *Soil and Sacrament*.

86. Shamu Sadeh interview.

87. Rebecca Bloomfield interview.

88. "Shira" interview.

89. Shamu Sadeh interview.

90. New moons are traditionally celebrated in Judaism. Rosh Chodesh ("Head of the Month") celebrations mark both the new moon and the beginning of a new month.

91. Participant observation, Isabella Freedman Library and Lake Miriam, July 1, 2015.

92. "Sam" interview.

93. "Debby" interview.

94. "Zack" interview.

95. See Sigalow, *American JewBu*.

96. As discussed in the introduction to this book, there are also valid critiques of the ways that Americans, and white Americans in particular, adopt Eastern religious traditions. The ways that Sam and Zack indicated that they were studying Hinduism and Buddhism suggests that Adamah's efforts to name the origins of these ideas and practices were helping fellows learn and engage these traditions with some awareness of these concerns. See Jain, *Peace Love Yoga*; and Lucia, *White Utopias*.

97. "Maya" interview.

98. Janna Siller interview.

99. I have written about the *sadeh* and the floods elsewhere; for further discussion, see "Farming on the Front Lines."

100. Participant observation, *sadeh*, July 10, 2015.

101. Participant observation, *sadeh*, July 10, 2015. The blessing mentioned, in translation, is "Blessed are You, Adonai, Ruler of the Universe, Who sanctifies us with the mitzvot and commanded us concerning immersion."

102. "Rayna" interview.

103. Rebecca Bloomfield interview.

104. Shamu Sadeh interview.

105. A combination of the pandemic and the reorganization of Hazon into what is now Adamah brought a pause in the food conference.

106. אדמה ושמים חום האש צליל המים אני מרגיש זאת בגיפי ברוחי בנשמתי.

107. "Avodat Lev: Service of the Heart," *Adamah Reader*, 23.

CHAPTER 2

1. All the names of the participants at the health retreat have been changed to protect their privacy. In earlier versions of this chapter, the real names of the retreat leaders were used because the health retreat center was still in operation and their names were accessible on the website. That is no longer the case, so for this version, I have used pseudonyms for them as well.

2. The Hallelujah Diet is the name of both the book and the movement that developed around it. I will italicize the phrase when referring to the book and will use plain text when referring to the movement or the retreat center.

3. "Rev. George Malkmus," Hallelujah Diet website, accessed July 1, 2024, myhdiet.com/pages/remembering-rev-george-malkmus.

4. Malkmus with Shockey and Shockey, *Hallelujah Diet*, 44.

5. "Rev. George Malkmus."

6. Malkmus with Shockey and Shockey, *Hallelujah Diet*, 65, 39.

7. "Rev. George Malkmus."

8. Malkmus with Shockey and Shockey, *Hallelujah Diet*, 56.

9. Malkmus with Shockey and Shockey, *Hallelujah Diet*, cover.

10. Malkmus with Shockey and Shockey, *Hallelujah Diet*, 39, 95, 161. It is true that many of the nutrients from fruits and vegetables are retained through juicing, but nutrients and other benefits are also lost in the discarded skin, pulp, and fibers from those plants.

11. George Malkmus passed away in November 2023 at the age of eighty-nine after a fall ("Rev. George Malkmus").

12. As of 2024, the store in Gastonia closed; the only headquarters remaining is in the United States; and there are no active retreat centers.

13. Various informal conversations, Hallelujah Diet Health Retreat, June 21–26. All interviews in this chapter are from this time period at the Hallelujah Diet Health Retreat.

14. "Home," Hallelujah Diet website, accessed August 31, 2015, www.myhdiet.com.

15. Malkmus with Shockey and Shockey, *Hallelujah Diet*, 184.

16. Metcalfe, *Address on Abstinence from the Flesh of Animals as Food*, 6–7.

17. Shprintzen, *Vegetarian Crusade*, 62.

18. Sack, *Whitebread Protestants*, 190.

19. Sack, *Whitebread Protestants*, 188.

20. Graham, *Treatise on Bread*, v, 42–45, 10, 18.

21. Graham, *Lecture to Young Men on Chastity*, 38, 59–60.

22. Nissenbaum, *Sex, Diet, and Debility in Jacksonian America*, 4.

23. White, *Counsels on Diet and Foods*, 303–4.

24. White, *Health*, 20, 30.

25. Graham, *Lecture to Young Men on Chastity*, 35.

26. Buettner, *Blue Zones*. The claims made by Buettner in *The Blue Zones* have been critiqued by Saul Justin Newman and others.

27. Nissenbaum, *Sex, Diet, and Debility*, xv.

28. Nissenbaum, *Sex, Diet, and Debility*, xv.

29. Sack, *Whitebread Protestants*, 185.

30. Malkmus with Shockey and Shockey, *Hallelujah Diet*, 80.

31. Sack, *Whitebread Protestants*, 190–91.

32. Malkmus with Shockey and Shockey, *Hallelujah Diet*, 79.

33. Malkmus with Shockey and Shockey, *Hallelujah Diet*, 91, 92.

34. Malkmus with Shockey and Shockey, *Hallelujah Diet*, 93, 94, 60.

35. Malkmus with Shockey and Shockey, *Hallelujah Diet*, 129, 141.

36. Malkmus with Shockey and Shockey, *Hallelujah Diet*, 161.

37. Malkmus with Shockey and Shockey, *Hallelujah Diet*, 114, 113, 53, 37.

38. In the summer of 2015, when I attended the retreat, the Hallelujah Diet was in the midst of a branding shift. In July 2014, the emails from the organization started coming from "Hallelujah Diet" instead of "Hallelujah Acres." The "health retreats" were formerly known as "lifestyle centers." Andrea explained that this change was due to the fact that they are teaching a diet, not farming.

39. "Andrea" interview.

40. "Andrea" interview.

41. "Lori" interview.

42. "Calvin" interview.

43. "Lori" interview.

44. "Danni" interview.

45. "Faith" interview.

46. "Mike" interview.

47. "Cathy" interview.

48. "Kendall" interview.

49. "Kendall" informal conversations.

50. "Erica" interview.
51. "Andrea" interview.
52. "Tom" interview.
53. Griffith, *Born Again Bodies*, 5.
54. Blazer, "Hallelujah Acres," 69.
55. Griffith, *Born Again Bodies*, 212.
56. Annie Blazer verified via email with me that "Tom" and "Andrea" were the retreat leaders she referenced in her chapter.
57. "Tom" interview.
58. The other Hallelujah Diet Health Retreat that was active in 2015 was run by Christians.
59. Ariel, *Evangelizing the Chosen People*, 220–21, 225.
60. Stern, *Messianic Judaism*, 3, 4.
61. Ariel, *Evangelizing the Chosen People*, 227–29.
62. "Tom" interview.
63. "Andrea" interview.
64. "Andrea" interview. In this case, Andrea used "Israel" to mean the people/nation of Israel, rather than the modern state of Israel, but they also flew both American and Israeli flags outside the health retreat house.
65. The two Messianic Judaism books that Andrea gave me to take home and think about call this claim into question. But I also recognize that my situation may be a unique case given my identity as both a Jew and as someone interested in religion.
66. Participant observation at morning devotions, Hallelujah Diet Health Retreat, June 21–26, 2015.
67. "Tom" interview.
68. Griffith, *Born Again Bodies*, 211.
69. "Erica" interview and "Cathy" interview.
70. "Andrea" interview.
71. Klippenstein, "Imagine No Religion," 391.
72. Pike, *New Age and Neopagan Religions in America*, 8–9.
73. Klippenstein, "Imagine No Religion," 401.
74. Pike, *New Age and Neopagan Religions in America*, 100–101.
75. "Erica" interview.
76. "Kendall" interview.
77. "Danni" interview.
78. "Oils of the Ancient Scripture," Young Living Essential Oils website, accessed April 22, 2025, www.youngliving.com/us/en/product/oils-of-ancient-scripture.
79. "Tom" interview.
80. Blazer, "Hallelujah Acres," 72.
81. "Lori" interview.
82. Malkmus with Shockey and Shockey, *Hallelujah Diet*, 68.
83. Campbell, foreword to *The Hallelujah Diet*, 24.
84. Malkmus with Shockey and Shockey, *Hallelujah Diet*, 89, 49.
85. Malkmus with Shockey and Shockey, *Hallelujah Diet*, 52.
86. "Mike" interview.
87. "Kendall" interview.

88. "Cathy" interview.
89. "Calvin" interview.
90. "Lori" interview.
91. "Mike" email correspondence.
92. "Erica" email correspondence.
93. "Tom" interview.

CHAPTER 3

1. Participant observation, Baldwin Family Farms, June 4, 2015.

2. In the United States, all cattle spend at least some of their time on pasture eating grass, but 95 percent of cattle are "finished" or "fattened" on grain, which means they spend the last 25–30 percent of their lives on feedlots eating grain-based feed. Grass-fed or grass-finished cattle spend their entire lives on pasture eating grass. The USDA used to certify grass-fed beef but revoked this certification in 2016. Tara L. Felix, Jessica A. Williamson, and David Hartman, "Grass-Fed Beef Production," PennState Extension, updated May 13, 2024, extension.psu.edu/grass-fed-beef-production.

3. V. Mac Baldwin interview, December 10, 2015.

4. Land-grant universities are often critiqued as "land-grab universities" because these fifty-two schools were built on 11 million acres of Indigenous land that was taken, or grabbed, from approximately 250 tribes, bands, and communities through 160 "violence-backed treaties and seizures." Robert Lee et al., "Land-Grab Universities," *High Country News*, accessed April 22, 2025, www.landgrabu.org/.

5. Baldwin interview, December 10, 2015.

6. "About Baldwin Family Farms," Baldwin Beef website, accessed December 29, 2021, www.baldwingrassfedbeef.com/shop/pc/viewContent.asp?idpage=16.

7. "The Baldwin Beef Story," Baldwin Beef website, accessed July 9, 2024, www.baldwingrassfedbeef.com/shop/pc/The-Baldwin-Beef-Story-d16.htm.

8. Baldwin interview, December 10, 2015.

9. There is a category of laws colloquially known as "ag-gag laws," which have been passed in many states. These laws have varied purposes, but they often seek to prevent people from posing as employees to record practices within factory farms and slaughterhouses and release the recordings to the public, which is a documented practice of the animal rights organization PETA (People for the Ethical Treatment of Animals).

10. General Assembly of North Carolina, Session 2015, "House Bill 405: Ratified Bill," accessed July 31, 2024, www.ncleg.net/Sessions/2015/Bills/House/PDF/H405v4.pdf. After sections of the act were struck down in 2020 by US district judge Thomas Schroeder, the Fourth Circuit Court of Appeals struck down the portion of the 2015 Property Protection Act that prevented animal rights groups from "newsgathering" while leaving other portions of the bill intact in February 2023 ("Split Federal Appeals Court Blocks NC from Stopping PETA's 'Newsgathering' Actions," *Carolina Journal*, February 23, 2023, www.carolinajournal.com/split-federal-appeals-court-blocks-nc-from-stopping-petas-newsgathering-actions/). North Carolina attorney general Josh Stein and the North Carolina Farm Bureau Federation asked the US Supreme Court to take the case, but the court declined to do so in October 2023 ("SCOTUS Rejects Case

Involving NC 'Ag-Gag' Law," *Carolina Journal*, October 16, 2023, www.carolinajournal.com/scotus-rejects-case-involving-nc-ag-gag-law/).

11. I hadn't expected to meet V. Mac that day, never mind engage him in an hour-long conversation, so I didn't have my tape recorder with me. This vignette is based on the notes I took while he spoke. Participant observation, Baldwin Family Farms, June 4, 2015.

12. "About Us," Gideons International website, accessed July 16, 2024, www.gideons.org/about.

13. Participant observation, Baldwin Family Farms, June 4, 2015.

14. Adam et al., "Christian Case for Farmed Animal Welfare," 1.

15. Wirzba, *Food and Faith*, 121.

16. Adam et al., "Christian Case for Farmed Animal Welfare," 5.

17. "The Positive Traditions" focus on examples of animal welfare in the Bible and human diets before the flood, which has a tendency to lead to vegetarianism. This was discussed in chapter 2.

18. McDaniel, "Practicing the Presence of God," 137.

19. McDaniel, "Practicing the Presence of God"; Linzey, *Animal Theology*; Clough, *On Animals*.

20. McDaniel, "Practicing the Presence of God," 137.

21. Other industries such as cosmetics and pharmaceuticals are also cited often as modern systems wherein animals are treated as mere commodities.

22. Singer, *Animal Liberation*, 186, 191.

23. Adam et al., "Christian Case for Farmed Animal Welfare," 8–9.

24. Descartes, "Letter to More."

25. Darwin, *Descent of Man*, 394–95.

26. Singer, *Animal Liberation*, 95.

27. Pachirat, *Every Twelve Seconds*, 3–4.

28. Kirby, *Animal Factory*, xiv, 32.

29. Felix et al., "Grass-Fed Beef Production."

30. Foer, *Eating Animals*, 33.

31. Kirby, *Animal Factory*, xiv.

32. Mathews and Johnson, *Alternative Beef Production Systems*, 2.

33. Fraser, "Caring for Farm Animals," 553. For a similar approach to understanding the biblical pastoralist ethics related to land, see Davis, *Scripture, Culture, and Agriculture*, as well as chapters 1 and 4 of this book.

34. Fraser, "Caring for Farm Animals," 553, 554.

35. Baldwin interview, December 10, 2015. This is a reference to Psalm 50:10, which reads, "For every beast of the forest is mine, the cattle on a thousand hills" (ESV).

36. "Article 61," North Carolina Department of Agriculture and Consumer Services, accessed April 22, 2025, www.ncleg.gov/EnactedLegislation/Statutes/PDF/ByArticle/Chapter_106/Article_61.pdf.

37. Participant observation, Baldwin Family Farms, June 9, 2015.

38. Baldwin interview, December 10, 2015.

39. Tobacco farming often involves the use of chemical pesticides and fertilizers, and tobacco depletes soil nutrients because it requires more nitrogen, phosphorus, and potassium than other major crops. See Novotny et al., "Environmental and Health Impacts."

40. LeVasseur, "Introduction," 1.

41. Berry, *Unsettling of America*, 7.

42. Wirzba, *Food and Faith*, 29, 24–27.

43. Van Wieren, *Food, Farming and Religion*, 14–15, 31.

44. Baldwin interview, December 10, 2015.

45. McDaniel, "Practicing the Presence of God," 141.

46. Baldwin interview, December 10, 2015.

47. Baldwin interview, June 4, 2015. It is not clear which biblical creation story he is referencing, but plants are created early in both Genesis 1 and 2.

48. Baldwin interview, June 4, 2015.

49. "Why Charolais (Char-Lay) Cattle," Baldwin Beef website, accessed December 31, 2021, www.baldwingrassfedbeef.com/shop/pc/viewContent.asp?idpage=17.

50. Baldwin interview, June 4, 2015.

51. This is an industry term for cattle that are grass-fed and pasture-grazed but then feed on grain the last 90–160 days before slaughter. I had been a vegetarian since 2011, so I did not try any of Baldwin Beef's products and can neither authorize nor contest V. Mac's claims about the taste of the meat.

52. Lim et al., "Consumer Preference for Grass-Fed Beef," 459.

53. "Why Charolais (Char-Lay) Cattle."

54. "Information about Our Grass Fed Beef," Baldwin Beef website, accessed December 29, 2021, www.baldwingrassfedbeef.com/shop/pc/About-Our-Beef-d9.htm.

55. Baldwin interview, June 9, 2015.

56. "Whole Foods Market Commits to Full GMO Transparency," Whole Foods Market website, March 8, 2013, media.wholefoodsmarket.com/whole-foods-market-commits-to-full-gmo-transparency/. The USDA published its own labeling standard, the "National Bioengineered Food Disclosure Standard," in the *Federal Register* in December 2018, which required the disclosure of bioengineered or genetically modified organisms if they were detectable in the final product (www.federalregister.gov/documents/2018/12/21/2018-27283/national-bioengineered-food-disclosure-standard). Whole Foods continues to maintain a higher standard and requires all non-GMO claims on product labels to be "third-party verified or certified" ("GMO Labeling," Whole Foods Market website, accessed July 16, 2024, www.wholefoodsmarket.com/quality-standards/gmo-labeling).

57. This information comes from the US Food and Drug Administration, and it has determined animal feed and human foods with GMOs to be safe for consumption ("GMO Crops, Animal Food, and Beyond," FDA website, accessed July 16, 2024, www.fda.gov/food/agricultural-biotechnology/gmo-crops-animal-food-and-beyond). The alternative food movement includes people who are concerned about GMOs and disagree with the FDA's assessment.

58. When I visited on June 4, 2015, V. Mac had just been audited by one certification agency, and it determined that it would cost him $1,650 for the certification.

59. Baldwin interview, June 4, 2015.

60. See Pachirat, *Every Twelve Seconds*; and A. Gross, *Question of the Animal and Religion*, as examples of critiques of USDA-inspected slaughterhouses.

61. "All-natural" is not a term regulated by the USDA. "Beef FAQs," Baldwin Beef website, accessed January 17, 2016, www.baldwingrassfedbeef.com/shop/pc/viewContent.asp?idpage=3 (page inactive).

62. "Beef FAQs."

63. Baldwin interview, June 4, 2015.

64. Baldwin interview, December 10, 2015. The National Institutes of Health Office of Dietary Supplements notes that study results related to omega-3s as a tool for cancer prevention have been inconsistent and vary by cancer in addition to other factors like gender and genetic risk ("Omega-3 Fatty Acids: Fact Sheet for Health Professionals," National Institutes of Health Office of Dietary Supplements, accessed July 16, 2024, https://ods.od.nih.gov/factsheets/Omega3FattyAcids-HealthProfessional/.

65. The NIH fact sheet does not contain information that would corroborate this claim but does say that "consumption of fish and higher dietary or plasma levels of omega-3s are associated with lower risk of heart failure, coronary disease, and fatal coronary heart disease" ("Omega-3 Fatty Acids: Fact Sheet for Health Professionals").

66. The NIH fact sheet does mention that omega-3 fatty acids have some anti-inflammatory properties ("Omega-3 Fatty Acids: Fact Sheet for Health Professionals").

67. "Beef FAQs."

68. "Recipes and Health," Baldwin Beef website, accessed January 17, 2016, www.baldwingrassfedbeef.com/shop/pc/viewContent.asp?idpage=4.

69. Baldwin interview, December 10, 2015; "Recipes and Health."

70. Baldwin interview, December 10, 2015.

71. Baldwin interview, December 10, 2015.

72. Baldwin interview, June 9, 2015.

73. The kosher chicken slaughter demonstration did not end up being part of this book because it was organized through a synagogue in Durham, North Carolina, rather than through one of the religious alternative food movement organizations discussed here.

74. Baldwin interview, June 9, 2015.

75. Baldwin interview, June 9, 2015.

76. Baldwin interview, June 9, 2015.

77. Baldwin interview, June 9, 2015.

78. Baldwin interview, June 9, 2015.

79. Baldwin interview, June 4, 2015.

80. Though I was worried about going to the actual slaughterhouse, I did reach out to Abdul Chaudhry in 2015 to try to arrange an interview, but I did not hear back.

81. Baldwin interview, June 4, 2015.

82. Baldwin interview, June 4, 2015.

83. Baldwin interview, December 10, 2015.

84. Despite V. Mac's best efforts, I remain a Jew whose interest in Jesus is purely academic.

85. Baldwin interview, June 4, 2015.

86. I suggested that Jews and Muslims don't view slaughter or the kosher and halal systems in relation to sin, but he was unconvinced. I did manage to point out the fact that kosher and halal slaughter procedures are not identical.

87. Baldwin interview, June 4, 2015.

88. This is also not how Jews understand kosher slaughter.

89. Chandia and Soon, "Variations in Religious and Legal Understandings," 715.

90. In 2024, that citation is no longer on the website banner.

91. Baldwin interview, December 10, 2015.

92. Baldwin interview, December 10, 2015.

93. Baldwin interview, December 10, 2015. I did not speak to the team leader or anyone at Whole Foods, so this story represents V. Mac's perspective on how Whole Foods came to carry Baldwin Beef.

94. Baldwin interview, December 10, 2015.

95. "Our Customer," Baldwin Beef website, accessed January 17, 2016, www.baldwingrassfedbeef.com/shop/pc/viewContent.asp?idpage=49 (page inactive).

96. Romans 8:28 (ESV).

97. Baldwin interview, December 10, 2015.

CHAPTER 4

1. When I was at Pearlstone Retreat Center in 2015, it was an independent retreat center under The Associated: Jewish Federation of Baltimore. Pearlstone merged with Hazon (the umbrella organization of Adamah, featured in chapter 1) in 2023, and the entire organization is now called Adamah and the Pearlstone Retreat Center is the Pearlstone Campus of Adamah. In this chapter, I refer to Pearlstone as "Pearlstone Center," "Pearlstone Retreat Center," or simply "Pearlstone," as it was called in 2015.

2. In 2022, the Chesapeake Conservation Corps became the Chesapeake Conservation and Climate Corps after the Maryland General Assembly passed the Climate Solutions Now Act ("Our Story," Chesapeake Conservation and Climate Corps Website, accessed April 21, 2025, https://cbtrust.org/chesapeake-climate-corps/). In 2015, it was still known as the Chesapeake Conservation Corps, so that is what I use here.

3. My visit in 2013 was a preliminary step toward my more in-depth research in 2015. I volunteered on the farm that year as a private individual and didn't conduct any interviews, so that visit will be mentioned only to provide information about the farm prior to the *shmita* year.

4. All the names of the Pearlstone employees who are no longer with Pearlstone or are in different positions in the organization have been changed to protect their privacy. The only name I did not change was the name of the executive director, Jakir Manela, who is now the CEO, because he was and is a public figure associated with Pearlstone.

5. "Gabe" interview. All of the interviews cited in this chapter are from my 2015 visit at Pearlstone Center.

6. As is the case with the transliteration of many Hebrew words, there are various options for transliterating the Hebrew word שמיטה. I will use *shmita* because this is the spelling used by most of the texts and projects related to shmita in the United States. When I am quoting other sources, I will maintain the transliteration used in the texts. Popular variations include *shemita* and *shemittah*.

7. For information on the calculation of the sabbatical (and jubilee) years, please see Zuckerman, *Treatise of the Sabbatical Cycle and the Jubilee*.

8. For more information about the Jewish community farming movement, see my "Growing Food."

9. "Pearlstone History," Adamah website, accessed July 20, 2024, adamah.org/retreat-centers/pearlstone-baltimore/pearlstone-history/.

10. "Pearlstone History."

11. Jakir Manela interview.

12. "Pearlstone History."

13. In 2017, the management of the Camp Milldale property was delegated to Pearlstone by The Associated: Jewish Federation of Baltimore. This expanded the footprint of Pearlstone to 180 acres. Because this chapter is about Pearlstone in 2015, I restrict my discussion to the 7 acres that Pearlstone managed at that time. I discussed some of the restoration work that Pearlstone has been doing on the former Camp Milldale property in "Jewish Farming and the Climate Crisis."

14. I was able to visit Pearlstone many times after the 2014–15 shmita year, including a visit during the 2021–22 shmita year for an ongoing project on Jewish community farming, but my analysis in this chapter is focused on the 2014–15 shmita year to align this chapter chronologically with the others in this book.

15. Lyrics from "*Shmita*: Rest and Release" set to the tune of "Hey Ya!" by Outkast, lyrics by Natalie, music by Outkast, Pearlstone Center, October 2014/5775. This is the second verse of the song and the chorus.

16. I use "land of Israel" here because the boundaries of the area where shmita is required are not the same as the boundaries of the modern state of Israel.

17. There have, of course, always been Jews working in agriculture, but they have always been a minority within the broader Jewish community. For more information on the history of Jews in agriculture in the United States, see chapter 1.

18. "Nora" interview.

19. For a more thorough overview of this textual tradition and the historical implementation of shmita, see my article "'Shmita Manifesto,'" which was based on an earlier version of this chapter. Much of the analysis of shmita texts and the history of shmita's implementation in the United States appeared in similar form in that article.

20. Exodus 23:10–11 (JPS).

21. Leviticus 25:4–5 (JPS).

22. Newman, *Sanctity of the Seventh Year*, 15.

23. Leviticus 25:20–22 (JPS).

24. Each shmita cycle is seven years, with six years of growing annual and perennial crops and then the seventh shmita year. In the shmita cycles, the Israelites would need to grow enough food in the sixth year to store what they needed to eat alongside perennial crops throughout the entire seventh year. In addition, they would also need to store some of those sixth-year crops for the beginning of the eighth year, which would technically be the first year in the next shmita cycle of seven years.

25. Newman, *Sanctity of the Seventh Year*, 16. This interpretation is again related to understandings of the biblical texts regarding the covenant between the ancient Israelites and their God and the role of the land of Israel in that covenant. In the contemporary era, understandings of the ideal relationship between Jews and the land of Israel are contested in and outside the Jewish community.

26. Deuteronomy 15:1–11, 31:10–13; 2 Kings 19:29–30; Jeremiah 34:13–14; Nehemiah 10:32; 2 Chronicles 36:21.

27. There is some disagreement over whether the jubilee year occurs in year forty-nine or in year fifty of the cycle. For more information, see Zuckerman, *Treatise of the Sabbatical Cycle and the Jubilee*.

28. Leviticus 25:13–18, 23–55. Shmita cycles were tracked better than *yovel* cycles through history, so while there is agreement on when the shmita years are, there is no consensus on when the *yovel* years are in the modern era.

29. Newman, *Sanctity of the Seventh Year*, 19–20.

30. Benstein, *Way into Judaism and the Environment*, 190.

31. Blidstein, "Man and Nature in the Sabbatical Year," 50.

32. As Jews settled in what was then Ottoman Palestine in large numbers in the late nineteenth century, a legal discussion related to shmita arose there, and the rabbis determined that the best way forward was to permit a *heter mekhira* (sale permit), which enabled Jewish farmers to sell their land to non-Jews for the shmita year, which then exempted them from shmita restrictions. For more information, see my article "'Shmita Manifesto,'" 308–9; and Kook, *Rav Kook's Introduction to Shabbat Ha'Aretz*.

33. Jakir Manela interview.

34. In 2024, Nati Passow was working as director of operations and finance at the Jewish climate organization Dayenu. "Our People," Dayenu website, accessed July 20, 2024, https://dayenu.org/who-we-are/#our-people.

35. Passow, "Shemita as a Foundation for Jewish Ecological Education," 4.

36. Passow, "Shemita as a Foundation for Jewish Ecological Education," 3.

37. Jakir Manela interview.

38. Pearlstone later merged with Hazon in 2023, becoming one organization under the name Adamah, but in the Shmita Project era and during the 2014–15 shmita year, Pearlstone and Hazon were separate organizations.

39. "Shmita Project Overview," Hazon website, accessed August 15, 2015, http://hazon.org/shmita-project/overview/. The website and the mission statement were updated in advance of the 2021–22 shmita year, but the 2015 version is preserved here because these were the goals of the shmita year discussed here.

40. I discuss *Envisioning Sabbatical Culture* in more detail in "'Shmita Manifesto,'" 315–17.

41. Deutscher, *Envisioning Sabbatical Culture*, ii, 23, 35–36.

42. I discuss the *Hazon Shmita* שמיטה *Sourcebook* in more detail in "'Shmita Manifesto,'" 317–18.

43. Deutscher et al., *Hazon Shmita* שמיטה *Sourcebook*, 65.

44. Jacobs, "Jewish Environmentalism," 451.

45. Benstein, *Way into Judaism and the Environment*, 189.

46. Participant observation at Adamah Farm Fellowship, July 2015.

47. The album is titled *Release: Songs for Shmita*. It is available at https://hazon.bandcamp.com/album/release-songs-for-shmita.

48. As discussed in chapter 1, I visited Adamah in the summer of 2015, which was the same shmita year summer described here at Pearlstone. For more information about shmita at Adamah, please see "Adamah in the Shmita Year," Hazon website, accessed July 31, 2024, http://hazon.org/shmita-project/adamah-in-shmita/.

49. "Natalie" interview.

50. "Daniel" interview.

51. The game description is based on summaries included in the interviews with "Daniel," "Natalie," and "Nora."

52. Jakir Manela interview.

53. "Nora" interview.
54. Jakir Manela interview.
55. "Mission & History," Pearlstone Center website, accessed August 10, 2015, http://pearlstonecenter.org/mission-history/. The mission of Pearlstone changed after the merger with Hazon, and the mission statement from 2015 is no longer on the website.
56. "Mission & History."
57. "Rachel" interview.
58. "Mission & History."
59. "Nora" interview.
60. Jakir Manela interview.
61. Pearlstone has since acquired a camp that sat adjacent to its land and now grows food on an ever-expanding number of acres, many of which are dedicated to "UPick" fields where community members can head into the fields to harvest their own berries.
62. The farm is now USDA organic certified, but it was not in 2015 ("Pearlstone," Adamah website, accessed July 21, 2024, https://adamah.org/retreat-centers/pearlstone-baltimore/our-land/).
63. "Our Farm," Pearlstone Center website, accessed August 10, 2015, http://pearlstonecenter.org/ourfarm/. After the shmita year, the goals and produce grown on the farm changed; the updated website reflects those changes.
64. "Our Farm."
65. Jakir Manela interview.
66. "Jake" interview.
67. "Ava" interview.
68. "Sydney" interview.
69. Two hens later died because of fox and raccoon attacks, so the flock stood at sixteen in June 2015 ("Natalie" interview).
70. "Gabe" interview.
71. "Gabe" interview.
72. "Sydney" interview.
73. "Ava" interview.
74. "Sydney" interview.
75. It is possible that people complained but not to me, both because I carried around a tape recorder and because I am one of the lucky people whose skin does not react to poison ivy through an explosion of red blisters.
76. "Sydney" interview.
77. "Sydney" interview.
78. I asked Sydney why all the invasive species seem to be Japanese. She explained that Japan has a similar climate, so many Japanese plants that are introduced into Baltimore thrive there.
79. "Sydney" interview.
80. "Sydney" interview.
81. Jakir Manela interview.
82. "Daniel" interview.
83. The calendar garden is a circular arrangement of triangular raised beds, each labeled with the name of a Hebrew month and filled with plants related to holidays that occur during that month.

84. "Nora" interview.

85. "Nora" interview.

86. Participant observation at Shmita Fest, Pearlstone Center, June 14, 2015.

87. "Nora" interview. As I mentioned above, there were fewer animals, but there were still animals on-site during the shmita year.

88. "Jake" interview.

89. "Gabe" interview.

90. "Gabe" interview.

91. "Sydney" interview.

92. "Sydney" interview.

93. "Daniel" interview, in which he cited Anderson, *Imagined Communities*.

94. "Daniel" interview.

95. "Ava" interview.

96. "Natalie" interview.

97. "Daniel" interview.

98. Jakir Manela interview.

99. Jakir Manela interview.

100. "Jake" interview.

101. Jakir Manela interview.

102. "Gabe" interview.

103. "Jake" interview.

104. "Gabe" interview.

105. Jakir Manela interview.

106. "History of Pearlstone," Pearlstone Center website, accessed January 16, 2022, www.pearlstonecenter.org/wp-content/uploads/2019/09/history-poster.pdf.

107. Jakir Manela conversation.

108. "History of Pearlstone."

109. "Gabe" interview.

110. Jakir Manela interview.

111. "Nora" interview.

112. "Ava" interview.

113. "Jake" interview.

114. Jakir Manela interview.

115. "Hazon Merges with Retreat Centers," *Detroit Jewish News*, July 15, 2021, https://thejewishnews.com/2021/07/15/hazon-merges-with-retreat-centers/.

116. "Shmita Project," Hazon website, accessed January 16, 2022, https://hazon.org/shmita-project/overview/.

117. For an analysis of shmita in the 2021–22 sabbatical year, see my article "Stimulating Shmita."

CONCLUSION

1. Participant observation, Isabella Freedman Jewish Retreat Center Kitchen and Adamah Kaplan Family Farm, Adamah Farm Fellowship, July 2015.

2. Adamah is a USDA organic-certified farm, so it has to abide by USDA standards for compost. These standards require that the compost piles maintain a temperature between 131°F and 170°F for three days. The temperature of the piles is checked regularly at Adamah.

3. Participant observation, Kaplan Family Farm, Adamah Farm Fellowship, December 2015.

4. Douglas, *Purity and Danger*. Douglas amended some of her initial arguments about Leviticus in the preface to the Routledge Classics Edition in 2002, but her amendments were related to her understanding of how animals were categorized and not to her overall argument about the laws and purity.

5. There are exceptions. Ritual foods, especially those used in Communion, still require an attention to purity.

6. Fishkoff, *Kosher Nation*. The status of pork as taboo is complicated, as the rejection or consumption of pork often serves as a marker of Jewish identity. See Rosenblum, *Forbidden*, for further discussion of this particular taboo.

7. Psalm 118:22 (JPS).

8. For more information on the role of religion in the development of cultured meat, see my article "Religion, Animals, and Technology."

9. Carter, *Spirit of Soul Food*, 4, 140–43, 150–51.

10. Penniman, *Farming While Black*, 1.

11. Francis, *Laudato Si'*.

BIBLIOGRAPHY

PRIMARY SOURCES

Interviews

*Adamah Farm Fellowship,
Falls Village, CT*
"Amy." July 8, 2015.
"Ari." July 10, 2015.
"Debby." July 2, 2015.
"Elisa." July 9, 2015.
Janna Siller. July 8, 2015.
"Max." July 9, 2015.
"Maya." July 9, 2015.
"Miri." July 10, 2015.
"Rayna." June 30, 2015.
Rebecca Bloomfield. July 7, 2015.
"Rose." June 29, 2015.
"Sam." July 1, 2015.
Shamu Sadeh. July 8, 2015.
"Shira." July 8, 2015.
"Zack." July 7, 2015.

*Baldwin Family Farms,
Yanceyville, NC*
V. Mac Baldwin. June 4, June 9,
and December 10, 2015.

*Hallelujah Diet Health Retreat,
Lake Lure, NC*
"Andrea." June 25, 2015.
"Calvin." June 24, 2015.
"Cathy." June 26, 2015.
"Danni." June 24, 2015.
"Erica." June 23, 2015.
"Faith." June 24, 2015.
"Kendall." June 23, 2015.
"Lori." June 24, 2015.
"Mike." June 24, 2015.
"Robert." June 26, 2015.
"Tom." June 25, 2015.

Pearlstone Center,
Reisterstown, MD
   "Ava." June 18, 2015.
   "Daniel." June 17, 2015.
   "Gabe." June 19, 2015.
   "Jake." June 17, 2015.

Jakir Manela. August 5, 2015. Telephone.
   "Natalie." June 17, 2015.
   "Nora." June 19, 2015.
   "Rachel." June 19, 2015.
   "Sydney." June 18, 2015.

Participant Observation

Adamah Farm Fellowship
   June 28–July 10, 2015
   December 29, 2015–January 1, 2016
     (Hazon Food Conference)

Pearlstone Center
   June 14–19, 2015

Baldwin Family Farms
   June 4, 2015
   June 9, 2015
   December 10, 2015

Hallelujah Diet Health Retreat
   June 21–26, 2015

SECONDARY SOURCES

Adam, Margaret B., David L. Clough, and David Grumett. "A Christian Case for Farmed Animal Welfare." *Animals* 9, no. 12, article 1116 (2019): 1–13.

Alkon, Alison Hope, and Julian Agyeman. "Introduction: The Food Movement as Polyculture." In *Cultivating Food Justice: Race, Class, and Sustainability*, edited by Alison Hope Alkon and Julian Agyeman. Cambridge: MIT Press, 2011.

Anderson, Benedict. *Imagined Communities: Reflections on the Origin and Spread of Nationalism*. Revised ed. New York: Verso, 2006. Originally published in 1983.

Ariel, Yaakov. *Evangelizing the Chosen People: Missions to the Jews in America, 1880–2000*. Chapel Hill: University of North Carolina Press, 2000.

Bahnson, Fred. *Soil and Sacrament: A Spiritual Memoir of Food and Faith*. New York: Simon and Schuster, 2013.

Bender, Courtney. *Heaven's Kitchen: Living Religion at God's Love We Deliver*. Chicago: University of Chicago Press, 2003.

Benstein, Jeremy. *The Way into Judaism and the Environment*. Woodstock: Jewish Lights Publishing, 2006.

Bernstein, Ellen. *The Splendor of Creation: A Biblical Ecology*. Cleveland: Pilgrim Press, 2005.

Berry, Wendell. *The Unsettling of America: Culture and Agriculture*. San Francisco: Sierra Club Books, 1977.

Blanchette, Alex. *Porkopolis: American Animality, Standardized Life, and the Factory Farm*. Durham: Duke University Press, 2020.

Blazer, Annie. "Hallelujah Acres: Christian Raw Foods and the Quest for Health." In *Religion, Food, and Eating in North America*, edited by Benjamin E. Zeller, Marie W. Dallam, Reid L. Neilson, and Nora L. Rubel, 68–88. New York: Columbia University Press, 2014.

Blidstein, Gerald Jacob. "Man and Nature in the Sabbatical Year." *Tradition* 9, no. 4 (1966): 48–55.

Broad, Garrett M. *More Than Just Food: Food Justice and Community Change*. Oakland: University of California Press, 2016.

Buettner, Dan. *The Blue Zones: 9 Lessons for Living Longer from the People Who've Lived the Longest*. Washington, DC: National Geographic Society, 2008.

Campbell, T. Colin. Foreword to *The Hallelujah Diet*, by George Malkmus with Peter Shockey and Stowe Shockey, 23–25. Shippensburg: Destiny Image Publishers, 2006.

Carter, Christopher. *The Spirit of Soul Food: Race, Faith, and Food Justice*. Urbana: University of Illinois Press, 2021.

Chandia, Mahmood, and Jan Mei Soon. "The Variations in Religious and Legal Understandings of Halal Slaughter." *British Food Journal* 120, no. 3 (2018): 714–30.

Clough, David. *On Animals*. London: T&T Clark, 2012.

Darwin, Charles. *The Descent of Man and Selection in Relation to Sex*. Originally published in 1871. Princeton: Princeton University Press, 1981.

Davis, Ellen. *Scripture, Culture, and Agriculture: An Agrarian Reading of the Bible*. Cambridge: Cambridge University Press, 2009.

Descartes, René. "Letter to More." February 5, 1649. In "Selected Correspondence, 1619–1650," edited by Jonathan Bennett, Some Texts from Early Modern Philosophy (website), pp. 212–16. www.earlymoderntexts.com/assets/pdfs/descartes1619_4.pdf.

Deutscher, Yigal. *Envisioning Sabbatical Culture: A Shmita Manifesto*. New York: 7 Seeds, 2013.

Deutscher, Yigal, Anna Hanau, and Nigel Savage, *The Hazon Shmita שמיטה Sourcebook*. New York: Hazon, 2013.

Douglas, Mary. *Purity and Danger: An Analysis of Concept of Pollution and Taboo*. London: Routledge Classics, 2002. Originally published in 1966.

Fenyvesi, Shamu Sadeh. "Befriending the Desert Owl." In *Ecology and the Jewish Spirit: Where Nature and the Sacred Meet*, edited by Ellen Bernstein, 27–31. Woodstock: Jewish Lights, 1998.

Fishkoff, Sue. *Kosher Nation: Why More and More of America's Food Answers to a Higher Authority*. New York: Penguin Random House, 2010.

Foer, Jonathan Safran. *Eating Animals*. New York: Back Bay Books, 2009.

Francis. *Laudato Si': On Care for Our Common Home*. Vatican City: Libreria Editrice Vaticana, 2015.

Fraser, David. "Caring for Farm Animals: Pastoralist Ideals in an Industrialized World." In *A Communion of Subjects: Animals in Religion, Science and Ethics*, edited by Paul Waldau and Kimberly Patton, 547–55. New York: Columbia University Press, 2006.

Fuller, Robert C., and William B. Parsons. "Spiritual but Not Religious: A Brief Introduction." In *Being Spiritual but not Religious: Past, Present, Future(s)*, edited by William B. Parsons, 15–29. New York: Routledge, 2018.

Gottlieb, Robert, and Anupama Joshi. *Food Justice*. Cambridge: MIT Press, 2010.

Graham, Sylvester. *A Lecture to Young Men on Chastity. Intended Also for the Serious Consideration of Parents and Guardians*. Boston: George W. Light, 1839.

Graham, Sylvester. *A Treatise on Bread, and Bread-Making*. Boston: Light & Stearns, 1837.

Griffith, R. Marie. *Born Again Bodies: Flesh and Spirit in American Christianity*. Berkeley: University of California Press, 2004.

Gross, Aaron. *The Question of the Animal and Religion: Theoretical Stakes, Practical Implications.* New York: Columbia University Press, 2015.

Gross, Rachel B. *Beyond the Synagogue: Jewish Nostalgia as Religious Practice.* New York: NYU Press, 2021.

Haraway, Donna. *Staying with the Trouble: Making Kin in the Chthulucene.* Durham: Duke University Press, 2016.

Herscher, Uri D. *Jewish Agricultural Utopias in America, 1880–1910.* Detroit: Wayne State University Press, 1981.

Hodder, Ian. *Entangled: An Archaeology of the Relationships between Humans and Things.* Malden, MA: Wiley-Blackwell, 2012.

Hulsether, Lucia. *Capitalist Humanitarianism.* Durham: Duke University Press, 2023.

Imhoff, Sarah. *The Lives of Jessie Samfpter: Queer, Disabled, Zionist.* Durham: Duke University Press, 2022.

Jacobs, Mark X. "Jewish Environmentalism: Past Accomplishments and Future Challenges." In *Judaism and Ecology: Created World and Revealed World*, edited by Hava Tirosh-Samuelson, 450–63. Cambridge, MA: Harvard University Press, 2002.

Jain, Andrea R. *Paace Love Yoga: The Politics of Global Spirituality.* New York: Oxford University Press, 2020.

Kirby, David. *Animal Factory: The Looming Threat of Industrial Pig, Dairy, and Poultry Farms to Humans and the Environment.* New York: St. Martin's Press, 2010.

Klippenstein, Janet M. "Imagine No Religion: On Defining 'New Age.'" *Studies in Religion/Sciences Religieuses* 34, no. 3–4 (2005): 391–403.

Kook, Abraham Isaac. *Rav Kook's Introduction to Shabbat Ha'Aretz.* New York: Hazon, 2014.

Kranson, Rachel. *Ambivalent Embrace: Jewish Upward Mobility in Postwar America.* Chapel Hill: University of North Carolina Press, 2017.

Krone, Adrienne. "Farming on the Front Lines: Jewish Environmentalisms and Kinship in the Chthulucene." *Worldviews: Global Religions, Culture, and Ecology* 26, no. 1–2 (2021): 148–61.

Krone, Adrienne. "Growing Food: Ecological Ethics in the Jewish Community Farming Movement." In *Feasting and Fasting: The History and Ethics of Jewish Food*, edited by Aaron Gross, Jody Myers, and Jordan Rosenblum, 273–86. New York: NYU Press, 2020.

Krone, Adrienne. "Jewish Farming and the Climate Crisis." *The Revealer*, October 7, 2021, https://therevealer.org/jewish-farming-and-the-climate-crisis/.

Krone, Adrienne. "Judaism and Climate Change." *Religion Compass* 18, no. 4 (2024). https://doi.org/10.1111/rec3.12491.

Krone, Adrienne. "Opening the Tent: Jewish Veganism as an Expression of an Ecological Form of Judaism." In *Jewish Veganism and Vegetarianism*, edited by Jacob Labendz and Shmuly Yanklowitz, 117–30. Albany: SUNY Press, 2019.

Krone, Adrienne. "Religion, Animals, and Technology." In "Religion, Animals, and X," edited by Aaron Gross and Katherine Mershon. Special issue, *Religions* 13, no. 456 (2022): 1–17.

Krone, Adrienne. "'A Shmita Manifesto': A Radical Sabbatical Approach to Jewish Food Reform in the United States." *Scripta Instituti Donneriani Aboensis* 26 (2015): 303–25.

Krone, Adrienne. "Stimulating Shmita: Revisiting Louis Newman's *The Sanctity of the Seventh Year* Forty Years Later." *Journal of Jewish Ethics*, forthcoming 2025.

LeVasseur, Todd. "Introduction: Religion, Agriculture, and Sustainability." In *Religion and Sustainable Agriculture: World Spiritual Traditions and Food Ethics*, edited by Todd LeVasseur, Pramod Parajuli, and Norman Wirzba, 1–24. Lexington: University Press of Kentucky, 2016.

LeVasseur, Todd. *Religious Agrarianism and the Return of Place: From Values to Practice in Sustainable Agriculture*. Albany: SUNY Press, 2017.

Lim, Kar H., Wuyang Hu, and Rodolfo M. Nayga Jr. "Consumer Preference for Grass-Fed Beef: A Case of Food Safety Halo Effect." *Journal of Agricultural and Resource Economics* 46, no. 3 (2021): 447–63.

Linzey, Andrew. *Animal Theology*. Urbana: University of Illinois Press, 1995.

Lofton, Kathryn. *Consuming Religion*. Chicago: University of Chicago Press, 2017.

Lucia, Amanda J. *White Utopias: The Religious Exoticism of Transformational Festivals*. Oakland: University of California Press, 2020.

Magid, Shaul. *American Post-Judaism: Identity and Renewal in a Postethnic Society*. Bloomington: Indiana University Press, 2013.

Malkmus, George, with Peter Shockey and Stowe Shockey. *The Hallelujah Diet: Experience the Optimal Health You Were Meant to Have*. Shippensburg, PA: Destiny Image Publishers, 2006.

Marx, Karl. *The Economic and Philosophic Manuscripts of 1844*. New York: International Publishers, 1964.

Mathews, Kenneth H., and Rachel J. Johnson. *Alternative Beef Production Systems: Issues and Implications*. United States Department of Agriculture, April 4, 2013. https://ers.usda.gov/sites/default/files/_laserfiche/outlooks/37473/36491_ldpm-218-01.pdf?v=43218.

Mauss, Marcel. "Techniques of the Body." *Economy and Society* 2, no. 1 (1973): 70–88.

McDaniel, Jay. "Practicing the Presence of God: A Christian Approach to Animals." In *A Communion of Subjects: Animals in Religion, Science and Ethics*, edited by Paul Waldau and Kimberly Patton, 132–45. New York: Columbia University Press, 2006.

McDannell, Colleen. *Material Christianity: Religion and Popular Culture in America*. New Haven: Yale University Press, 1998.

Mehta, Samira K. "'I Chose Judaism but Christmas Cookies Chose Me': Food, Identity, and Familial Religious Practice in Christian/Jewish Blended Families." In *Religion, Food, and Eating in North America*, edited by Benjamin E. Zeller, Marie W. Dallam, Reid L. Neilson, and Nora L. Rubel, 154–72. New York: Columbia University Press, 2014.

Mercadante, Linda A. *Belief without Borders: Inside the Minds of the Spiritual but Not Religious*. New York: Oxford University Press, 2014.

Metcalfe, William. *An Address on Abstinence from the Flesh of Animals as Food, Delivered in the Bible-Christian Church, Philadelphia, June 8th, 1840*. Philadelphia: Board of Publication of the Church, 1840.

Morton, Timothy. *Hyperobjects: Philosophy and Ecology after the End of the World*. Minneapolis: University of Minnesota Press, 2013.

Newman, Louis E. *The Sanctity of the Seventh Year: A Study of Mishnah Tractate Shebiit*. Chico, CA: Scholars Press, 1983.

Nissenbaum, Stephen. *Sex, Diet, and Debility in Jacksonian America: Sylvester Graham and Health Reform.* Chicago: Dorsey Press, 1988.

Novotny, Thomas E., Stella Aguinaga Bialous, Lindsay Burt, Clifton Curtis, Vera Luiza da Costa, Silvae Usman Iqtidar, Yuchen Liu, Sameer Pujari, and Edouard Tursan d'Espaignet. "The Environmental and Health Impacts of Tobacco Agriculture, Cigarette Manufacture and Consumption." *Bulletin of the World Health Organization* 93, no. 12 (2015): 877–80.

Orsi, Robert A. *Between Heaven and Earth: The Religious Worlds People Make and the Scholars Who Study Them.* Princeton: Princeton University Press, 2004.

Pachirat, Timothy. *Every Twelve Seconds: Industrialized Slaughter and the Politics of Sight.* New Haven: Yale University Press, 2011.

Passow, Nati. "Shemita as a Foundation for Jewish Ecological Education." In *Jewish Education News.* New York: Coalition for the Advancement of Jewish Education, 2008.

Penniman, Leah. *Farming While Black: Soul Fire Farm's Practical Guide to Liberation on the Land.* White River Junction, VT: Chelsea Green Publishing, 2018.

Pike, Sarah. *New Age and Neopagan Religions in America.* New York: Columbia University Press, 2006.

Rosenblum, Jordan D. *Forbidden: A 3,000-Year History of Jews and the Pig.* New York: New York University Press, 2024.

Sack, Daniel. *Whitebread Protestants: Food and Religion in American Culture.* New York: Palgrave, 2000.

Schmidt, Leigh Eric. *Consumer Rites: The Buying and Selling of American Holidays.* Princeton: Princeton University Press, 1997.

Schorsch, Jonathan. *The Food Movement, Culture, and Religion: A Tale of Pigs, Christians, Jews, and Politics.* Cham, Switz.: Palgrave Macmillan, 2018.

Shprintzen, Adam D. *The Vegetarian Crusade: The Rise of an American Movement, 1817–1921.* Chapel Hill: University of North Carolina Press, 2013.

Sigalow, Emily. *American JewBu: Jews, Buddhists, and Religious Change.* Princeton: Princeton University Press, 2019.

Singer, Peter. *Animal Liberation: The Definitive Classic of the Animal Movement.* New York: HarperCollins Publishers, 2009. Originally published in 1975.

Stern, David H. *Messianic Judaism: A Modern Movement with an Ancient Past (A Revision of Messianic Jewish Manifesto).* Clarksville, MD: Lederer Books, 2007.

Tapper, Aaron Hahn. *Judaisms: A Twenty-First Century Introduction to Jews and Jewish Identities.* Oakland: University of California Press, 2016.

Tirosh-Samuelson, Hava. *Judaism and Ecology: Created World and Revealed World.* Cambridge, MA: Harvard University Press, 2002.

Tsing, Anna Lowenhaupt. *The Mushroom at the End of the World: On the Possibility of Life in Capitalist Ruins.* Princeton: Princeton University Press, 2015.

Van Wieren, Gretel. *Food, Farming and Religion: Emerging Ethical Perspectives.* London: Routledge, 2018.

Waskow, Arthur. *Down to Earth Judaism: Food, Money, Sex, and the Rest of Life.* New York: Quill, 1995.

Waskow, Arthur. *Seasons of Our Joy: A Modern Guide to the Jewish Holidays.* Philadelphia: Jewish Publication Society, 1982.

Weisenfeld, Judith. *New World a-Coming: Black Religion and Racial Identity during the Great Migration.* New York: NYU Press, 2017.

Wertheimer, Jack. *The New American Judaism: How Jews Practice Their Religion Today.* Princeton: Princeton University Press, 2018.

White, Ellen G. *Counsels on Diet and Foods.* Silver Spring, MD: Ellen G. White Estate, 2018.

White, Ellen G. *Health, or, How to Live: Number One.* Battle Creek, MI: Steam Press of the Seventh-Day Adventist Publishing Association, 1865.

Wirzba, Norman. *Food and Faith: A Theology of Eating.* Cambridge: Cambridge University Press, 2011.

Zeller, Benjamin E. "Quasi-Religious American Foodways: The Cases of Vegetarianism and Locavorism." In *Religion, Food, and Eating in North America*, edited by Benjamin E. Zeller, Marie W. Dallam, Reid L. Neilson, and Nora L. Rubel, 294–312. New York: Columbia University Press, 2014.

Zuckerman, B. *A Treatise of the Sabbatical Cycle and the Jubilee: A Contribution to the Archaeology and Chronology of the Time Anterior and Subsequent to the Captivity: Accompanied by a Table of Sabbatical Years.* New York: Hermon Press, 1974.

INDEX

Adam, Margaret, 97–98
Adamah Farm Fellowship, 3, 8, 14–33 passim, 145, 147; activism of, 37–38; blue moon celebration at, 55–56; Christian divinity students, visit by, 54–55; and free-range religion, 48–57, 82; gender balance of, 32; and halakhah, 48–50; mikvah for, 58; music at, 49–51; and pluralism's effect, 51–54, 56; religious innovation at, 55–57; and shmita, 129; transformative experience at, 58–60; worship practice at, 50–51
Agricultural Development and Preservation of Farmland, North Carolina Article 61, 102
agricultural history: Jewish, 34–35; in the United States, 34
agriculture: Jewish, 34–35; and religion, 8; restorative, 103; sustainable, 27, 29, 32–60, 102. *See also* LeVasseur, Todd; Van Wieren, Gretel

agriculturalists: industrial, 102; Jewish, in nineteenth century, 34–35
Agyeman, Julian, 2, 7
alcohol, abstention from, 23
Alkon, Alison Hope, 2, 7
Allen Harim, 111
Alliance for the Chesapeake Bay for the Trees, 135
alternative food systems: at Adamah Farm Fellowship, 40–48; on Baldwin Family Farms, 105–13; consumers of, 105; frequent invisibility of religion in, 116–17; in the Hallelujah Diet, 71–82; at Pearlstone Center during the shmita year, 130–36; religious, 2, 24
alternative medical treatments, 85; biblical and scientific authority for use of, 85; essential oils as, 85; in the mainstream, 156–57
American individualism and agricultural communitarian enterprises, 35
AmeriCorps program, 134

Am Olam (Eternal People), 34
animal consumption, effects on humans, 68. *See also* meat consumption
animals: and ability to believe in God, 99; certification for care of, 108; husbandry and welfare, 31, 94; as machines and commodities, 98; and modern ethics, 101; people caring about, 105; sentience and souls of, 98–99
animal sacrifice, 114–15. *See also* halal slaughter
animal slaughter, halal, 114–15. *See also* kosher slaughter
anthropocentrism, 5, 20, 125, 129
Aquinas, Thomas, 98
Ariel, Yaakov, 83
Aristotle, 98
Ashrei, 33
Associated: Jewish Federation of Baltimore, 142
aster flowers, 136
Augustine of Hippo, 98
Avodat Lev, 24, 34, 48–49, 147

BA. *See* Beit Adamah
Bahnson, Fred, 54
Baldwin, Peggy, 1, 93, 95, 101, 109, 110
Baldwin, V. Mac, 1–2, 12, 93–104; conversations with Abdul Chaudhry, 114–16; grass farmer, 104–18; marketing to secular markets, 116; principles reflecting commitment to customers, 117–18, 151, 154, 156
Baldwin Beef, 1, 11, 15, 19, 93–96; all-natural label explanation, 107–8; history of, 97. *See also* Baldwin, V. Mac: conversations with Abdul Chaudhry
Baldwin Family Farms, 1, 22, 25, 93; breeding chickens on, 110–11; free-range religion at, 113–16; "hen houses" on, 111; and management of habitat and woodlands breaks, 104; marketing of, 106; soil sampling on, 101–18; and use of chicken poop, 110
Baltimore, Jewish community in, 25, 130–31, 133, 142

Baltimore City Public Schools, 138
Baltimore County Department of Environmental Protection and Sustainability, 135
Baptisia australis, 136
Baptists, 22, 62
Barley Max, 62, 66
beef: from alternative production systems, 100; grass-fed, 104; health benefits of, 109; hormone supplementation of, 108; protein benefits of, 104; USDA certified, 25
Beit Adamah (BA), 30–31, 46, 50
Bender, Courtney, 18
Benstein, Jeremy, 126, 129
Bernstein, Ellen, 36–37, 163n35
Berry, Wendell, 102
Bible, 25–26; as compared with science, 88; as a source for nutritional advice, 90
Bible verses, and food practices, 6, 16, 25–26, 46, 27, 33–34, 37, 63, 82, 87, 114, 116, 125, 161n5
biosecurity, 111
Blazer, Annie, 79–81, 88
Blidstein, Gerald, 126
Bloomfield, Rebecca, 30, 32, 40, 55, 58,
blue wild indigo (*Baptisia australis*), 136
breed-mixing of cows, accidental, 113
Broad, Garrett, 10
Buddhist tenets, 56
Buettner, Dan, 70, 166n26

caffeine, abstention from, 23, 71, 75
CAFOs (confined animal feeding operations), 100, 108
Calvin, John, 98
Campbell, T. Collin, 89–90
Camp Milldale, 122, 144, 173n13
cancer, 78; alternative treatments for, 85; traditional treatments for, 89
capitalism, 15, 129, 137
Carrboro Farmers' Market, North Carolina, 117
Carson, Rachel, 70
Carter, Christopher, 157

Cartesian mind-body dualism, 68
Caswell County, North Carolina, 103
cattle, grass-fed: and medicinal value of bones, 109; and pasture-raised 12
certifications, third-party, 105–6; administrative time involved, 107; for animal welfare, 108; cost of, 106; lack of, for grass-fed beef, 108; non-GMO, 105–6
Charlotte, North Carolina, 65
Charolais cattle, 1–2, 93; breeding; 112–13
Chaudhry, Abdul, 96, 114, 171n80
Chaudhry Halal Meat Company, 2, 106, 114–15, 117
Chesapeake Bay Trust, 135
Chesapeake Conservation Corps, 119, 139
chickens, 110–12; waste as fertilizer, 95
Christianity, 4, 10, 13, 15, 17, 19, 25, 82–84, 86, 96, 105, 118, 153; and animals and meat eating, 2, 97–99, 114–15; and land stewardship, 101–3; Protestant, 13, 64, 79
Christian diets, 65, 71, 81, 158; ecojustice and, 103
Christian theology, 153
climate change, 5, 20, 31, 36–37, 122, 153, 157
Clough, David, 97–98
Coalition on the Environment and Jewish Life, 36
compost, 21, 24–25, 30, 34, 47, 32, 53, 147–51, 155, 177n2
coneflower, green-headed (*Rudbeckia laciniata*), 136
confined animal feeding operations (CAFOs), 100, 108
consumerism, 15
cover-cropping, 134
cucumbers, 21, 40, 46, 61, 156

Darwin, Charles, 99
Descartes, René, 99
Deutscher, Yigal, 128, 153
Diaspora, 36, 124, 127, 135
diet culture, devotional, 79
diet plans, concessions to, 72–73

Donaldson, Michael, 78
Douglas, Mary, 18, 152, 177n4

eco-kashrut, 36
ecological life: and interdependence, 33, 42, 57; restoration of, 135
Edenic state of perfection, 62
Eden Village Camp, 18
environmentalism, Jewish, 18, 24–25, 29, 34–38, 127, 130
environmental justice, 6–7, 9, 30–31, 35, 37, 39, 157
essential oils, 85
Ethiopian Hebrew congregations, 5
evangelical Christianity, 82–83

factory farms, 26, 97, 100, 108
Falls Village, Connecticut, 27
Fannie Lou Hamer's Freedom Farm Cooperative, 157
Father Divine's Peace Mission Movement, 4–5
fertilizer, 95
fibromyalgia, 78
flooded fields, use of, 57–58
Foer, Jonathan Safran, 100
food, desacralized, 153
food, living and dead: definitions of, 74; proportions allowed in Hallelujah Diet, 73
food and foodways, study of, 18
food insecurity, 31, 157
food justice movements, 6–9, 24; religious, 24, 31, 35, 39, 47, 59, 144, 157
food movements, alternative religious, 2–9, 14, 88; Adamah impact on, 59; and carcinogenic additives, 5; and genetically modified organisms (GMOs), 5; history of, 23–24; and Israelites, ancient, 25–26; and Jewish immigrants, 4; monoculture versions of, 2; tension between religious participants in, 94. *See also* Adamah Farm Fellowship; Hallelujah Diet Health Retreats; Pearlstone Retreat Center

food systems: Adamah, 29, 40–45; American industrial, 2–3, 19, 152; and morality, 46, 71; sabbatical, 128; sacred relationship with, 128; utopian, 5
Francis (pope), 157
Fraser, David, 101
free-range, definition, 12
Fuller, Robert C., 13

gender identity, 32
genetically modified organisms (GMOs), 105
Gideon's International, 1–2, 97; 101
Global Animal Partnership, 108
goats: milking on Shabbat, 50; milk of, 49–50
God's Love We Deliver, 18
Gottlieb, Robert, 6
Graham, Sylvester, 4, 68–70; *Lecture to Young Men on Chastity*, 69
grass: cereal ryegrass, 104; crabgrass, 104; Kentucky 31 fescue, 104; V. Mac Baldwin and; 103
Griffith, R. Marie, 18, 79–81, 84
grocery stores, 25. *See also* Kroger; Publix; Whole Foods Market
Gross, Rachel, 14
Grow and Behold (kosher meat market), 59
Grumett, David, 97–98

halakhah (Jewish law), 48; at Adamah, 50
halal slaughter, 1, 25, 106; and absolution of sin, 115; outdated understanding of, 114–15; USDA-certified beef, 25
Hall, David, 18
Hallelujah Acres, 63–64; God's Way to Ultimate Health seminar, 65
Hallelujah Diet, 11–15, 64–65; alignment with biblical foundations, 74–75, 85–86; as alternative medicine, 62, 77–78; ban on animal products, 75; brand supplements, 65; "cheating" potential while on, 74; in contrast to New Age practices, 85–86; essential oils and, 64; historical context for, 65; human lifespan and, 91; as an individual effort, 85; and liquids, 67; living and dead foods, 73–75; naturopathic remedies and, 64; origins of, 62–63; religious support for, 66–67; scientific support for, 65–66. *See also* Hallelujah Diet Health Retreats; Malkmus, George
Hallelujah Diet Health Retreats, 10, 13, 16, 19, 22–24, 61–62, 64–65; breaks at, 62; expense of, 65; free-range religion at, 82–91; juicing vegetables at, 61–62
halo effect, 104
Hanau, Anna, 128
Haredi. *See* Judaism: Haredi
Havdalah ceremony, 27–29, 32
Hazon, 43, 145; 159n4
Hazon Food Conference, 59, 127
health minister training, 77
Heber Brown's Black Church Food Security Network, 157
herbicides, as unsustainable and ineffective, 135
Herscher, Uri, 35
Hessel, Dieter, 103
Hodder, Ian, 21
homesteading work session, 43–45
Hulsether, Lucia, 15
humans, and relation to animals, 99
Hydroboost, 67

Imhoff, Sarah, 10
intelligent design, 90
Interdependence Day, 33
invasive species, 134–35
Isabella Freedman Jewish Retreat Center, 3, 24, 30–31, 38, 41–42, 47, 51, 145, 151; vegan food options, 23, 59
Islam, 2, 5, 10, 15, 25, 82, 114–15, 140

Jain, Andrea, 14–15
Japanese dodder, 135
Japanese stiltgrass, 135–36
Jewish communities, 51–55

Jewish environmentalist movement, 18, 24, 29, 31, 34, 36–38, 121–24, 127–28, 130, 145, 153
Jewish Farm School, 145
Jewish food movement, expansion of, 59
Jewish identity, 32, 140–41; fear and shame about, 56
Joshi, Anupama, 6
joy, 57
Judaism, 13; agrarian, 32; Conservative, 160n34, 164n84; contemporary disengagement from agriculture, 124; and ecology, 36, 53; Haredi, 32, 53–54; Orthodox, 12, 32, 53, 54, 153, 160n34; practicing and prioritizing Judaism, 141; Reform, 12, 22, 32, 38, 82, 153, 160n34, 164n84; Renewal, 18, 36, 38–39, 48, 53, 55, 129, 164n84. *See also* Messianic Judaism

Kaplan Family Farm, 33, 58
Kayam Farm at Pearlstone, 18, 122
Kellogg, John Harvey, 4; and Battle Creek Sanitarium, 71–72
Kellogg, W. K., 4; and Corn Flakes, 71
kibbutzim, of Israel, 4, 34, 36
Kingsolver, Barbara, 46
Kirby, David, 100, 103
Klippenstein, Janet, 86
kosher, 19, 21, 29, 36, 47, 50, 52, 59, 143–45, 152–54; mashgiach, 51
kosher slaughter, 9, 31, 171n73; outdated understanding of, 115, 171n86
Kranson, Rachel, 35
Kroger, 25, 94, 106, 117

labor and accomplishment, connection between, 43
Lake Lure Hallelujah Diet Health Retreat, 64, 76–92
Lecture to Young Men on Chastity, A (Graham), 69
LeVasseur, Todd, 8, 35, 102
Linzey, Andrew, 98
Lippman Kanfer Prize for Applied Jewish Wisdom, 144

lived religion, 18
living food, 63–64
locavores, 45–46
Lofton, Kathryn, 15
Lookout Point, Appalachian Trail, Connecticut, 27
Lucia, Amanda, 17
Luther, Martin, 98

Mah Tovu, 48
maintenance of relationships, 80–81
Malkmus, George, 62–65; and diet concessions, 74; and living foods, 73–74; on effects of impure food, 70–71; and meat production, 75; on morality of food choices, 71, 84; prohibitions on eating animal products, 75–77, 84; and science, 88–91
Malkmus, Paul, 64
Malkmus, Rhonda, 63–66, 70
Manela, Jakir, 18, 122–23, 127, 130, 132–33, 137, 142–45, 172n4
Marx, Karl, 43
McDaniel, Jay, 98
McDannell, Colleen, 15
meat consumption, and human health, 69, 75, 80, 84, 86, 108–16
meat industry: breeding cows in, 112; centralization of processing, 5; environmental effects of, 88; and meat fat content, 100
medical practitioners, as authorities, 85, 88–89
Mehta, Samira, 18
Mercadante, Linda, 13
Messianic Judaism, 10, 22, 64, 82–84; and adoption of Jewish practices, 83; and engagement with Christian theology, 83. *See also* Judaism
Metcalfe, William, 67–68
Mishnah, shift in, 126
Modeh Ani, 48
monoculture, 2, 26, 153, 156
morality, dietary choices and, 84
music: at Adamah, 59; at Pearlstone, 138

nature-agriculture continuum, 136
neopagans, as compared with New Agers, 86
New Age: and potential to lead away from Christianity, 86; remedies, 85–87; as religion, 86–87; and spirituality, 13, 17, 24, 38, 82–85
New Agers, compared to Hallelujah dieters, 86–87
Newman, Louis, 125–27
Nissenbaum, Stephen, 69–70

omega-3, 104, 109, 112, 154
Orsi, Robert, 15–16, 18, 26
Oseh Shalom, 33

Pachirat, Timothy, 100
Parsons, William B., 13
Passow, Nati, 127–28, 153, 174n34
pastoralist ethic, as alternative philosophy, 101
pasture-raised, definition, 12
pawpaw trees, 136
Pearlstone, Jack, 122
Pearlstone Retreat Center, 7–9, 14–15, 18–19, 22, 24, 119; acquisition of Camp Mildale property, 144; animal program changes, 133; attitudes toward other religions, 140; and Jewish community gardens, 142; education at, 139, 141–42; free-range religion at, 136–43; innovation and environmentalism at, 130; Kayam Farm at, 122; overview, 122–23; relationship with Judaism, 140; shmita-themed game, 130–32; and shmita year, 25, 129, 132–36, 143; and singing, 138; Tu B'Shvat celebrations, 131. *See also* Adamah Farm Fellowship
Penniman, Leah, 157
Pew Research Center, 13–14
pickles, 15, 20–21, 30
Pike, Sarah, 86
Pollan, Michael, 46
polyculture planting method, 134–36
Property Protection Act (North Carolina), 96

providence, 103–4
Psalm 84, 33. *See also* Ashrei
Publix, 106

Rabbi Judah the Prince, 126
raspberries, picking of, 40–41
Riesterstown, Maryland, 3. *See also* Pearlstone Retreat Center
religion, free-range: as an amalgamation, 16; defined, 3, 12
religions: experiences of, 16; institutional, 12; intertwined, 10. *See also* Christianity; Islam; Judaism
religious exoticism, 17
religious recombination, 10
religious studies, 10–15, 46, 79, 152
riparian zone, 134
Roloff, Lester, 62
Rubin, Jordan S., 109
Rudbeckia laciniata, 136

Sack, Daniel, 68, 71
sacrifice. *See* animal sacrifice
SAD (Standard American Diet), 6, 63, 71–72; as "Satan's Alternative Diet," 63
sadeh (field), 57–58
Sadeh, Shamu, 30, 32–34, 37, 42, 47, 54–55, 57, 59, 161n7
Savage, Nigel, 128
Schachter-Shalmi, Zalman, 36
Schmidt, Leigh Eric, 15
Schorsch, Jonathan, 7
Second Great Awakening, 68
Second Temple, destruction of, 126
Seder Zeraim, 126
Seventh-day Adventists, 68–70
Shabbat, 12, 14, 27–28, 45, 49–51, 58, 137; experience of, 140; Kabbalat, 51; meat on, 19; menu for, 51; prohibitions for, 50–51
shacharit prayers, 33. *See also* Avodat Lev
Shalom Center, 18, 129
Shambhala Buddhism, 9, 138
Shema, 33, 48, 162n23
shmita, 6–10, 23, 25, 37, 46, 59, 137; and agricultural restoration, 133–36; as

alternative to capitalism, 129; benefits shared with non-Jewish staff, 137; as cultural currency, 146; flexibility of practice, 137; as an imaginary ideal, 124; as more than a calendar year, 128; overview of concept, 3, 124; Pearlstone's implementation of, 119–21, 129, 137; and perennial plants as food source, 125; as Sabbath for the land, 125; shift in after the destruction of the Second Temple, 126–27; sourcebook for, 129; textual basis of, 124–26

Shmita Fest, 138

Shmita Prizes, 145

Shmita Project, 59, 128–29, 145

Shomrei Adamah (Keepers of the Earth), 36

Shoresh (Toronto), 18

Siller, Janna, 30, 32, 53, 57–58

Singer, Peter, 99

social conservatism, 22

socialism, 35

social justice, 3, 6–7, 9, 24, 29–30, 35–36, 38, 151, 157

Soul Fire Farm, 157

Standard American Diet. *See* SAD

Stern, David, 83

Surprise Lake Camp, 36

Tabor, Mike, 36

Tanakh, 19, 25–26

Teva Learning Center, 31, 36, 122; Seminar on Jewish Environmental Education (2012), 18–19; Seminar on Outdoor, Food and Environmental Education (2013), 128

Tirosh-Samuelson, Hava, 36

Topsy Turvy Bus, 31, 128, 161n11

tza'ar ba'alei chayim (suffering of living creatures), 37, 163n42

United States Department of Agriculture (USDA), 2, 100; and Baldwin Beef, 108; certifications by, 105, 106–7; trust in, 105–6

unprocessed food, 45–46; compared to industrial processed food, 46

Van Wieren, Gretel, 8, 103

veganism, 6, 16, 23–24, 51, 65–67, 81, 87, 90–92, 156

vegetarianism, 67–68

Wake Forest University School of Divinity, 54–55

washing greens, 52–53

Waskow, Arthur, 18, 36, 129, 153, 162n34

weeding and pest control, 40, 42–43, 58, 120

White, Ellen, 4, 68, 71; and meat consumption causing "animalism," 69–70; and dietary practices of Seventh-day Adventists, 4, 68

Whole Foods Market, 2, 25, 76, 94, 97, 115–17; and Global Animal Partnership, 108; and GMO transparency, 105; and halal beef, 106; relationship with Baldwin Family Farms, 117

Wirzba, Norman, 98, 102–3

Yanceyville, North Carolina, 1, 93–94

yovel (jubilee) year, 126

Zeller, Benjamin, 46

www.ingramcontent.com/pod-product-compliance
Lightning Source LLC
Chambersburg PA
CBHW021857230426
43671CB00006B/422